Job
of
Arc

ABOUT THIS BOOK

"A rare inside look at a non-offending parent's struggle with guilt, aloneness, shame and despair, and learning how to cope with these negative emotions. Demonstrating how to build a life for the victims that have been harmed so globally by the abuse, it is a story of the triumph over people's trauma and movement of a family into recovery."

Dr. Jay D. Woodman, Ph.D. *Clinical and Consulting Psychology*

"Five stars. An absolutely powerful story, beautifully told. Having the ability to pick this up and connect with another parent who has walked in my shoes has been an amazing source of strength for me. This is an excellent book for other parents, students, and individuals within the system who are working to protect our children. A must-read."

K. F. *Non-Offending Parent of a Sexually Abused Child*

"Required reading for all the perpetrators in our program. Furthermore, I think it ought to be required reading for everyone who works with cases of child sexual abuse in any profession."

John Brogden, Director *Association for Sexual Assault Prevention*

"This book painfully and poetically describes the two years after the author discovered that the man she fell in love with and married was a pedophile. What happens to this family after the secret is out and they start to rebuild their dreams is not only maddening but a beautiful testament to courage, love, and determination."

B. Lynn Heil, R.N. *Emergency Room Triage*

"Highly recommended: A unique story of personal, ecclesial and family narratives for all whose lives have been touched by pedophilia. This book forces the reader to take seriously the possibility of the pervasive nature of evil in a postmodern world. In the depth of its theological grounding, *Job of Arc* is also appropriate for professionals who work with pedophiles – and for the abusers themselves."

Rev. Peggy A. Way, Ph.D. *Pastoral Care and Counseling*

"This is not just a story for non-offending parents. This is a story for women who just can't 'like' their ex-husbands, for men who despise their bosses, and for people who hate the way southerners drive south of DC on I-95. This is an important story."

Elizabeth Wilson Jack *Critic*

"The thing I fear most has happened to me,
And whatever I dread comes true.
For me there is neither peace nor quiet;
I cannot find rest, for trouble has come."

Job 3:25-26

Job of Arc

Reflections on Pedophilia
& Intergenerational Abuse
Their Effects & Our Response

Sophia Ruah

HUMMINGBIRD & HERON, NASHVILLE, TENNESSEE

ISBN 978-1-935271-13-0

April 2009
Cover Photograph by Victoria Alexandrova, http://vikavalter.com
Foreword by Martha Whitmore Hickman
Question Generation by Nathan Eubank
Edited by Tracy Lucas at Four Square Creative
The author gratefully acknowledges permission to use quotes from: John Brogden,
B. Lynn Heil, Martha Whitmore Hickman, Elizabeth Wilson Jack, Jill S. Levenson,
Syracuse Cultural Workers "Tools for Change" @ www.SyracuseCulturalWorkers.com,
Peggy A. Way, Susan Ford Wiltshire, and Jay D. Woodman.

Printed in the United States of America on acid-free paper.

HUMMINGBIRD & HERON
P.O. Box 210183
Nashville, Tennessee 37221

"If we could read
the secret history of our enemies,
we should find in each one's life
sorrow and suffering enough
to disarm all hostilities."

Attributed to
HENRY WADSWORTH LONGFELLOW

In Loving Memory

of

Laura

Thank You

To
Martha
Almost Mother

To
Edward
For giving me reason to write

To
Bridgett
For speaking the words that got me started

To
Deborah and Doc
For helping me stay alive long enough to finish

To
Al, Bev, Craig and Laura
For counting me among the widows and orphans

To
Lora, Stonewall, and Susan
For encouraging me to persevere

To
Betsy, Jeff, and Jim
For proffering fitting words at perfect times

To
Paula and Tracy
For making last year fun

And to
Peggy
Mentor and Friend

CONTENTS

PROLOGUE

In the spring of 2005, our family's psychologist suggested I write letters for two of my sons to have after my death. Conner's letter turned into a book of "his stories" that he had asked me to write for his graduation present from high school. Edward's letter took the form of an explanation for my anticipated suicide. I wanted him to understand that none of what had happened, or was about to happen, was his fault.

By Holy Week, Edward's letter had grown to thirty-five pages in length. Then, within days of each other, two things happened. My mother said that if I was going to write a book, I had better get busy and do it, and my daughter, Bridgett, made a comment that clearly was the title of something. All the title needed was a book to go along with it.

It was on Easter morning, then, that I began to type this chronicle; Edward's letter became *Revelations,* the second section of this book. The chapters of *Revelations* which tell the story as it occurred are written in the present tense. The chapters which precede and follow the ones in present tense, *Background* and *Afterwards,* were added later in response to numerous requests that I explain how arrived at the point in my life that I came to marry Jack, and what happened after the story ended. Both those sections were recorded subsequent to the events they describe, and as a result are written in the past tense.

The passages in italics found at the beginning of each section (*Job, Trouble Comes, The Goddess,* and *Wisdom*) are my own version of parallel passages found in the biblical book of Job. They reveal both similarities and differences between his life and time and my own, between women's lives and men's. The Glossary in the Study Guide contains a variety of terms that may be unfamiliar to some readers. Those words are denoted by an asterisk (*) upon their first occurrence in the text.

At my children's request, our names and identifying information have been changed. Other than that, the events described, though greatly truncated, are true.

FOREWORD

This is not a book for the faint-hearted. It is, in many ways, a
love story, but it is heavy going. A woman in midlife has two
marriages behind her and a son by her first marriage, and has under
the auspices of a state Department of Children's Services taken,
cared for, and sent back into the world a procession of hard-to-
place children. She has dreams of fostering a continuing parade of
such children and has three already adopted, whom she loves when,
against all expectation ("Two failed marriages is enough.") she
meets and falls in love with a bright, attractive, compassionate man
who is in charge of a store that sells recyclable building materials.
He has been married, has a foster son. They share their dreams –
to parent many abused children. They marry; she is blissfully happy
until one day in church, he informs the congregation that he has a
long-time history of being a child molester. Everyone is duly
shocked, except his wife, to whom he revealed his story after one of
her adopted sons told her he had seen his dad engaging in
inappropriate behavior with a younger brother.

Her confidence in her husband, and in herself, is shattered.
The lives of the other two boys she has adopted are thrown into
disruption, and in various ways they act out their anger and fear –
they love their Dad and now what?

"Now what" takes many pages of harrowing description of
legal and personal maneuvers with the Department of Children's
Services, and with officials of the church she has loved and for
which she is an ordained part-time minister, which turned against
her. How can she keep her faith intact and be the mother her
boys need – getting them continuing psychiatric care and caring
for herself as well? When I asked her if she couldn't omit some of
the run-ins with agencies she said, "For every upsetting episode I
included I left two others out."

"Please, forget the suggestion," I murmured.

But if the constant episodes of disturbed children and inept
bureaucracies gets you down, here is another suggestion: if you
have had all the gloom and doom you can stand, including the
detailed plan of this gifted and loving mother to carry out – as a

kindness to those she would leave behind and because she has had all the doom and gloom she herself can stand – the best scenario to kill herself, when you have read more than enough about violated safety plans and untenable treatment plans than you can stand, take a leap, skip about one hundred pages, and go to the beginning of Part 3. Prepare to read there some of the most heartening Good News pages – about honoring your own Truth, about signs of Grace and daily Manna from Heaven that change the way the wind blows, about her own experience of The Goddess, where her story fits into the journey of Job, how she came to believe, as her own personal good news, that she was in fact lovable, and that the man she calls Jack loved her as much as he, with his own experience of child abuse, was able – as we who have loved her and grieved with her already knew. We hope with her and with her children who have already experienced their own lives as transformed – for a truly fulfilled life, not, alas, with Jack, whom we have also grown to love and who is trying to accept his life out of his past, but who knows who may yet enter her life with matching dreams, and with courage and persistence and love enough to encircle the world?

MARTHA WHITMORE HICKMAN
AUTHOR OF *Healing After Loss*
FEBRUARY 7, 2006

In the Beginning...

♦ ♦ ♦

"The story of your life, Sophia, is
the feminization of Job."

BRIDGETT
Personal Communication

♦ ♦ ♦

JOB

There once was a woman who lived in the land of Gaia, and her name was Job. While all who knew her agreed that her judgment tended to err on the side of Grace and Love, making her by no means blameless for the things that followed, she had lived her life trying to be faithful to her calling and her God. And by birth, or adoption, or fostering, or marriage, seven sons and three daughters had been mothered by her.

Also in her possession were five horses, six dogs, twenty-three hens and two roosters, one jack and two she-donkeys, and a barn full of cats. She had a car that ran most of the time, a postage-stamp farm with a miniscule farmhouse, and a job in town to help pay for them. She had friends she valued above money, but lived from paycheck to paycheck. All these things added up together made her, like most women, not very great or powerful at all in the eyes of the world. She could have been any woman, anywhere, at any time.

This is her story.

CHAPTER ONE

The Man of My Dreams

I never thought it would happen to me. Not that I thought it wouldn't, you understand. I didn't think I was special, or blessed, or deserved to be spared misfortune. I just never thought it would. It was kind of like not thinking you're going to run out of gas. If you thought about it, you'd plan ahead. You'd stop at the next exit and fill up the tank. You'd even stop at the anytime teller if you needed to. It's when you *don't* think about things that you run into trouble. I had not even considered it as a possibility, so when it happened, I was completely unprepared.

Even Bridgett, who had known me for years, was taken aback. When I told her, she sat down, stunned. "Your husband, Jack? Your *husband*, Jack? But, you don't trust anybody. If it could happen to you, it could happen to *anyone!*" And she was right. It could happen to you.

◆ ◆ ◆

Other than the innate lack of trust Bridgett was referring to (my deep and abiding conviction that we are, all of us, capable of evil and are therefore deserving of at least a little suspicion and caution), I am, in most respects, just like everyone else in the world. When I go, I hope to leave the world a better place than it was when I arrived. I have dreams and fears, as do you. Like other people you know, the circumstances of my life that make me different from you are less important than the universalities we share in common. Commonalities as well as differences abound.

As is true for many of the people of the world, I was born and grew up in a small town; in my case this was the county seat of a county so sparsely populated that its entire population would fit into the football stadium closest to where I live now – seven times. Like most people, I had parents, siblings, grandparents, cousins, aunts, and uncles. I was loved by some members of my family, tolerated by others, and outright disliked by a few. I got into trouble now and then, was sure that I was misunderstood, and probably was. I was, in most ways, like most people. My most significant difference from others was that unlike almost everyone else I knew, I had an easier time with schoolwork than my classmates. I didn't acclimate to public education well (by first grade I was already so hard-headed I had to stand in the corner for refusing to print when I already knew how to write in cursive), and it didn't help my socialization any when my first grade teacher decided I needed to skip ahead a couple of grades so that I was two years younger than everyone else in my class. Much of the time, I was sad and lonely. Trees and books became my very best friends.

By the time I was seven years old, I was in the fourth grade and had read every Charles Dickens novel our library possessed. He was my favorite author until my teacher assigned Madeline L'Engle's newly published *Wrinkle in Time*. In her bright young outcast Charles Wallace I found someone I could relate to even more easily than I identified with Dickens' succession of miserable waifs. Later that year, a school vision screening revealed that it was no wonder I lived through the books that I read, since I could not see much farther than the pages of the book you hold now in your hands.

It was also as a result of that vision screening that I discovered most people do not see two of everything. Since I had always seen that way, I just assumed everyone did – we do, after all, have two eyes – and kids only know what they experience and what they're told. It's not the sort of thing that comes up in casual conversation ("And how many of everything do *you* see?"), so it never occurred to me to think that my experience was anything other than normal. My vision was for the first time corrected from its natural state, and I walked out of the optometrist's office amazed to discover that it was possible to see individual leaves on trees. A whole new world opened up before my 20/450 eyes.

My seventh year was also the year I started singing in the church choir and became aware of what I believed to be a call into the ministry. It was a year in which my life shifted on its axis. Though I had started reading on one side of the local library with the goal of reading all the way across the room, after I finished L'Engle's books, my reading interests shifted to the sections on mathematics, science fiction, religion, and philosophy. I was too young to understand a lot of what I read, but I kept reading anyway. In a larger city I might not have been so unusual, but in our tiny community it would be fair to say that as children go, I was odd.

By the time I reached high school, the band had become my primary social outlet. A year after graduation, a member of the trumpet section asked me to marry him, and I accepted. I was seventeen and beginning my second year in college; he was eighteen. It was a difficult marriage, as young marriages often are. Three years later, four months pregnant and a senior in college, I finally realized that my husband was addicted to cocaine and marijuana. That explained a great deal, most notably where all the money was going, and why sometimes he thought I was the greatest thing to walk the earth, but minutes later despised me entirely. After he destroyed the contents of our house during my sixth month of pregnancy and I knew my prenatal child and I were in danger, I fled. I stayed in hiding until after my son John was born. When he was six months old, my first husband and I were divorced. I was twenty-one.

The second time I married, just over two years after my first marriage ended, my choice was an old family friend. Though I had known him since I was a child, I had never witnessed one of his rages until we were driving towards the hotel where we were to spend our honeymoon night. I was terror stricken, but had just said "till death do us part" for the second time, and at the age of twenty-three, I didn't know what an annulment was. I hung in there in that marriage until six years later, when my two stepsons, who lived with us, were finally old enough to drive. When an ulcer perforated and my blood pressure skyrocketed, my friends were afraid I was going to die if I did not get out. So was I.

By the time that marriage failed, I had given up on relationships altogether. Twice, I had married men who were abusive in one way or another. Twice, I had chosen partners who continued the dynamics of my relationship with my own birth father, who died when I was twelve. (Thirty-eight years after his death, I am contending still with his legacy of Posttraumatic Stress Disorder* with its recurrent nightmares and depression that often lead to suicidal ideation.) Twice, I had chosen badly and was unable to fulfill my commitments. I took my word and my faith seriously, and I wasn't going to risk saying "till death do us part" another time. Determined never to make the same mistake again, I resolved not to marry for a third time.

For the next sixteen years, I was faithful to that decision. When I was ordained into the ministry in the summer of 1987, I was bound by an ordination vow of "celibacy in singleness and fidelity in marriage," (my denomination's way of excluding gays and lesbians from ordination without having to come right out and state their intention) and within a few months I read that every cell in the human body regenerates over a seven-year span. I decided I wanted that symbolic new start. I had been bouncing for years from one relationship to the next, seemingly more out of a reaction to my past than by choice. I wanted a clean break with what went before, and a chance to start over. I dedicated myself to becoming a new person, faithful to my vow. If I could be faithful for just seven years, I would have the chance for a new beginning. Then, if I ever again chose to give myself to someone, it would be in a renewed body, unadulterated by my past.

By the time the Christmas holidays arrived, the nightmares I had been having since childhood had increased, both in intensity and in frequency, until on December 23, 1987, for the first time the images I saw even intruded on my waking hours. Initially, I believed I was hallucinating, and was overwhelmed with despair. At the time, I was doing a clinical pastoral education * (CPE) internship as a chaplain at the VA Hospital, and was serving part time as the pastor of a local church. I didn't know why I felt so bad. I even felt bad about feeling bad. Finally, one of the CPE supervisors asked me, "Why are you so ashamed of your feelings? Don't you realize you came by them honestly?" I was shocked. The possibility that *anything* wasn't my fault had never occurred to me, because I thought I was responsible for *everything*. Driven into therapy by the need to prevail over my depression so I could stay alive until John reached adulthood, I began to face the demons that lived within my mind.

In some ways, it is unfortunate that real life is not like a movie. You can't hit "replay" over and over until everyone involved agrees on seeing the same thing. Members of my immediate family do not have the same memories I do and, like so many whose lives have been touched by abuse in one way or another, I found that my story was not believed by those I needed to believe it the most. Even the parts that others did remember were different in their eyes. "You're always making such a big deal out of everything," my brother said when I asked him about it later. "And besides, you've got it all wrong. He didn't beat us every day, he beat us *twice* a day, and it wasn't anything like you're making it out to be. It was okay, because we were bad and we deserved it."

I couldn't figure out what small children could have possibly done to deserve the punishment I remembered, and would hear my father's voice in my memory joking with his friends. "My motto is 'whip your children every day,'" he would say. "If *you* don't know the reason why, *they* do," and everyone would laugh. They probably thought he was kidding. I thought they knew he was telling the truth.

The problem was that there were many days when I did *not* know what I had done, and trying to figure it out was driving me crazy. "Please, help me be a good girl," I would pray. "I just want to be a good girl." But I was never good enough. And those were just the things that went on in the light, things he did not try to hide. After dark, the sexual abuse would begin.

I struggled to understand if what I thought had happened was true, why no one had stopped it. I wrestled with what I had done to deserve what happened to me. I must have been bad. It must have been my fault, and I deserved to be punished. Because of his threats that I would be killed if I told, I feared that since I had told, my death was imminent. As a child, I had every reason to believe that my father would, in fact, carry out his threat. As an adult, I grappled with the fear that I had totally lost my sanity, because my underlying belief was that if what I kept reliving in my mind had actually happened, I would be dead. Since I had told and hadn't died yet, I must be crazy. Or if it was true, then since I had disobeyed the prohibition about telling, but was still alive, I was certain that I needed to kill myself before anyone else could get to me and do something even worse. I had been trained to self-destruct rather than tell the secret. I believed the only way to be safe from what was sure to come was to be dead.

I tried to put together the picture of how the abuse could have gone on unchecked for so long. My father controlled everything about our lives, keeping us almost completely isolated. He had a job that allowed him to be with us virtually twenty-four hours a day, year round. Friendships were discouraged. Individuality was forbidden. He even controlled what we ate and drank, putting the food on our plates from the head of the table. No matter what it was or in what quantity, we were compelled to eat it. On "television night," our once-weekly ritual, he popped the popcorn, poured the drinks, and gave one to each child and to my mother. Every week, before she finished half of hers, my mother would fall asleep so soundly that my father would have to pick her up and carry her off to bed. There is no way I can ever prove my theory that he was drugging her, but while my mother slept, my father was free to do whatever he wanted. So were his friends, one of whom was the man who would become my stepfather.

Within months of my father's death from a heart attack when I was twelve, the friend's wife died of cancer. Shortly afterwards, the two surviving spouses married. My stepfather stepped in right where my own father left off. Only after he married my mother did he reveal himself to her for who he truly was. It turned out his first wife had not been as "clumsy" as everyone thought. Her broken arms and bruises were the result of his beatings. When my mother was at home during their marriage, he would beat her up, too. Frequently, my mother's job took her away, and during those times, my stepfather's physical abuse was not all I suffered while thinking I was protecting my younger siblings. He told me he would leave the others alone if I would do whatever he wanted, so I did. For over thirty years, I have had nightmares of his rapes. Eventually, I learned my submission was futile; my stepfather lied. He didn't leave them alone at all.

Finally, one night he attacked my mother one too many times. As the oldest child home, I called the police and had him arrested. He was taken from the jail to a psychiatric hospital, where he was diagnosed as paranoid schizophrenic*. Shortly afterwards, he and my mother were divorced. One day he went to the elementary school, picked up his children, my stepbrother and stepsister, and took them to another state. I never even got a chance to say goodbye. Knowing I was powerless to protect them ever again, I grieved as though I had lost my own children. Years later my stepbrother told me I had been right to grieve. He and his sister were both raped and beaten for years, until he finally grew so tall and strong that one night when his father came to him, he was able to strike a blow hard enough to knock his father out. Only after that did his father finally leave them alone.

I was in college before my stepfather finally died. He literally drank himself to death. When I heard of his passing, I was sorry – not that he had died, but that I had not gotten to see him cold and dead on the slab. I wanted confirmation that it was over. I wanted to *know* he was dead. He is the only person I have ever known who invaded my body space merely by being alive.

Eventually my mother remarried – this time to a wonderful and gentle man – and I talked to her about the things I remembered regarding her first and second husbands. Her initial reaction was everything I could have hoped for. She said that she was sorry, that she had never known. She told me that when she was a child she had also had her trust betrayed, though not by an immediate family member. She said she, too, had never told a soul. I felt affirmed. I believed that if she had known, she would have protected me. The feeling did not last long. Within days she called me back, having talked to my brother and sister in the meantime. My brother, who had already left home before my mother married for the second time, had told her he did not believe that anything had happened to me; he thought if something *had* happened, I would have told him so at the time. My sister had told my mother that she didn't remember anything happening either, though she did offer to go into counseling to see if any memories arose. The catch was that she wanted me to promise on the front end that I would not be angry with our mother if she remembered that anything bad had happened to her. It was a promise I would not make; I could not give that guarantee. And in retrospect, my mother added, she thought that what her abuser had done to her wasn't really all that bad, either. She did have a crush on him at the time, after all.

It was as though our history, my mother's and mine, was rewritten over a weekend, and my relationship with my biological siblings has never been the same again. Looking for confirmation, I went to see my younger stepbrother. I asked if he remembered anything. "You were my hero," he answered. "You took everyone else's blows for them." I asked about one incident in particular that troubled me, which involved both our fathers at the same time. "I've spent my whole life trying to forget," was his reply. Living with me, he said, was the happiest time of his life, because he knew I would protect him. I felt sad that I could not say the same. Living with his father was not the happiest time of mine.

As I struggled with all these things in therapy, my mother went to see my doctor. He was convinced after talking to her that she had never known what had happened to me. Still, even after talking to him she did not believe me, though she did say that she was confused as to why I would lie about these things when I had never lied about anything else. She even said to me, "It would take less time for him to treat you for abuse than to convince you that it had never happened." In spite of the fact that my father emotionally abused her so severely that she, too, has nightmares about him still, she insisted that my father, at least, "would never have done those things to [me], because he loved [me]." Though we were all intimidated and bullied by him, no one in the family dared speak badly about him, even thirty years after his death. That I did made me an embarrassment and a disgrace.

I kept on in therapy, and my life took on a new purpose: to make sure that the things that happened to me as a child did not happen to anyone else. I may have learned as a child that I was helpless and powerless to protect myself, but as an adult I was *not* powerless to protect others. I realized that I kept living over and over again what had happened to me in my childhood, and that I kept choosing partners who were like the men I had grown up with. They felt familiar to me, "comfortable" in a way I couldn't explain. Somehow, it seemed I kept trying to resolve my old unfinished business by going through it time after time. *This time*, it will be different. *This time*, I will be able to make it work. It was as though the feelings I experienced around men who abused were old friends whose presence I equated with love.

If I couldn't do anything to change my own past, I could at least do something to change another child's present and future. I wasn't sure how to make a better choice in a life partner, but I knew I could make no choice. I could live alone and care for other children who had been abused. My friend Deborah, who is a forensic interviewer at one of the Child Advocacy Centers, tells me that frequently, no matter how horrible their abuse was, children answer the question, "What was the worst thing that happened?" by saying "My mom didn't believe me," or "My mother did not do anything to protect me." I was not going to make the same mistake. I was determined that if children told me they were being hurt, then I would put a stop to it. I would believe them. I was going to do it right. Though I could not keep every child from being wounded, I resolved to protect as many as I physically could. I put a poster printed by the Syracuse Cultural Workers above my desk: "Always hold firmly to the thought that each one of us can do something to bring some portion of misery to an end."[1] That thought was my comfort and my goal. I couldn't do everything, but I could do something. I lived by it.

As the years went by, so did many children. Three foster daughters, Lucy, Bridgett, and Letta, came and went and then frequently came and went again. I adopted my youngest three sons, Edward, Ben, and Connor, all of whom had special needs*. A couple of years after I adopted Edward, he was diagnosed with a lethal, hereditary kidney disease. The diagnosis meant my youngest son, who had lived to play football, could never play any contact sport again. Although on the outside Edward looks like a normal kid, the frailty of his kidneys has affected every aspect of his life and psyche ever since his diagnosis. Since he also suffers from severe Attention Deficit Hyperactivity Disorder* (emphasis on hyperactive) as well as Obsessive-Compulsive Disorder* (emphasis on drives-me-crazy), his doctor and I hoped to get him to fixate on eating the right things, for his kidneys' sake. So far, it hasn't worked. For the first couple of years after we found out he had polycystic kidneys*, he literally didn't grow an inch. Then, he shot up to be tall and thin, blond-haired and blue-eyed.

Edward's older biological brother, Ben, who has a multitude of psychiatric difficulties, grew to be even taller and thinner, with noticeably lighter blond hair and deeper blue eyes. Ben's emotional disturbance is so severe that by the time he was eight and Edward was six, the two of them had been placed for adoption five times. Unfortunately, the longest any adoptive family had been willing to keep them both was two weeks. Several placements had wanted to keep Edward; none of them was willing to keep Ben. This was due in large part to Ben's violent expressions of a psychiatric diagnosis that was not (by any stretch of the imagination) his own fault.

Ben's primary diagnosis was Reactive Attachment Disorder*, a form of Posttraumatic Stress Disorder that develops in the first eighteen months of life. As a reaction to things that happened to him during his infancy he never developed the ability to attach to others (or in his case, even to things), and therefore he never developed much of a conscience. He could be physically violent to anything or anyone with no apparent guilt or shame ("Okay, Ben, you're on time out. You cannot hit Edward." "I can hit him if I want to; he's MY brother."), as easily as he could tell a lie, which he did with an absolutely straight face ("How can you tell if Ben is lying?" "His lips are moving," we would joke). Because children like Ben lack the ability to identify with how their actions affect others, Reactive Attachment Disorder with its related Conduct Disorder* in children almost always leads to being a Sociopath* in later life.

Edward had always tried to be the "good boy" in an attempt to minimize the consequences he suffered from Ben's behavior, but no matter how good Edward tried to be, no one human could have been good enough to compensate for Ben's violence towards his caregivers. Edward's attempts to be perceived as the "good one" ranged from trying to anticipate whatever an adult might want and offering to do it before he was even asked, to interactions such as this one:

"Mom, Ben hit me!"

"Edward, I was watching you. He did not hit you."

"He almost did!"

"Edward, what are you talking about? He wasn't even close to you."

"Well, HE WAS THINKING ABOUT IT!"

And Edward was probably right. It was fairly typical of Ben to spend time plotting how to get away with hurting his brother and caregivers. At one point, he even took to hitting Edward in the head, because he figured out if he did that, he wouldn't have to worry about Edward's kidneys, Edward's hair would hide the bruises, and he knew Edward was too afraid of him to tell. If Ben had not bragged to his teacher about how clever he was, we might have never found out.

Conner, older than the other two, had been adopted several years before they came along.   He suffers from severe Posttraumatic Stress Disorder, Intermittent Explosive Disorder* (which looks to an outsider as though periodically his wiring gets crossed and shorts out, and he uncontrollably explodes with anger that is not in proportion to the precipitating events), and has a functional level of about seven and a half years old.   Although I have never known him purposely to tell a lie – ever – he will tell you in a heartbeat, "I'm not talking about that."   He frequently misunderstands or misinterprets data.   Anything that has ever happened once "happens all the time."   For example, one year at Christmas, he got sick.   Since then, he has insisted every year that he "always gets sick at Christmas."   Pointing out years in which that did not happen makes no difference, because once, of course, it did.

Although his appearance does not immediately divulge his cognitive difficulties, Conner will likely remain for the rest of his life in the stage of "concrete operations," which is just a fancy way of saying that his thinking is, for all practical purposes, set in concrete.   For Conner *every* activity is concretely right or wrong. There are no shades of gray in his thinking.   There are no instances in which something might be the right thing to do in one circumstance but not in another.   This meant that once he got to high school, days off from school became a major crisis.   He insisted that any day either he or his brothers did not have school should be a day off for everyone.   It was completely beyond his ability to understand that if he had one day off, Ben and Edward would have a different day off.   Since the calendar was set by the school board, everyone had the same total number of days, but Conner never understood.   It wasn't fair for him to have the day off if his brothers did not, and he wouldn't stand for it.

Though Conner is not biologically related to Ben and Edward, he has, for the large part, loved being their big brother.   And though they are now taller, big he is.   When he first arrived, Conner was a tiny boy with failure to thrive*, and he hardly grew for years.   When he started taking meds that made it possible for him to better control his impulsive behavior, they had the side effect of making him gain weight until he weighed more than his two brothers combined.   With a Native American grandmother, his short, thick stature and dark hair, eyes, and skin make him stand out from his brothers.

All three of these young men, the youngest of my children, were adopted with "adoption assistance*" contracts. These contracts between adoptive parents and the state promise that, in return for the adoptive parent taking on the responsibility inherent in parenting the child considered "hard to place*," the state guarantees payment for any expense related to conditions that existed prior to the adoption – up to and including 365 days of hospitalization per year. The catch is, these expenses must be anticipated and specifically written into the contract prior to the adoption being finalized. For us, that means that Edward's kidney disease, which clearly existed before the adoption since it is hereditary, is still not a covered expense. Because we did not know he had it at the time of his adoption, we did not know to write the transplant he will need into his contract. The idea is that the state will cover any condition you adopt the children "in spite of." Conditions you find out about later are not included because *any* parent might find out his or her own birth children have exceptional needs after the birth. In theory, these contracts make it possible for people like me, who are willing to adopt difficult children but have no way to pay their considerable expenses, to provide permanent homes for children who might otherwise spend their lives languishing in foster care*.

Over the years, the older children grew up, got jobs, left home, and took off to college. Snow-loving John, five years Conner's senior and a short young man with light brown hair like mine, went to college in Montana and became a member of the Western Buddhist Order. After graduation, he moved to England to live a semi-monastic life there. Andrew and James, John's older Nordic stepbrothers, went to college in California and North Carolina and afterward became an artist and a computer wiz, respectively.

Next older was Letta, who came to live with me when she aged out* of the foster care system with nowhere to go. One of the counselors working with her knew me, and called to ask if I would take her in. At the time of the call Conner was the only one living at home, so I had beds available. Of course, I said yes. Letta, too, had been tragically abused, and suffered from one of the most extreme forms of Posttraumatic Stress Disorder: she had been diagnosed as having developed multiple personalities, each of which experienced part of her abuse. (Originally called Multiple Personality Disorder*, this diagnosis is now known as Dissociative Identity Disorder.) Letta was, I have to tell you, a lot of fun to live with; she was, to say the least, unpredictable.   Conner especially was crazy about her. With black hair and beautiful deep brown eyes and skin, she eventually went west to Utah and got a job she loved, working as a nanny.

Bridgett had preceded Letta, having come to stay with us while I was working at the high school she attended. Though before I met her she had been diagnosed as schizophrenic* with psychotic episodes, it did not take long before I realized that what she was experiencing were actually flashbacks of being abused by a neighbor years before. It was a much more hopeful diagnosis. One day, she showed up in my office with a packed bag, saying, "Can I leave this here during school today? I'm never going home again, but if you have to tell, I'll understand." She was wrong. She wasn't understanding at all when I called her folks and arranged for her to be admitted for drug treatment. When she came out of rehab, her parents were not prepared for her to return home, and she came to live with me. Even shorter than I am, she is brilliant and kind, and has naturally curly blond hair that changes colors with her moods. Bridgett eventually went to college in Tennessee, had a little boy of her own, and became a nurse.

Lucy was my first foster child, and is the oldest of all my children, tall and thin with dark brown hair. She came to live with me when she was in the eighth grade, and John was just eighteen months old. When I was asked to take her, I was told, "We have a mentally retarded, behaviorally disordered, sexually active fourteen-year-old, and no other foster home in the county will take her. We think you'd be perfect for her." It was only later that they told me they needed a home for her right away because her mother had a gun and was threatening to kill her. Though she has come and gone from my home several times over the years, she has never moved very far away. Since reaching adulthood, Lucy has been able to support herself using her considerable skills as a "maintenance man," and I've decided anyone who can fix my car, my appliances, and do her own taxes has *at least* average intelligence.   She calls if she needs anything. When she married, she even asked Edward to be her best man.

There was a twenty-four year span between the ages of Edward and Lucy.   Thus, our family was comprised of such a variety of shapes, sizes, races, and ages that we could easily have posed for a Norman Rockwell cross-sectional portrait of Americana.   We didn't have a lot of money, but somehow we always got by. Everything I did was an effort to be faithful to what I understood my calling to be, as a pastor, as a counselor, as a mother. My goal was never to do anything I would be ashamed for my children to know about, and never to lie to them if I did.

Almost exactly seven years after my ordination, I went out to lunch with a friend a few times, and during that time, I had a series of dreams. In the first one, I dreamed I was getting married to a man in a wheelchair, in a tent, in a backyard. My impression was that the man had a broken leg, though I wasn't sure. The dream was so vivid that when I awoke, sobbing with joy at being truly happy for the first time in my life, I knew in great detail every aspect of the house, the backyard, and my wedding dress. I had never seen such a dress, but I knew it.

Later that week, I was driving through town when I saw a sign in the window of a store I had never been in because it looked expensive. The sign said, "Going Out Of Business - 90% Off." I figured at a discount like that, even I could look. When I went in, the store was almost empty, but one of the few things they had left was the dress. It wasn't a wedding dress, but it was THE dress. They had only one. It was my size. At 90% off, it was just under a hundred dollars, and I bought it, even though I couldn't really justify spending that much money. I decided I would keep it, and that hanging in my closet, it would be my hope chest. It would give me hope to remember that once I had a dream that someday, I would be happy.

After several more dreams like that in the next week or so, I had the last dream in the series. In the final dream, I was given a choice. Like the biblical Jacob at the end of his first seven years working for Rachel, I had spent the previous seven years working (in my case, mostly in therapy) on the legacy of terror in my mind. In this last dream, I was presented with the option of marrying the friend I had enjoyed lunch with a few times, or waiting seven additional years for someone else. If I made the choice to marry then, I was to understand that while it would not be bad, it would be like Jacob and Leah – tolerable, and close to what I wanted, but not quite what I was looking for. Or, I could wait and work another seven years until my real match came along. I thought it was a bizarre dream, since my friend and I weren't even really dating at the time, but then one day he took me to look at a house he was thinking about buying. It was the house. THE house, from the dream. The backyard was the same. The house, all the way down to the laundry room, was the same. I was stunned, at a loss as to what to think, but I kept holding on to the dreams. My friend and I did not see as much of each other after that, but the hope kept me going.

Four more years into the fourteen, my house was hit by a tornado, "an act of God," as they say. The kitchen in back of the house was destroyed. The torrential rains that followed the tornado washed my backyard into a mudslide that flooded the room, while the rain itself drenched the appliances and cabinets after the roof caved in. Byron, my insurance agent, explained I would actually have been better off financially if the appliances had shorted out and started a fire. In that case, they would have been replaced, because I did have fire coverage. Unfortunately, since I did not live in a flood plain, I did not have coverage for water damage. That meant my coverage would not be sufficient to replace all of my appliances or cabinets. In addition, it turned out that the roof on that part of the house was substandard. It took all the money from the insurance settlement just to bring the roof up to current codes, leaving me almost nothing with which to rebuild the interior of my kitchen. There was some federal disaster money I could use, but that was not enough to cover it either.

As a result, I started going to a place called "Reduce! Reuse! Recycle!" slowly picking up one thing at a time to rebuild the interior of the kitchen. It was essentially a more-or-less organized collection of junk that would have otherwise ended up in the dump, and the items were priced so low that even the poorest of the city's residents could afford them. A good-hearted recycler had started the non-profit organization over a decade before, and it had mutated and moved several times over the years it had been in existence.

To get to its current location, customers had to drive through one of the worst housing projects in the city. Drug dealers would try to flag cars down, often standing in front of moving vehicles in an attempt to gain their business. Eventually, I mastered the art of never looking directly at any of them and driving slowly but steadily forward, leaving time for the dealers to get out of the road.

Once customers got to Reduce! Reuse! Recycle!, they had to wind their way through the maze of charred mobile home carcasses that preceded the gate, then pass through eight feet of chain link topped by razor and barbed wire. Inside the gate, a myriad of appliances, building materials, and anything else that could be salvaged attacked your eyes. The collection was loosely organized: carpet, windows and countertops in an outside shed. Showers, tubs and toilets in the yard. Sinks on racks. Doors and cabinets in a row of mobile homes so decrepit shoppers constantly feared the possibility of falling through the floor. Hardware and paint were in the only building with heat, which also housed the offices. The guard dog was ferocious. The only person who could approach him was the guy who ran the place, and it was clear from the dog's behavior that this man was the love of his life. He lived for that man, and would have died for him.

Slowly, very slowly, I began to see why. I really liked "The Reduce! Reuse! Recycle! Guy," as he was called by customers and employees alike. He was tall and striking in appearance. Completely bald but sporting a black goatee, he towered more than a foot above the top of my head, his dark good looks in sharp contrast to my fair complexion and waist-length, graying hair. He was witty and intelligent, with an explosive and contagious laugh that would roll around like thunder in the distance until it finally erupted from deep within his chest. He was from an esteemed and wealthy family and had worked for several years as an architect, but he had given it all up to run this place. Making it run well was his passion. He was respected by his court-ordered community service workers*, and was well-liked by all. He ran a non-profit that I believed was a very good cause, and since I had worked for non-profits and good causes for most of my life, we found we had much in common. At first, I loved talking to him about those causes and buildings and faith, but eventually I discovered I loved talking to him about anything at all.

Sometimes, I would find myself dragging the kids there even when we didn't really need anything in particular.   My three youngest boys, the last ones left at home, also liked The Reduce! Reuse! Recycle! Guy, and thought it was hilarious that he always referred to me as his girlfriend.   "Be nice to her," he would say to the community service workers who worked there.   "She's my girlfriend."   He gave them instructions that no one else was to wait on me, and would be annoyed on those occasions when he found out that one or another of them, meaning well, had done so.

After the September 11, 2001 planes crashed into their targets, my feeling that life is tenuous at best was exacerbated, and I decided that taking greater risks was in order.   I was also beginning to be aware of the fact that my fourteen years of celibacy would be up in mid-November.   Amazed at my own bravado, I asked one of the Reduce! Reuse! Recycle! employees one day, "Is he married?"

The answer was, "No."

"Is he straight?"

The answer was, "Yes."

"Is he dating anyone?"

The answer was, "I don't think he is right now."

"Do you think he would go out with me if I asked?"

The answer was, "ASK HIM!"

On October 30th of that year, when The Reduce! Reuse! Recycle! Guy told yet another group of community service workers to be nice to me, because I was his girlfriend, I responded for the first time with something other than a grin.   "You've been saying that for three years," I said, "and you've never even asked me out the first time."

"That's because I believe that in this day and age, the woman should ask the man out first," he replied.   "And if you did, I'll tell you what will happen on our first date.   I'll pick out a movie, and you can choose where we go to eat."

"No," I said, "that's not what will happen.   I'LL chose the movie, and YOU can choose where we eat."   And so it was, that since we were both committed for the following night, Halloween, our first date was on the first of November.

By the time Thanksgiving was upon us, I had fallen head over heels for Jack, The Reduce! Reuse! Recycle! Guy. My feelings for him were as much a surprise to me as they were to everyone who knew me – well, "everyone" with the exception of my dog, Ananda, who seemed to be just as happy to see Jack every time as I was. An architect by training, Jack loved buildings and houses just as much as I did. He was a "special-needs" foster parent, as was I. Jack's foster son, Gabriel, was an effervescent young black man with Hemophilia* and AIDS* contracted from a blood transfusion while he was a student in my best friend's kindergarten class some fifteen years before. Neither Gabe nor his dad seemed to think there was anything strange about my unusual family, and when the time came for Gabriel and his fiancé to select the officiant for their wedding, I was honored when they chose me.

Like me, Jack wanted a dozen children altogether, although he didn't want to count in that number the ones I had parented before we met; he wanted a dozen of his own. We shared faith and values. We had met due to an "act of God." It just seemed a match made in heaven. And, in all fairness, I set him up.

"What would you like for Christmas?" I asked one evening, explaining that our family rule was that all Christmas lists had to be turned in by Thanksgiving Day. After that, I explained, nothing on the list could be mentioned again because at its mention, it would be taken off the list. It was a rule I had come up with over twenty years before, because it kept me from going crazy every time one of the kids saw a new toy advertised in the holiday madness, and tried to convince me to buy it. I asked him, knowing that he would almost certainly reciprocate by asking me what I wanted, just to be polite.

"Hmmm. I think I'd like a tri-fold wallet," he replied, "and what would *you* like?" I told him that what I wanted for Christmas was for him to marry me.

We were sitting on the couch in my living room at the time. The fire was going, the reflection of the flames flickering in the stained glass windows. He sat there for a moment. Then, he broke the silence with the words, "I'm not The One. You think that I am The One," he explained, "but I'm not. I am just like John the Baptist, giving you hope and telling you that The One is coming, but it's not me." I was devastated. He assured me that he wasn't involved with anyone else, he wasn't gay, and he had never even looked at another woman during the years he was in his first marriage. He said it wasn't anything about me at all; he just wasn't ready to get married.

I had known it was hasty to ask him. Though Jack and I had known each other for three years, we had only been dating for a few weeks. Still, I was wrestling with the repercussions of my fourteen years of celibacy. In large part because of my past, the sanctity of the marriage bed was extremely important to me. I was falling desperately in love with Jack, but was determined not to violate my ordination vows. Though I was grateful that he was not pressing me to violate my boundaries, my humanity was catching up with me as well. I did not want to be courting; I wanted to be *married*. By the next morning, I was ashamed that I had told him what I wanted, to say nothing of the depth of my hurt. I did not know if I could continue to date him and still remain faithful to my vow. I was wounded by his response to my invitation. I was not sure if I ever wanted to see him again.

At that point, I had not yet told any of my co-workers that I was dating, and now that Jack had said "no," well, I was too embarrassed. But for some reason, that day at work Brenda came up to me. "I don't know what this means," she said. "I don't know what you're thinking about doing. I only know that I am supposed to tell you to go for it." I couldn't believe it. She said it had come to her in prayer, that she was supposed to tell me to "go for it," whatever "it" was. I wasn't sure how to respond, and didn't tell her anything about my dilemma.

The next time I talked to Jack, before I could tell him what Brenda had said, he told me he had gotten the strangest phone call at his work. A pastor who had been in the Reduce! Reuse! Recycle! store to make a donation some months before had called him that day, out of the blue. The pastor said that a message had been "laid on his heart" for Jack. The message he was supposed to give him was, "Walk by faith and not by sight."

"Go for it," Brenda told me. "Walk by faith and not by sight," the pastor said to Jack. I took it as a sign. Even Jack took it as a sign. And so it was that in December, we were married in the home of two friends, a tiny, intimate, simple, beautiful wedding. I wore the dress from the dream. Jack wore the tux his father had worn on the day he married Jack's mother. The best man brought the rings. A friend of mine performed the ceremony. Her husband provided the reception, complete with cake and champagne. My foster daughter, Bridgett, was there, and Jack's foster son, Gabriel, and Jack and I each brought two friends. I could not have asked for anything more wonderful.

In the candlelight that evening, as Jack slipped my wedding dress from my shoulders and it dropped to the floor, I knew that moment was what I had saved myself for all of those fourteen years. From that first wedding night together, the nightmares I had experienced almost every single day since I was a child ceased. Nowhere in my life did I feel more safe than I did in Jack's arms. All it took was his touch to calm me, to soothe my troubled spirit. The despair that had started to lighten in the days I was falling in love with him now lifted altogether.

CHAPTER TWO

Going for Refuge

The next two years, while not by any means what one would consider easy living, were still the happiest of my life. Our first Valentine's Day, 2002, I couldn't have been more content. I awakened to this poem from Jack:

Morning Thoughts

A light, a spark, begins the day
I glance across and hear her say,
"Good morning, Dear!" – a whispered call –
I wake beside my all-in-all.

Such joy, such bliss, my heart swells full,
My soul responds to morning's pull,
A sweet caress, a hug, a kiss,
Drawing close my loving Ms.

Flowing hair and supple skin
Sweetly clothe the girl within
Wise consideration, fun
Flow from my beloved one.

Stimulation, ecstasy
Shared by you to pleasure me.
Rapt conjunctions, truest love,
Blessed by God, The Lord, above.

Happy Valentine's Day! Love, Jack

In my denomination, pastors are appointed to congregations. With the advent of spring I was informed that after a total of twenty-five years at Kellogg's First Church (the last fifteen of which I served with no remuneration as one of the part-time associate pastors), I was to be appointed in the summer of 2002 with pay as the sole part-time pastor of Solid Rock Church, in a small town about thirty miles away. I had been miserable at First Church ever since the current senior pastor had come, and was eager for the first time in many years to try something new.

On my way to look at Solid Rock for the first time, I watched for signs in the neighborhood bearing those precious words, "for sale." I had been looking to get out of the city for years, ever since I moved to town at the end of my second marriage; Sunday afternoons were often spent driving around surrounding counties with the boys, scrutinizing farms for sale. The past six or seven years, we had been looking in earnest. I had several criteria: the farm had to be at the end of a dead end road; it had to have a supply of fresh water; it had to be situated so that there was at least one place on the property where a house could be built so that from the house, nature was all we could see; and it needed to be fenced and cross-fenced, so that we could have farm animals. The last criterion was the only thing negotiable, since fencing could always be done later. And last but not least, if such a property could be found, then somehow I had to be able to afford it.

So it was that I was looking for properties close to the church where I was about to be appointed. Nothing appealed to me on the way to Solid Rock, but instinct and curiosity led me to drive down a one-lane road that branched off from the main road directly across the street from the church's driveway, just to see what was to be found there. Eight-tenths of a mile later, at the very end of the road, was a "for sale" sign. It turned out there had once been a sign at the beginning of the road across from the church, but it had been knocked into a ditch by the mowers. If I hadn't driven down the road, I would never even have seen that the property was available.

The farm had a tiny house, only about a thousand square feet (not counting porches). It had been the honeymoon cottage of a couple who had lived there for all fifty years of their marriage, until they both died in their eighties. The property itself encompassed forty acres. The entrance was from the east, opening into a small valley. Wildflowers I didn't know the names of grew everywhere, and in that first short visit I saw deer, wild turkeys, and hummingbirds zipping through the marsh of cattails where bushes heavy with fragrant, unfamiliar orange blossoms grew. The sweet smell of clean air perfumed by honeysuckle infused me. There was a spring-fed creek that meandered through the valley, gurgling cheerfully between the railroad trestle at the top of the hill along the southern property line and the top of the ridge on the north, while a pump house at another spring sent water coursing towards the cottage. The property ran all the way from hilltop to hilltop, and a symphony performed by chirping crickets, croaking frogs, and singing birds filled the hollow. The western end of the property was bordered by a fence, which was also at the top of a hill. There was a potential house site from which nothing but that piece of property could be seen, and there was a huge storage building. Though it was not fenced or cross-fenced, it met all my other criteria. I called Jack, full of excitement at the possibility. Maybe it could be as good for us as it had been for the couple who had lived there so many years.

The perfect property I had spent years looking for was itself only the vehicle for another part of my dream: a house built in the country where I could provide a home for as many more children as I had beds. I knew from experience that the foster care system was a disaster, and wanted to get as many children out of it as possible. For almost all my adult life I had rotated as many children through my home as I possibly could, and my dream house was large enough to adopt a dozen more. I had designed it and redesigned it in my mind at least a hundred times over that twenty-plus year span, and I had been collecting building materials for it for almost that long as well. I had doors, windows, cabinets, sinks, tubs, toilets (eight of them!), lighting fixtures, and plumbing parts. I had collected so much stuff I hardly had places to store it all.

Jack and I started into negotiations with the sellers, who had already turned down more than one offer of less than their asking price. Even with our combined incomes from my new part-time job at Solid Rock, my full-time job and Jack's, there would still be no way for us to qualify for a loan. I was not at all sure we could pull it off, but Jack promised, "I will work two jobs if we need it – three if I have to. We could finance it for fifteen years. That's not long. We can do *anything* for that long, and then it will be paid off." The deal we offered the sellers was this: we would pay their asking price, if they would provide owner financing. Eventually, they agreed, and a month and a half before my job at Solid Rock was officially to begin, we bought the property at the end of the road. We named it "The Refuge." It would be a refuge for motherless children and young adults. Money would be tight, but together we could make it – as long as nothing went wrong.

The move promised to be monumental. The house on the farm was smaller than either of the houses Jack and I lived in prior to the wedding. As a matter of fact, it was only about a third the size of our two houses combined. In addition, I had a storage building I had been renting to store all the building materials I had been accumulating. All of it had to be moved to the farm.

Prior to the move, I had accepted a new full-time job working as one of the supervisors for the child abuse hotline the state was developing. It was to be a crucial part of the Department of Children's Services* new Statewide Intake Unit. Ever since I had taken home my first foster child, Lucy, over twenty-three years before, I had hated the foster care system with a passion. I was hoping desperately that the fledgling Intake Unit would address some of the things that upset me the most about it. Given my upcoming job change, I decided that what made the most sense was to go ahead and take two months off between jobs to orchestrate the move and to pack. For the entire two months, I did little else. I thought it would never end.

As soon as our move to the new property was complete, we had the wedding ceremony of Jack's dreams. We rented a huge tent, which Jack and the boys set up all by themselves, in the field that would eventually become the livestock paddock. I kept expecting Jack to break a leg before the service, since a groom in a wheelchair had been a part of my dream from seven years before, but he had broken one of his legs about the time I had the dream, so I thought that might explain it. On the day of the wedding, friends came bearing gifts of food for the potluck. Family members came from far and near. Children and grandchildren were in abundance. Many friends read the different parts of the wedding service. Instead of rice, those who loved us threw cupfuls of wild flower seeds. It was a wonderful occasion. As much as I loved the first service, Jack, who desperately wanted a large celebration, loved the second.

Although I had taken two months off to pack our two households and coordinate the move to the new farm, Jack had taken off only two weeks for the move and wedding preparations themselves. Unfortunately, within a week of the wedding, we were both faced with economic surprises. Mine came in the form of a phone call from the district church office. Members of Solid

Rock Church, where I had already started preaching, had written the Bishop with complaints. These ranged from the fact that I preached too much about loving everybody no matter who they were, and not enough about hell, to my favorite complaint, which was that all those children I brought to church had different fathers, and I wasn't married to any of them.

While this was true enough, I had to admit, I thought I should have gotten credit for the fact that they also had different mothers, and I *wasn't* any of them. The rumor, apparently, was that I had adopted my own illegitimate children to cover up for my indiscretions. But the final straw, I was told, was that what they seemed to be saying was that it was bad enough that the Bishop had sent them a woman, but then they had found out I was a Democrat, and they were Republicans, and it just wasn't going to work. Apparently, my being married to a Republican was not enough of an endorsement of my willingness to "sleep with the enemy" to compensate for my party affiliation. So, after buying a farm that we could not begin to afford without the additional income from the church, we found ourselves living in a place that was above our means, and because of the farm's proximity to the church we had to drive by Solid Rock every time we went anywhere. For months afterwards, I cried every time I passed it by and was reminded of what had happened.

Then Jack got his surprise, when he returned to work after the wedding. It turned out that while he was gone, the board had "reorganized" him out of a job. The two weeks he was off had apparently been very busy ones for Reduce! Reuse! Recycle! Although prior to his vacation he had been asked to destroy the agency's financial records (a bizarre request), he suspected foul play, and had not done so. Mysteriously, in his absence, a fire started in the room next to the office where his computer was, but the fire department arrived and put out the fire before it reached the office. After the fire, there was a break-in, and the hard drive from the computer had been stolen. Not the computer itself, just the hard drive. Then, when he got back to work, there was a "thank you for all you've done, but your services are no longer needed" letter on his desk. His severance package, which included "Rhett," the guard dog no one else could handle but who had fortunately come to love his new expanded family, would not last us long. I had no money coming in from the church, and it was going to be a month before I got my first check from my new full-time job.

Jack and I talked at length about what kind of a job it would make sense for him to have. For several years before the wedding, he had been making a minimal salary in order to perform what was essentially a ministry for those he worked with. On the one hand, we desperately needed the money that he had the potential to make as an architect. On the other hand, we also needed him to be nearby to the farm to help out with the kids, and that was a ministry in and of itself. One of the things that had attracted me to him initially was the skill he demonstrated in working with the probationers serving as community service workers at Reduce! Reuse! Recycle! and I wanted my boys to benefit from those gifts as well. We decided that even with all the financial pressure facing us, it was more important that he do the "right" thing than to make more money.

All five of us were stressed out by the move and all the changes, to say nothing of the pressure of being broke. None of us was having an easy time of it. The children were trying to finish up the last couple of weeks of the school year at their old schools thirty miles away, which meant a great deal of daily driving. Conner was about to finish high school, and was already worrying about the changes he was facing. The younger two boys were not looking forward to saying goodbye to all of their friends at their old schools. Jack got a new job doing maintenance at a church camp whose property bordered ours, and was trying to get used to that change as well.

Then one day Conner had a terrible accident. I had adopted him just before he turned ten, by which time he had a multitude of emotional wounds from his childhood that even now have yet to heal. The abuse he suffered while he was in the foster care system was one of the reasons I hated what Children's Services does to children: after being physically tortured, starved, and sexually abused in his birth home, he was then moved *twenty-one times* in the five years he was in the state's custody. The foster parents in many of those homes abused him, as well. What his birth family didn't do to him, "the system" did.

By the time I got him, Conner didn't believe anyone would keep him. Due to the abuse he suffered as a child, which was complicated by his many moves while in the care of the state, he has never trusted anyone he has not known for a long time. All of those factors complicated the results of the accident. Conner, with his limited cognitive ability and Intermittent Explosive Disorder, punched out some windows in frustration, and in the process unintentionally cut through an artery in his arm.

Conner was bleeding profusely, and I was afraid it was likely he would bleed to death before we could get him to a hospital. Because he will not let strangers touch him, I knew we would never be able to get him into an ambulance with people he did not know. Not only that, he was also already legally an adult, and despite the condition he was in, was declaring his intention to refuse treatment of any kind. Out of desperation, Jack and I physically wrestled him into the car. With Jack driving, I sat in the back seat with Conner, trying to keep him in the car, to keep a belt as a tourniquet on his arm, and praying that by the time we got to the hospital, he would be passed out but not yet dead, so that they would be able to work on him. For the entire trip I was terrified, and was greatly relieved when we made it to the hospital without him bleeding to death.

In the aftermath of the accident, we were anguished to discover that our health insurance was not accepted by the county hospital to which we had first taken him. That possibility had never occurred to me. It turned out a feud was going on between the insurance company and a number of regional hospitals. The hospital in our new county was one of those that had refused to buckle. The bill was many thousands of dollars, to say nothing of the cost of the ambulance ride he had taken when he needed to be sedated and transferred from the county hospital to a larger medical center, almost an hour away. That ride, too, was not a covered expense. Since Conner was over the age of twenty-one, he no longer received adoption assistance, and we had no way to pay the bill – on top of the fact that we continued to get further and further behind each month due to the changes in our jobs. I had already declared bankruptcy once when Conner had over $52,000 in uncovered psychiatric hospital bills a number of years before, and it was too soon to do so again. I was at a loss as to what to do. In a generous act of kindness, Kathy, a friend who had known the boys and me for many years, made a gift to us of the money to pay the hospital and ambulance bills and to get caught up again.

Then for a period of time, things slowed down. Jack and I settled into a routine, as did the boys. We all grew to love living on the farm, which we struggled to hold on to, even though everyone we knew said it was not reasonable to do so. I just couldn't let go of my dream, and the boys loved living in the woods almost as much as I did. Jack kept working at the camp next door. I kept working in town, and was re-appointed, with no pay, to First Church, where I was serving before the disaster at the end of our road.

Every day, I grew more and more in love with Jack, who seemed my ideal soul mate. He had a couple of odd habits, like drinking about twenty cups of coffee a day and flinching whenever I would move my arms expansively. He paused before each sentence to concentrate. Finally, he was diagnosed with ADHD, though he was more attention-deficit, and less hyperactive than Edward. Once he started taking medication for it, his coffee intake dropped by over a dozen cups a day and his occasional moodiness seemed to even out. At the beginning of our marriage, listening to him snore at night had made it difficult for me to sleep, since I kept waking up when he stopped breathing. Then he started using a C-Pap machine for his sleep apnea, breathed better while he slept, and we settled right in together. I was in some ways just like our dogs, especially Rhett, who would watch out the door for him with excited expectation, waiting for him to get home from work. On the days I got there first, I would find myself doing that, too. After all the years of being a single parent, the whole house, tiny as it was, seemed to burst with joy for me when he was there.

Jack's job at the camp gave him quite a bit of flexibility in scheduling, since it didn't matter a whole lot when the maintenance was done, and that flexibility helped us out enormously. As I was the midnight supervisor of the child abuse hotline, I slept during the days, and Jack was able to pick up the slack in caring for the boys and the farm. After fourteen years as a single parent, having Jack to rely on seemed to be a Godsend. I was especially grateful for his help in the arena of ferrying the boys to and from their many doctors, therapists, tutors, and school. Not only could Edward ride the bus to the camp after school during the school year, but also once summer school started, Jack was able to take him there, pick him up, and then carry him to the camp to hang out until I woke up in the afternoon. Without Jack's help, working midnights would have made the summer schedule absolutely impossible for me to swing.

Jack had seemed almost perfect before the wedding, and as time went on, he looked more so to me every day. Daily, I was amazed that we disagreed so little. All I could attribute it to was the years each of us had spent alone prior to our marriage. Each of us seemed just as determined as the other that *this* marriage would last. *This* marriage would be successful. We worked every day at making our marriage work. Even with the children we shared, we set aside a time every week just for ourselves. Sunday afternoons were sacred times, and I looked forward to them all week long. Jack was immensely strong and there was no task around the farm we could not master with his help, so that just his presence was a comfort to all of us, each of whom been abused in one way or another. Around Jack, we felt safe, and little by little, we let our defenses down. Life with Jack was just plain fun. Even chores were more fun for me when we did them together, whether it was fixing the toilet or constructing a stall for the animals.

So far, we had collected twenty-three hens, two roosters, and a pair of donkeys I adopted from one of the local rescue operations. Wishing for horses I could not afford, I got David and Annie instead. They were sweet, though occasionally temperamental, and Annie was VERY pregnant. For weeks, she looked as though she was going to pop at any minute. By the time she delivered, we had chosen the perfect name for the foal. With apologies to Cervantes, he was to be named Donkey Oaty. When she was born, we had to rethink our decision. She became Donkey Oaty-Belle. Jack and I were totally enamored with our first mutual grandchild. After the donkeys came, my sister-in-law, Betsy, sent me an e-mail with an attachment of little known facts, and the notation "Pay close attention to number 5!" Number 5 read, "More people are killed each year by donkeys than in plane crashes." I resolved to be careful.

Christmas came and went, then winter and spring. On our second Valentine's Day, in 2003, I awoke to a house covered with tiny notes. All day I found them in the least expected places. Thinking I had found them all, that night, turning off the light before we went to bed, I discovered, "You light up my life." Though we had no money to go out to celebrate, Jack's notes were the sweetest Valentine's Day gifts I ever received.

Our second summer on the farm, I saw an ad in the paper for registered Arabian horses for sale or trade, and begged Jack to go look at them with me. We had no money to buy, but maybe we could trade, and I had longed for Arabians ever since I was divorced from my second husband sixteen years before. In that divorce I was so desperate to get out that I agreed to his getting everything he wanted, including the farm and the horses. I had missed them ever since.

When I called Wilma, the breeder, to ask about what she had, one of the fillies she described was everything I dreamed of: a bay foal with four white stockings and a large white star. Her name was Liberty because she was born on the fourth of July. I was in love with her even before I saw her, and when I did see her, I loved everything about her. She was a joy just to look at and she moved like a dream. It made me happy just to watch her. The only thing that troubled me was that in my mind's eye, she kept falling down and not getting up. She wasn't doing it in real life – I just kept seeing it in my mind. I kept telling myself it was just what I was afraid of, because I didn't believe I deserved anything so beautiful. I was smitten.

Wilma needed fences, and we wanted horses. The deal we made was that we would trade five days of running fence, and all the supplies we had, for five horses, one for each of us. Ben, who was between Conner and Edward in age, was in a psychiatric facility at the time. He said he didn't like horses, anyway, but five would give me an extra one in case he or a friend ever did want to ride with us. Five days of hard labor, by the four of us who were at home, for five horses. Wilma and I were both getting a great deal. Jack, Conner, Edward, and I each picked out the horse we wanted. Liberty was my choice. Jack's choice was named Starling, and he found great comfort in the fact that she shared a birthday with his deceased sister. Starling was a beautiful bay yearling with a large white star.   Conner selected a rose gray filly with one white sock named Rose.   Edward got a dark bay filly with one white sock named Sable.   The last one I chose was Starling's younger sister, a gray filly with black mane and stockings named Silver Lining. We must have chosen the five hottest days of the summer to run the fence, but when we were done, we were ecstatic.   It seemed that ever since I had fallen in love with Jack, everything I had ever wanted or hoped for was falling into place.   It seemed nothing could go wrong.

The Day's Own Troubles

◆ ◆ ◆

"Sometimes I think of the suffering of those we love
as a crowbar, prying open a space between us
to ease the way toward letting them go.
Other times I hold on for dear life."

SUSAN FORD WILTSHIRE
Seasons of Grief and Grace

◆ ◆ ◆

TROUBLE COMES

Now there came a day when most of Job's sons and daughters were grown and on their own, and only the three youngest of her adopted sons were still members of her household. And one night a messenger came to Job and said, "The man you brought into your house is under the control of the Adversary, and your sons and daughters, and your grandsons and granddaughters are in danger, and I alone have escaped the danger to tell you."

Hardly had the words grown cold in the mouth of the first messenger, when another came to Job and said, "One by one, the possessions that mean the most to you have been torn away. You have lost partner and friends, community and pets; you have lost your job and your home and your church. Even your Love of Life has been stolen from you. One by one, you have lost everything that brings you joy, you have lost them all, save only the children it is your responsibility to care for. I alone have escaped the danger to tell you."

Throughout all this misfortune, Job held fast to her belief that even her adversary had a place at the table of God. Then her friends said to her, "Do you still hold fast to your integrity? Admit that we are right. Curse your misunderstanding of God and let your misguided faith die!"

But Job said to her friends, "Shall we take our own place at God's table, and not acknowledge that all others are welcome there as well? Shall we claim God's Good for ourselves, and then deny God's Grace for all?" In all this, Job never gave up her faith in the Goodness of God, and would not pay lip service to those who would have her abandon her belief.

And when Job's friends saw her, they did not recognize her; they lifted their voices and wept. They tore their robes and dressed in sackcloth, pouring ashes upon their heads. Some sat Shiva* silently with her while she grieved, but there were others who had been her friends who fled from her presence. They spoke not a word, nor did they come to her. After seven days and seven nights, Job opened her mouth, and said, "Why is life given to she who longs for death? And why is death denied me? For the thing that I feared most has come upon me, and what I dreaded above all else has been realized in my life. There is no peace, no quiet for me; I cannot sleep or even rest, for trouble has come."

CHAPTER THREE

The Tide Turns

After a gentle, peaceful period when everything in my life seemed on the surface to be calm, a few weeks ago First Church, where I have grown into adulthood and raised my children, began to address some of its underlying problems. The woman who is the current senior pastor has managed in one way or another to offend most of the congregation, and for months, people I love and who have been my friends for years have been leaving the church in droves. A mediator had to be called in to help resolve issues, and at one of the meetings just recently, one of my friends said aloud that she had been sexually abused many years ago by one of the former pastors. Things got a lot worse, fast. The man's friends swore he would never have done such a thing, and faced with her distress, I did something I had never intended to do. I told his defenders to leave her alone, because I believed her. When they asked why, I revealed that I believed her because something had also happened between that pastor and me.

I had been young and naive at the time, between my first and second marriages. I was twenty-two; the pastor my friend was accusing was more than twice my age. Both of us were divorced. He was "older and wiser" – or so I thought. When my infant son was sick and had to be hospitalized, the pastor gave me a ride from the hospital. We stopped by his house, and I never made it home that night. The affair went on for months, until I found out by mistake that I was not the only one, as he had led me to believe. I discovered that "this is something special just between us" did not mean "it is only happening between us." It meant "don't tell anyone else because it is a secret between us." When I told one of the pastor's defenders that, he kept asking me, time and again, "Did you consent?"

Over and over, I kept replying, "He purposely misled me. I would never have consented if I had known the truth."

Finally, the man was yelling at me over the phone, "BUT DID YOU CONSENT?"

While he was yelling, I kept thinking *I'm only telling you because I want you to leave her alone. I just want you to know that what she is saying is indeed possible. Something could have happened to her, the way she said. Something happened to me. And not only did something happen to me, but since I spoke up, I have found out it happened to others that I didn't know about, as well – women who were student interns, other women in the congregation. She could be telling the truth. Just leave her alone.*

Sometimes the whole situation at church leaves me so frustrated I have to fall back on lessons I learned years ago, when one of my kids went to alcohol and drug treatment. For years afterwards, I went to Al-Anon. *I am powerless over this church and all the people in it,* I keep reminding myself. *Easy does it. Just let it go.* I missed the meeting at which my friend made her disclosure because I had to work, and several leaders in the church told me I would not be allowed to attend the next meeting, saying I should not bring up in public what happened to me. I called the mediator, who said I would have to decide for myself just how public I wanted my past to be. I am really sorry I brought it up at all. It is hard to go to church, when I feel so ashamed.

Today, however, I don't have to feel bad when I go to church, because today Jack and I are skipping church altogether. Today, on our weekly visit to see our baby horses, we are going to finally bring Sable and Liberty home. We got the three older horses home months ago, but not Edward's and mine. They were way too young. Edward hasn't been nearly as invested in the waiting as I have been, but for the past five months we have driven the two hours each way every single Sunday, just so I could see my baby. My birthday is next weekend, and I just can't wait any longer. Wilma weaned both of the babies last week, and I am determined that they are going to come home today. Liberty is going to be my birthday present to myself.

It seems like everything is working against it being today keeps running through my head. So far, we've had to deal with the fact that Jack's decrepit old truck wouldn't start. Though it is his primary mode of transportation, it is exactly what you might expect a workboot-wearing, die-hard recycler to have: two-toned, wrecked after being stolen, hot-wired so you have to use a screwdriver to start it, dilapidated and tired, but most days its motor will at least still turn over. Jack doesn't throw *anything* away that can be reused. Once we finally got the truck going and on the highway, there were signs to take an alternate route because the interstate is closed. We got off the interstate onto a back road, only to discover that the one we chose was blocked due to a wreck. It is getting later and darker, and I really don't want to get the babies home after dark, but my desire to get Liberty in time for my birthday is making it hard for me to be objective. I keep saying to Jack that maybe all these things are signs we shouldn't do it today, but he knows how badly I want to get her home, so he keeps driving and telling me it will be fine. I ride next to him, thinking *he's such a sweetheart.*

Loading the fillies into Wilma's trailer in the dark terrifies them. We decide that since the trailer does not have taillights, Jack will pull the trailer home using Wilma's truck and I that will follow in ours. That way, other drivers will be able to see my taillights from behind, and at the same time I can keep an eye on the horses through the rear of the trailer in front of me. Part of the way home, I watch a disaster unfold. *Oh, my God, one of the horses has kicked open the back of the trailer. The weld on the center post holding the doors together has broken.* The door pops part of the way open. *Oh, Jesus, one of Liberty's legs is caught in the opening!* I honk in desperation, and it seems like it takes Jack half a mile to stop. I pull up behind him and look back, but it has only been about two car lengths. Not much damage is done to Liberty's leg, but I am in despair. We get her leg back through the broken door into the trailer, and tie the doors shut so it won't happen again. *I just can't bear the thought of turning back around and unloading them again at Wilma's, and no matter which way we go, we have to transport them in the same trailer.* We decide to keep going.

Two hours later, having finally crept home in the dark, Jack drives the truck into the meadow where the other horses are and turns it around so that the front of the truck faces the gate, and the rear end of the trailer faces the meadow. *Where is the flashlight? I've got to see how much damage was done to her leg.* I come around the back of the trailer with a flashlight. The light shining in the dark blinds and frightens them. I keep trying to see what Liberty's leg looks like, but even with the flashlight it is hard to tell in the dark. *Please, just hold still long enough for me to see.* The other horses are milling around, whinnying back and forth. It has been so long since we brought them home that the babies do not seem to recognize them, and the older horses do not seem to recognize the fillies, either. The youngsters in the trailer become more and more agitated. Jack, who has a way with horses, keeps speaking to them gently, but to no avail. Suddenly, with no warning, Liberty spins around facing the rear of the trailer. *Oh, God, she's trying to leap over the gate. We've got to get it open.*

Her head comes through the opening above the gate. We can't get her calm or back into the trailer. Her body plunges through the opening, and once again her leg is caught behind her in the broken door. This time her body is outside the trailer rather than in. The weight of her body pulls the gate open just far enough that her leg can slide down between the door and the center post with the broken bottom weld. *Oh, God, we've got to get her loose before she breaks that leg.* Panicked, Jack and I try to lift her body enough so that we can get the door open. When we do, she bolts loose, with Sable close behind.

In the dark, I keep trying to follow her with the flashlight. Every few minutes I can see her eyes shining in the dark, but cannot tell much about the way she is moving or if she is bleeding badly. "I can't see her anywhere, Jack. Can you see her? Wait a minute... There she is by the pond!" The minutes pass like hours, when suddenly Starling begins chasing the new inhabitants of her meadow. She is the oldest by a year, and is terrorizing the new babies, showing them she is the boss. *We've got to get them apart! We have created a disaster by unloading the babies in the dark.* Somehow, we've got to separate Liberty and Sable into the paddock, but we can't do much with Starling chasing them all over the place.

Horrified, I watch as Starling herds them past me in the dark, straight toward the hog-wire fence that separates the meadow from the paddock. They do not know the lay of the land, having never seen it in the light. *They don't even realize the fence is there!* Sable jumps clean, but Liberty doesn't make it, and her legs are tangled in the wire. Struggling to get free, she rips the same leg through the wire in her attempt to free herself. By the time Liberty is able to pull loose, her leg is in far worse shape than it was before.

Eventually, after what seems like hours, we get them separated. Each of Liberty's injuries has happened to the same leg. It is torn and bleeding, but she is by this time too panicked to let us near her. *Somehow, we have to catch her. She absolutely has to have antibiotics and a quick acting tetanus shot.* She won't let us. Exhausted and despairing, after hours of trying, Jack and I put out plenty of feed, water, and clean hay, and head for bed. Lying in the dark beside him, I am overwhelmed with the sensation of approaching doom. *I have hurt the horse I loved by bringing her home. If I had not wanted her, if I had been more patient, if I had left her at Wilma's, I am sure that exquisitely beautiful creature would have been fine.* Instead of being thrilled to have her home, I am miserable that my eagerness to get her home has caused her pain. I think of all the dreams I have had of her over the past few months falling down, after which I would wake up terrified, willing her to get back on her feet. *This is all my fault.*

That misery is on top of what has become the growing tension between Jack and me. Over the summer, it seems he has become more and more distracted by other things, and less interested in me. As long as we are working on a project of some kind, everything seems fine, but as soon as the project is done and we are alone, he starts looking for something else to do. He's started substitute teaching at all three schools in town – the elementary, the junior high, and the high school. In the evenings, he's been picking up shifts working for a caterer. Sunday afternoons, the one time that had been just for us, he's started subbing in a bell choir at another church. He's even started a bell choir for kids in the neighborhood at First Church. He fills up every available minute with some activity, but none of them gets the chores completed that need to be done around the farm. Rarely, if ever, do we have time together as a couple anymore. *No matter how much he denies it, it seems that he keeps choosing any other activity over being alone with me.* I keep trying to talk to him about it. Once, I confront him with the fact that most of the time it feels as though he would rather be fighting with Edward about anything than to be alone with me. *He may keep denying that anything is wrong, but it sure doesn't feel that way.*

The only thing that makes my loneliness tolerable at all is that the disastrous trip home for Liberty has resulted in an unexpected benefit. Because she has to have the dressing on her leg changed frequently and is being kept away from the other horses while her leg heals, she and I are growing more attached to each other every day. I can't wait to see her every time I go out, and she seems to look forward to our visits almost as much as I do. Her need for medical attention has brought about a bond I have not had with any other horse. Her eagerness to see me each day helps to fill the hole left by Jack's growing absence.

Earline, an old friend of mine from First Church, says that Jack and I are heavy on her heart, and she has been praying for us. Although I haven't told her anything about my sadness, she says it has come to her in prayer that we need to deal with what is going on "behind closed doors," as she put it. She says she doesn't know what that is, only that if we deal with it, our marriage will be better than ever before, but if we do not, we are in trouble. The only trouble I see is that recently there's *nothing* going on between Jack and me behind closed doors. While that certainly is a problem for me, I don't know whether that's what she's talking about or not. *Jack has seemed so distracted lately. I wonder what is going on that I don't know about.* When I tell Jack what she said, he looks shocked. Again, he denies that anything is wrong. He cannot explain why it is that I want more time together alone with him, and he wants less. "I just have too many other things to do," he says. I certainly can't argue the point. With our crew, there is always something to be done.

In addition to all the regular farm and household chores there are to do around the place, my kids are constantly in and out of the hospital, and Jack's foster son, Gabriel, is no different. That's just what you expect when you have special-needs kids like ours. The week before Christmas, it is Gabriel who is taking a turn in intensive care. Although his Hemophilia is life threatening, we have every reason to believe that he will recover from this particular episode within a few days. Jack is going to take a turn staying with him overnight in the hospital. *I am truly grateful they are going to have some time together. There is some underlying tension between Jack and Gabriel's wife, so that since Gabe's marriage and since Jack and I got married, they rarely get to see each other anymore. I miss Jack like crazy when he's not around, but I am glad for both of them that they are going to have the time alone.*

Christmas 2003, Jack's and my third Christmas together, is a wonderful celebration. First Church is one within a network of churches that provide food and shelter to homeless folks one night each week all winter. For several years our family has been privileged to host those who come the last Tuesday before Christmas. Last year, Christmas Eve was on a Tuesday and Ben was with us for the occasion. This year, sadly, he has not earned a pass, but Jack, Conner, Edward, and I go together. Each year, we give our guests Christmas bags for which we have been collecting things for months: decks of cards, toothpaste, long johns, shirts, socks, gloves, paper, pens, and stamps. A dozen homeless men spend one night each week all winter, so we've been buying things in dozens for quite some time. The most fun part of all is preparing the bags after the men fall asleep. Trying to guess which size each one is, we match clothing items with men and put their names on each bag. Wednesday morning, Christmas Eve, we wake our guests for breakfast with a "Merry Christmas!" and a bag of goodies from Santa. *This is the best part of the day.*

Christmas morning, after opening gifts at home, we celebrate Eucharist with the community I have worshipped with for almost thirty years. *I love to officiate for the Christmas morning service. I am really lucky that I have gotten to do this for over half the Christmases I've been here.* Occasionally I forget, but I always try to choose someone we wouldn't ordinarily think of to invite to the table. This week, I remember. When I pronounce the invitation, I reiterate what I have said to this congregation every time I have led this ritual for the sixteen-and-a-half years since my ordination. "This is not First Church's table; it is not our denomination's table. This is the Lord's Table, and everyone who is willing to accept the invitation has been invited. For the past two weeks, we have been hearing a lot about the capture of a dictator who has abused his power, much as Herod did in the story we remember today. As hard as it is for us to comprehend, even Saddam caught in his 'spider hole' has been invited, along with all his victims, for EVERYONE has a place at this table." And the congregation repeats, as they always do, "*Everyone* has a place at this table."

After church, we head off to celebrate over and over again as the day goes on. We take home-baked Christmas cookies as gifts as we travel from one friend or relative's house to the next. The cookies were baked the week before, and we take them to people who have been important in our lives. The boys' favorite part is always going to the home of the grandparents of Edward and

Ben's half-sister. The paternal grandparents of their maternal half-sister have grandparented my boys, too, though they are not any biological relation to them. Since Ben and Edward became a part of my family, Skip and Mary Jo have also included Conner among their grandchildren.

Skip and Mary Jo have a feast for every holiday, and this year is no exception. There is, as usual, a house full of extended family members, with gifts for every grandchild, no matter how they are connected to the family. The best part for me is not the gifts or even the food, though I have to admit that the feast is always spectacular. My favorite part is being in the midst of a family that welcomes my children, with all of their problems, with open arms. I get included as the mother of some of Skip and Mary Jo's grandchildren. *I love spending the day this way. In my house growing up, my father frequently stated he wanted his children to be seen and not heard, and preferably not seen. Skip and Mary Jo's house rates just below heaven.*

Walking through the front door of our seventy-year-old farmhouse the next morning, two years and one month after Jack's and my wedding, I see there is something wrong with Ananda. At first I can't tell what is happening. The dog has been my faithful companion, my best friend, for over eight years, ever since I rescued him from the animal shelter. Or perhaps it would be more accurate to say he rescued me. Two of my children had left that week, John for college and Conner for a behavioral treatment program, and for the first time in over eighteen years, I had been alone. Consumed with loneliness, I went to the shelter to see who was there.

In the midst of a hundred barking dogs, one alone stood looking at me, not barking at all. A huge yellow lab, he just stood there, while we looked at each other. He looked at me, and I looked at him. I looked at him, and he looked at me. Finally, when we had sized each other up long enough, I quietly asked him, "Would you like to go home with me and be my dog?" and he barked at last. Just once. I took that for a "yes," and went inside and claimed him, and he has claimed me, ever since. Like Charles Wallace in L'Engle's books I read as a child, I named my dog Ananda, the joy that like glue was holding my universe together.

THE TIDE TURNS   49

Eight Christmases later, kneeling beside him, I realize that he is having seizures. *He doesn't deserve this. I can't leave him here like this. Please, somebody, help me.* The seizures are so bad that I think I will have to take him to the vet to have him put down. I am sobbing, but have to leave for work. My heart is breaking. *He has been such a good dog, so faithful and so true, that I cannot let him suffer.* Jack offers to take him to the vet for me and to call me at work as soon as he finds out anything. When the call comes, it is almost more than I can bear. The diagnosis is cancer; the prognosis, bad – a year at the most. The vet offers Jack some medicine that will help with the seizures, but nothing will stop the progression of the disease. Sure enough, as the medication kicks in, it does ease the severity of the seizures. But Ananda's impending death is the first unmistakable sign I discern. Somewhere, somehow, the tide of my good luck has turned. My dream is turning into a nightmare.

CHAPTER FOUR

Behind the Mask

On the fifth day after Ananda's first seizures, my world falls apart. It is New Year's Eve, and I am looking forward to a quiet evening at home with Jack. Time alone with him has become rare and precious to me, and I am eagerly anticipating the weekend together. The kids have been packing their bags for a while, getting ready to go to Skip and Mary Jo's cabin at the lake to watch the fireworks. I am in the kitchen washing the supper dishes. Everything, on the surface at least, seems normal. Then it happens.

"Jack really likes penises," Conner says. "He touches Edward's penis all the time." It feels like the inside of my brain explodes. *Silence! Don't say a word!* Conner has come into the kitchen and is standing behind me, and he reports the fact in about the same tone of voice you would expect from someone saying, "We're having eggs and toast for breakfast." I have my back to him, and am trying desperately to regain control of my face, which I am sure is betraying my efforts to hide my horror.

"I didn't know that," I say, "thanks for letting me know." Trying to be calm, I ask if he has his meds. My mind is going wild, as I will my body to be still. I just keep thinking *I have to be calm. Maybe he just misunderstood something he saw. I don't want to upset them unnecessarily. I have to be calm.*

It seems like it takes forever, but the bags are finally packed, Skip and Mary Jo finally arrive, and Conner and Edward leave with them. Ben is still in a psychiatric facility, so at long last, Jack and I are alone. I keep trying to be calm and to think. *I can stall with a movie. That will give me time to figure out what to say next.* The whole time it is playing, my mind is going faster than I can keep up with it. I sit on one couch, with Jack sitting facing me. *I don't want to touch him. How can he sit there watching this movie, pretending everything is all right? Just keep trying to breathe.* I try to think about what to say and how to say it. My brain is trying to access everything I have ever learned about interviewing skills; at the same time I am trying not to despair prematurely.

I have spent my entire adult life trying to protect children from abuse. I have taken them into my home to get them out of a system that frequently abuses them as much as the homes they came from. I was a counselor for fourteen years before going to work as a supervisor for the state's child abuse hotline. I have been a pastor and chaplain part-time for seventeen years. I keep trying to remember everything I have ever learned about open-ended questions and being non-threatening and trying to obtain as much information as possible in an interview. *I need to find out everything I can in one sitting, because initial disclosures are often recanted in the light of the next day. If I can get him talking to me at all, I will need to find out everything possible before he has a chance to reconsider.*

Two desperate hours later, when the movie is finally over, with the man of my dreams facing me, I take a deep breath and begin. Telling him what Conner has said, I go on, "Do you have any idea what he could have been talking about?" That seems a safe enough way to begin, as the boy is as honest as the day is long, but often misinterprets things that he sees or hears. I have had enough time to come up with an opening that I hope will give Jack a chance to answer without immediately shutting down and closing me out.

For over twenty minutes, Jack says nothing. The longer the silence grows, the worse I know the truth must be. *If there were any easy explanation, if Conner really did misunderstand, I would have gotten it by now.* With my thoughts growing more desperate by the minute, I keep telling myself over and over that I have to be patient. I have to give him time to answer. *If I want to find out anything, I cannot attack him. If I want to find out anything, it is absolutely necessary that I be silent, that I be still. I have to wait until he speaks first.*

All the time, I keep hearing Laura's voice in my mind. Though she died a few years ago, I loved her dearly, and just like we hear memories of our parents speaking sometimes ("i before e except after c" I hear my mother's voice saying still) Laura's voice comes to me now, something she said to me over and over through the years. "You have to learn to love George Wallace," she used to say to me. "If you're ever going to learn how to love anyone, you have to learn to lo-o-ove George Wallace."

Laura had fought hard for her civil rights in Tuskegee, Alabama, and knew exactly how difficult it was to love George Wallace, the man who, as her governor on June 11, 1963, stood in the doorway of the University of Alabama with armed state troopers on either side of him, in a last-ditch attempt to keep people who looked like Laura from going to school with people who looked like me. For twenty years, from when I met her until her death, Laura used George Wallace to remind me that if we are ever to really love *any*one, we must learn to love *every*one. All these years, as I have tried to learn to love all of God's children, perpetrators have been the hardest for me: the epitome of evil – my personal George Wallace. It is Laura's voice I keep hearing as I sit on the couch desperately willing my body to be still. "If you're ever going to learn how to love anyone, you have to learn to lo-o-ove George Wallace."

Finally, after what feels like hours, Jack gets up, goes over to the door, picks up his boots, and puts them on. *What in the world is he doing? What does it mean?* Only when they are completely laced does he commence to speak.

"It has been going on for years," he begins. He tells me he believes he may be gay and has been trying to figure it out for himself without talking to anyone about it. Although he was able to restrain himself at the beginning of our marriage, his behavior had changed with my children over the summer, about the time our fortunes seemed to change. Through the fog in my mind, I hear my husband's voice describe wrestling with children, pretending to play, as the wrestling turns to touching, so that he can "test himself." He says he "tested himself" with Gabriel and with one of Gabe's cousins, too, many years before. Not only that, but in addition to the three children he is admitting having fondled, he says he has experienced "inappropriate thoughts" during virtually every outwardly appropriate interaction he has had with children since he himself was a child. He tells me that what Conner has noticed is true. "I would never put Edward in the position of having to testify against me. I'll plead guilty, because I did it. I can't stop," he says, "and I need help."

Oh, my God. Jack may think that he is gay, but he isn't gay or straight, either. His sexual preference isn't adults at all. It is children. The man I am married to is a pedophile*. I have married a child molester*. [2]

As I sit petrified, completely horrified and stunned, he tells me that he was silent for so long before he answered because he was deciding that for the first time in his life, he would tell the truth. He says he put his boots on before he started talking, because he was sure that once he started speaking, I would begin screaming and throw him out, and he would need his shoes on because the road was long. I am in shock.

All the time I am listening to him speak, I am thinking. *My life will never be the same again. Oh, God, if this is what he is admitting to, what else did he do that he isn't telling me? What does this mean for the boys?* I want it all to be a mistake, but I know it is not. *I would never knowingly have brought myself to get to know a perpetrator well, much less love one. Surely, the only way I could ever have changed my attitude about them as children of God was to have loved one first, and then found out he was an abuser of children later. Otherwise, I would never even have given one a chance.*

For many years, I have been grateful that as a member of the community of faith, it is not necessary for any one person to do all things. Together, if each one of us does his or her part, all things can be done, without any one person having to do it all. I have comforted myself with that thought for years, as I have prayed for victims of abuse, telling myself that I did not have to pray for the perpetrators because someone, somewhere, was doing that for me. I've been telling myself for years that it is enough that I do the part I can do.

I keep thinking about all the ways I have distanced myself from perpetrators over the years. When I was screening counseling requests at the agency where I worked before the wedding, I wouldn't even assign cases of perpetrators to other counselors in the same agency. I would just refer them out of our office altogether. I wanted the office where I worked to be a safe place for victims and did not want offenders anywhere on the property. And I have just found out I am married to one. *Oh, God, what have I done?* I am completely overwhelmed by grief and shock. We talk for hours, with Jack rambling on with answers. I hear myself saying, over and over, "help me understand" this part, or that one. The conversation goes on all night.

Each time Jack dozes off, my mind races. I have parented ten children at this point, including his son, but was aiming for more. *It will never happen now, I know.* The Refuge we have bought together to build the house of my dreams, a halfway house for youngsters transitioning from state custody to jobs and homes of their own, will probably be lost. *I cannot afford the payments on my own.* My dream house itself, for which I have been collecting building materials since before I met Jack, will never be built. *I'm going to lose everything.* But the most terrifying possibility is that as the non-offending parent, I will lose custody of Edward and Ben, the last two of my adopted children who are still minors. *When dealing with the state, one can never be sure what will happen.* I know, because I work there.

What Jack is describing would not have been against the law had it been two twelve-year olds horsing around while wrestling, but it is absolutely illegal if one of them is an adult. Even though I'm falling apart, the counselor in me kicks in: *Come on, you know that what he is admitting to you now might well be just the tip of the iceberg. You can do this. Just keep him talking. He has no idea what the ramifications are of what he is telling you.* I know well what is likely to happen.

How devious it was of him to prey on children who had already been abused. How despicable to victimize children who were already wounded. If Conner had not seen and told, who would have ever known? I think back to once when Ben was raped at a treatment facility, years before. The staff had attempted to cover it up, and if another child who had witnessed the rape had not told, no one would have ever known. When I tried to find an attorney who would be willing to represent Ben to sue the facility, each one I approached told me the same thing: Ben was so disturbed before the rape that we would never be able to prove he had been damaged by it.

In this case, too, that would have been true. Jack has been purposely choosing children who already have so many problems that his abuse would just create more. We would never be able to separate new symptoms from their pre-existing conditions. He cleverly chose children so disturbed that it would be hard to attribute their behavioral acting out to his abuse. He chose children who would latch on to absolutely anyone who said a kind word to them. He chose children known to be chronic liars. He chose to marry a single woman with three special-needs sons, so that when he chose to abuse them, no one need ever know.

Although at this point he is claiming he never actually raped any of the boys, he had clearly kept trying to break down their inhibitions, exposing himself to them, talking about sex, trying to touch them inappropriately, trying to get them to show him their pubic hair. He says that when Edward would come to the camp after school, he would purposely time taking his showers so that he could come out nude while Edward was there, or would ask Edward to bring him soap or a towel. He says he would insist Edward look at him while they were talking, or would entice Edward to skinny dip with him in the camp pool, hoping that he would be able to brush up against him "accidentally." Little by little, his intention was to normalize these abusive behaviors until he could get Edward to do whatever he wanted.

Oh, God, what would have happened if Ben had been home? He is so much sicker than Edward. There's no telling what Jack could have gotten away with. And who knows what he actually did get away with that he isn't telling me? Jack has chosen to prey on children who were already needy, with little sense of what was appropriate between adults and children. And they weren't just mentally ill; they suffered from life-endangering medical conditions, Polycystic Kidney Disease, Hemophilia, AIDS. Oh, God help me, what have I exposed my children to? What have I done?

When daylight finally breaks the sky, I call our family's psychologist. Doc has been my doctor, and my children's doctor, for almost twenty years. He is so important in our lives together that my children even name the days of the week by when they see him: Docday, Tuesday, Wednesday, Docday, Friday, Saturday, Sunday. While two of my foster children have never met him, my birth and adopted children have all seen him twice a week for years – Monday nights for family therapy, Thursday nights for individual. For seventeen of those years, I have seen him on Thursday mornings as well. He is the one I call first: "I need a safety plan*, and I need it now," I gasp, as I blurt out the short version of the night's discussion.

A safety plan is in order whenever children are at risk for abuse. It sets out the rules for interactions that will ensure the safety of the children. Even though I have written them for other families, I know that because I am involved in this situation there is no way I can be objective enough to know what to do for my own family. I trust our doctor completely in this regard. I will do whatever he says.

Doc sets the following parameters in place: Jack is to have no contact of any kind with our minor children or any former victims.

Jack is to have no unsupervised contact with anyone under the age of twenty-one. Jack needs to be moved out of the house before the children get home at the end of the weekend. Jack must immediately begin a psychological evaluation, and as soon as possible must begin attending a sex offenders' group for therapy, since group therapy has been proven to be more effective for treating sex offenders than individual therapy. In addition to these rules, which will define the safety plan, Jack must abide by all the regulations for sex offenders in our state, including periodic lie detector tests. These rules will remain in effect until Doc amends the plan in some way. It is the standard plan, with only one change: usually the requirement is no unsupervised contact with anyone under the age of eighteen. Doc says he doesn't want any gray area of possible confusion about whether someone looks like an adult but is not yet. That sounds good to me. I tell Doc that for my own sanity I need to file the report with Children's Services myself.

I call Deborah. She moved to Florida many years ago, but we still talk on the phone several times a week. *Please, tell me that you'll pray for me. Please, tell me I can survive what we both know is coming.* Deborah also works for a state agency that fights child abuse. Her job is to do forensic interviews of abused children and then to testify in court on their behalf. If anyone knows the ordeals my family is about to undergo, she does. "Breathe," she says. "Everything is unfolding as it should. If you did not love him, if he did not trust you, he might never have told anyone. He might have continued abusing children the rest of his life. The healing process is unfolding perfectly. Breathe." When I hang up, I immediately begin to put Doc's safety plan into place.

I go to work and type into the computer a report with my employer, the child abuse hotline of the state Department of Children's Services, against the man I have loved more than life itself. *Maybe doing the paperwork will make it more real.* I write out the report before I go, so I won't have to think once I get to the office. I have to type, because I cannot speak. Reports are assigned to investigators by county, so I type one report about my minor sons, since we live in one county, and another about Jack's son and nephew, since they live in the county we just moved from. In both reports, I type what Jack has told me: "Jack has admitted to having 'inappropriately touched probably over a hundred children.' A safety plan is in effect in which he has no access to children this weekend. He is willing to turn himself in on Monday morning, January 5, if someone will call to let him know where he needs to be and who he needs to talk to." It is easier to type the information into the database than to tell it to my friends and co-workers. I go tell my co-worker, Sarah, that I am submitting two reports to her, and ask her to do the history on them and take care of them after I leave. She asks if I am all right. "No." I shake my head. She puts her arms around me while I cry. *Thank you, Sarah. Thank you.*

I go outside the building where no one can hear me, and use my cell phone to call my supervisor. I tell her I am submitting the report, and I tell her what it says. I ask if, according to policy, the information can be protected from my co-workers. My supervisor tells me that while protection of files is normally provided for Department employees, it will not be provided for me. Because I work in the Intake Unit, access to the report cannot be restricted from the people I work with. Since state law requires every person who even suspects abuse of a child to report it, there will inevitably be more reports. And, since every time a report is made the Intake Unit does a history search on each person involved in the case, that means that eventually, everyone I work with will know. *Please, do something to protect this information. Please protect my privacy, and the privacy of my children. I can't take one more blow.* My supervisor tells me to go home, to take off all the time I need.

Before I get out the door, Sarah hands me a note: "Please know that you have a friend who is concerned about you – I can drive kids places, cook, clean (only for good friends!) so I expect to do things for you – You are in my prayers. I'll keep pestering you to see what you need. Much love, Sarah." Then, I escape.

I call my friend, Julie, and tell her the short version of what has happened. "Can you download me the forms I need to get Jack's power of attorney, and a quitclaim deed for our property?" She tells me that she will. I call another good friend, Brad, who works at the health department. He is able to arrange the details, and I take Jack with me for STD testing. Two years ago, we had gone to Brad for testing before we were married, but Jack has admitted by this time that his homosexual experimentation before our marriage involved a man with full-blown AIDS. *Come on, you can do this. Jack may be denying to you that he has had sex with anyone else during the marriage, but you cannot let yourself believe it. You have to keep making decisions based on the worst possible scenario.* You would never think you could cram so much into such a short period of time. And all the time, I just keep asking, "help me understand..."

Friday evening, we start moving Jack's things over to the camp where he has been working. No one is there for the winter, and the camp manager says it will be all right for him to stay there for a while. All the time we are moving his things, we keep talking. Over the weekend he tells me many things he says he has never told anyone. He tells me the story of how his father caught him with his next-door neighbor when the two of them were twelve-year-old boys engaged in normal adolescent sexual exploration. His parents' response had been to tell his best friend that he was never to come to their house or speak to their son again. He tells me of his terror that if his parents ever found out about his homosexual confusion, that the response they made to his friend would be the one they made to him, and that he, too, would be told to leave and never to return or speak to them again. He tells me he did not start acting out sexually with children until after his mother, father, and older sister all died, that they had been his external controls, and he simply has no internal controls at all.

He begs me to try to understand his hiding who he is and not to hate him. He asks, "Is there any way you can understand what it is like to long for a hairy, muscular chest to lean your head upon, and a pair of masculine, strong arms to hold you tight?"

All I can say is, "Of course I can understand, Jack. After all, that is exactly what I want, too. What I cannot understand is why you married me, if that is what you want." He keeps telling me he truly does love me, but I do not believe him. *He was only in love with the idea of being in love and having easy access to children at home.* He tells me that he married me because he wanted to be the man I saw when I looked at him, but I don't believe that, either. *I bet he only married me to get to my sons.* What I'm thinking, I don't say.

Jack tells me he believed that marrying me would make him stop the behavior that he hates in himself, behavior he is sure his parents would abhor. He says he thought that marrying into the community of which I am a part was marrying into the "appropriateness police," and that he would have to stop. He says he was sure that after our marriage he would never be able to touch a child inappropriately again because there would always be someone watching him. He says he thought that if he married me he would no longer want to act out at all, and that if by any chance after our marriage he still wanted to, then he thought he would not dare. *I guess he was wrong about marriage making him stop wanting to act out, but he is right about one thing. I will stop him. Not the way he means it, perhaps, but I will indeed make it stop.*

On the first Saturday night in January, I go by the hospital to talk to Gabriel, who is still an inpatient. In the early years of the AIDS epidemic, all the males in Gabriel's family, like most Hemophiliacs in those days, became HIV* infected through transfusions. We've never been sure whether it would be the Hemophilia or the AIDS that would kill him. This time, his hospital stay has been extended because they can't get the bleeding in his joints to stop, even with intravenous clotting factor. I love Gabe dearly but have had so much to do the past few days that I haven't made it by to see him since before Jack's confession, though we have talked a couple of times on the phone. He already has children of his own. *I wonder if Jack abused them, too.*

Gabe tells me a different story than the one Jack told. The abuse started long before Jack said it did, when Gabe was only nine, and it progressed far beyond Jack's admission. According to Gabriel, Jack's abuse began the very first time he spent the night at Jack's house. His story of that night starts out just like Jack's version: he was a little boy, alone and afraid since the death of his brother, who was also a Hemophiliac who contracted HIV from a blood transfusion. He wandered around Jack's house looking at all the beds, and then decided he wanted to sleep in Jack's bed with him. He had always slept with his brother and had not slept well ever since his brother's death. He curled up next to Jack, put his head on Jack's shoulder, and promptly fell asleep. At that point, their stories diverged.

Jack's version had always been that he was terrified to sleep all night, and had lain there with his arm around Gabriel's shoulder until light, thinking, "What have I gotten myself into?" Gabriel tells it differently. He says that some time in the middle of the night he woke up to Jack masturbating him. He says nothing like that had ever happened to him before, and that he was terrified to move, paralyzed. He says the abuse has continued ever since, up to and including during Jack's visit to the hospital last week. *Not only has Jack been unfaithful, but for the entire span of our marriage, he has been exposing me to HIV as a result of his raping Gabriel for years. For all I know, I may be HIV-positive and dying right now. Jack may have killed me.* I try to look calm, and to continue to listen to Gabe's story.

Gabriel tells me that his family has known that Jack was abusing him all these years, but that Jack would buy them gifts and otherwise enable their wants and needs, starting by taking him in after he wrecked his mother's boyfriend's car. His mother was mad and wanted Gabe out of her house. Jack stepped up like the hero offering to take him off her hands. Fully intending to abuse Gabriel, Jack still came off looking like the good guy. "If you need him to, he can come and live with me. I'll help you out."

Gabriel says that his mother, grandmother, and wife all hate Jack, and that his stepchildren and nieces and nephews all stay away from Jack "because he is a pervert." *Oh, God. I always thought when Gabe would say to Jack, "Come on, man, you know you want what I've got," that it was a normal adolescent running joke about comparative penis size. It was actually a crass comment about Jack's sexuality. Gabriel has been telling me all along, and I didn't get it.* Then he tells me that Jack even came to him for sex the week before our wedding, when I was so appreciative that Jack was not pressuring me to violate my boundaries. Now I realize why Jack was so willing to be patient. *I feel sick.* Gabriel tells me that he begged his father not to marry me. "You know what you are," he says he pleaded. "She is a good woman. Don't do that to her. Don't do this to her boys."

Gabriel, who is now my son as well as Jack's, says he was afraid to stop his dad, because he didn't want to lose his relationship with the only father he knew. He shakes with anger and fear when he talks about how used he has felt all these years. He says, "Dad called me, and asked me to lie to you about what happened, but I will not lie to you."

I ask, "Oh, Gabe, why didn't you tell me?"

He just looks sad and whispers, "I love you, Mom, and I know how much you love Dad. I'm sorry I didn't tell you sooner, but I didn't want to hurt your feelings."

Jack is waiting in the hall when I come out. He is hoping our son has lied to me. I am furious, and I tell him that is not what happened. I ask, "How could you have abused your own son, here in the hospital, in a hospital bed, with his body racked with pain?" Jack starts justifying his actions, saying he was just trying to give the young man some distraction, some relief from his agony. Incensed, I tell him how Gabriel felt about his actions, and ask again, "How could you? What in the world were you thinking? How could you abuse him here, when a nurse could have walked in at any minute? Don't you care anything about Gabe's feelings at all?"

Jack hung his head and quietly said, "That someone could have walked in was what made it so exciting."

Four days after my world fell apart, the first Sunday in January 2004, Jack and I go to church together, with Jack supporting me as much as I can bear to let him. Together we sit through church with my head upon his shoulder, as I weep. During the introductions, he stands up, and I feel hot and sick. Nausea washes over me. *Please, give me the strength to make it through this. There is no telling what he will say, even though I have begged him not to say anything.* The words that come out of his mouth are, "My name is Jack. You think you know me, but you don't. I am gay, and this is my wife, and she loves me."

People come up and gather round me, offering support, saying life will go on, and other inane things meant to make me feel better. *They only have what he has told them to go on. They have no idea what is really at stake.* After church, he talks to our friends, telling them he has been inappropriate with our sons and to keep their children away from him, because he never wants to put another child at risk again. He wants everyone to know he is a danger, because he loves the folks in that place, as much as he can, and wants everyone to be safe. He doesn't realize what I am thinking: *His kiss of love for them will be the kiss of death for all those relationships he holds dear.*

Many times over the weekend, I have tried to explain to Jack that I am unwilling to stay in the marriage if he is convicted of a felony, which is in and of itself a ground for a divorce in our state. He has no idea of the changes that status would bring for us, and I don't seem to be able to get him to hear me. The most significant change would be that convicted sex offenders cannot live in a home where there are minor children (other than their own biological children) for the rest of their lives; I have children and grandchildren unrelated to Jack who will be in and out of my home for the rest of mine. Convicted sex offenders cannot live or work within 1,000 feet of any facility, school, or park that provides programs for children, for the rest of their lives. Since our farm is less than 1,000 feet wide and shares a property line with the church camp on the other side of the hill, a felony conviction would mean that he could never again live where we do now, for the rest of his life. I'm not sure at this point that I will ever want to try living with him again, but if he is convicted of a felony I would never again be able to do so in the place that I love, for the duration of my days. When I have tried to explain these things, the only thing he seems to have heard was the single example, "I am not willing to live with a sign in my yard that says a convicted sex offender lives here." He hasn't been able to hear anything else. But if he doesn't get that boundary, he at least states that he understands my other boundary: I will not stay in the marriage if there is any violation of the safety plan, no matter how small. If he is serious about wanting forgiveness and a chance to start over, I will give him one chance to do so, but only one. I will not endanger my children further.

Monday morning, I get the quitclaim deed and the power of attorney from Julie. Then, I go home to pick up the man to whom I am, for better or worse, married. Before we leave the house, Jack gives me three letters, one each for Edward, Conner, and myself. Mine reads, in part:

> *Why you continue to care for and support me I may never fully understand, but I do understand this: you accept me as I truly am, even though that is not the way I presented myself to you from the time I first met you. I will always remember that and never be able to fully express my gratitude to you for that very simple act of love... The remorse I feel for my betrayal of your love for me is an enormous load to me, but your continuing devotion gives me hope that, like grieving, I will find a way to carry it easier and never forget the reasons why I have such regrets. I am sorry that I have not been the sort of partner you had hoped that I would be. I am sorry for the nightmare you have been forced to live and will live in for the near*

term... I will do everything in my power to help you through this time. I may have besmirched our marriage, but still want the chance to do the right thing as your husband... Jack

Together, Jack and I go to the bank, where there is a notary. He signs both of the documents and gives them back to me, to use whenever I need them. I have agreed not to file for divorce as long as there is no felony conviction and he does not violate the safety plan in any way, on the condition that he has signed both of these for me to use in the event that he violates either boundary.

From the bank, Jack and I go to the police station, so he can officially confess there. Because there are two counties involved, we decide to go to the police station in the county where most of the offenses have occurred. Jack tells the police officers that he wants an attorney, but they tell him one cannot be appointed until after he is charged, and that they cannot charge him with anything at this point. He has even worn sneakers instead of his customary boots and emptied his pockets before we came, so sure he is that he will be arrested on the spot. They tell us, "Real life is not like it is on television. It can take up to a year for charges to be filed."

Jack tells the investigator that he is so plagued with remorse that if he does not confess today, he will kill himself. Under those circumstances, they agree to take his confession even without an attorney. Before he goes in to talk to the investigator, Jack gives me a copy of his prepared confession. It reads in part:

There is more to this story and I am volunteering this information in order to clear my conscience and help lay a foundation for treatment which I believe could help me learn to better control my destructive behavior...

I am gay, but I have adamantly denied this simple fact up until New Year's Eve 2003, when my wife confronted me about comments made about me by her son Conner. Both Conner and his brother Edward were gone to their step-grandparents' lakeside cabin for the holidays, so there was plenty of time for a confrontation and interrogation.

I knew it was over. The sick behavior that had been haunting me for thirty years and which I had been trying to deny for the last fifteen years was going to have to come to an end. Thankfully, my wife is a pastoral counselor with 15 years experience in the counseling program where she used to work. While there, she tended to specialize in abuse cases and, for the last year and a half, has helped to set up and train people to run the state child abuse hotline.

Although she has never had any kind words for sexual predators, she has always been a strong advocate for the safety of their victims and a dedicated counselor when she has the chance to see them in her office. She decided to try to understand why I did the things I've done and support me in the process of healing, atonement and restitution/ rehabilitation which I will attempt, regardless of what this investigation determines and the court decides. I guess she loves me in spite of the way I've jeopardized the safety of our children and our home...

After they interview Jack, one of the officers tells me there is nothing he has confessed to that they would charge him with, since most of what he is describing has gone on, not with his hands, but between his ears. Jack's abuse of Gabriel prior to his turning eighteen is long past the statute of limitations. The officer tells me, "I've seen plenty of worse cases where the perpetrator has only been given probation. Don't expect much to happen." But they won't let us leave until they talk to Doc about whether or not it is safe to send Jack home, in case he commits suicide after leaving their office.

To call our doctor for the officers, I go with two of them to one of the rooms in the back. While I am waiting on hold for Doc to come on the line, I am reading things they have posted on the wall. I start laughing when I get to a list of Department of Children's Services "policies" that are, if not written anywhere, at least painfully true. They are so funny, I ask for paper and a pen and write my favorite three down. I put the paper in my pocket and keep it.

"False motivation is better than no motivation at all."

Chapter 1, page 11, DCS Management Handbook

"If anything is worth doing, it is worth doing half-way."

DCS Policy and Procedure Manual

"Paperwork is the embalming fluid of a bureaucracy. It gives the appearance of life where there is none."

Chapter 3, page 58, DCS Training Manual

When I start laughing, the officers remember I work for the Department and ask, "Why would you want to work there if you feel that way, too?"

I tell them, "I started working there when they put in the new Statewide Intake Unit. I hoped I could help make it better for children."

They tell me that as far as the police department is concerned, Statewide Intake, where I work, is a disaster. They ask me please not to tell anyone where I work that they have the jokes up. *Boy, that will be hard. These jokes may be funny, but where I saw them is even funnier.* Then, our doctor comes to the phone and I pass the handset to the officer in charge. I guess Doc tells them it is safe for us to go home, because they let us leave.

By the time Edward and Conner get home late on Monday afternoon, Jack is at the camp and I have steeled myself not to ask them the questions that are burning inside me. *It doesn't matter how desperately I want to know if the boys have been endangered, I must not ask them their version of what happened. I dare not risk affecting their testimony.* So, pretending that everything is normal, but knowing it will never be normal again, I take them to Doc's office at six o'clock in the evening so he can interview them and ask them what they know. Their stories and Jack's match exactly.

Edward says that Jack kept telling him, "This is what fathers and sons do." I have no idea if that *is* what Jack's father did to him or not, but Edward hadn't liked it, so every time Jack tried to touch him, he hit him. Conner concurs. Though Edward hadn't gone along with what Jack was attempting, in one respect his experience was just like mine with double vision as a child: until he was asked point blank, he hadn't realized he should tell someone. Like many families and therapists, we had talked about "safe touch, good touch, and bad touch" but Edward hadn't realized it meant *this.* Nothing he had heard prior to that point adequately communicated to him that father/son relationships weren't supposed to be like that. He only knew what he *experienced,* which he didn't like, and what he *heard,* which wasn't always what he was *told.* Edward says Jack even told him that if I ever asked, he was to tell me the truth. It could have been worse, much worse, but it is still terrible. It is the end of my life as I have known it.

CHAPTER FIVE

Not Much Left to Lose

The boys ask Doc what will happen to Jack now, but at this point it is much too early to know. When Doc replies, "He might go to treatment or he might go to jail," they just want to know how long it will be before he is allowed to come back home. Over and over throughout the years, we have talked about the fact that no matter what they do, no matter where they go, I will always be their mother. They immediately assume this family claiming will extend to their stepfather as well, and that no matter what Jack has done, he will be a part of our family forever.

They are such good boys. I am so proud of them. I am also heartbroken. I have no idea how to explain to them that an abusive marriage is not bound by the same rule our family has had for their adoptions; what is true for one may not necessarily hold for the other. After the session, they write a letter for me to give to Jack:

Dear Jack, All mistakes can be worked out. Sometimes it just takes a really long time. We still love you even though you made a mistake.

The attitude they have learned from me puts me in an untenable position, but they have learned the lesson well.

When I am finally able to talk to Doc alone, I fall apart. "How could I have missed it? How could I have been so blind? I thought this time I had finally chosen well. I thought Jack *was* The One. Given all of my history, how could I have chosen an abuser one more time?"

Doc says, "I'm not sure at this point whether you chose him, or whether he chose you."

I sob, "What did I miss? What signs were there that I ignored? Did you know and just not tell me?"

Doc keeps saying, "Anyone can be lied to, Sophia. He lied to me, too. He is a very good liar." He goes over all the things Jack did which make him unlike the typical pedophile, not the least of which was his regular participation in family therapy for the past two years. "He just didn't give much away," he reassures me. "And in spite of all the things he did which were terrible, he did do some things right.

He told the truth when you asked him. He took full responsibility for what he did. He did not make Edward out to be the liar."

We talk about Edward's love/hate relationship with Jack, but teenagers often have that type of relationship with their parents. We talk about issues that are likely to get worse for the boys as a result of Jack's betrayal. Trust, especially, has always been hard for both of them. Now, thanks to Jack, it will be even worse. He reassures me that I, too, have done many things right, the most important of which is that I immediately believed Conner and Edward, and took steps to protect them without delay. "But I *didn't* protect them," I wail.

"Anyone can be hurt once," he says. "The important thing is that they know you will keep them from being hurt again." It is little consolation.

I keep walking around in a daze, praying to anyone I think will listen: Jesus, God, Mary, Goddess, Saint Bridgid, Saint Michael the Archangel. *Please, God, help me. You know what it was like for your child to suffer. Please tell me what I need to say to Conner and Edward now. Please, Goddess, Creation was birthed in your womb. Tell me what the next thing is that Creation needs from me. Just tell me what the next thing I need to do is. Please, Mary, you were a mother; please give me the strength to mother my children now. Please, Bridgid, I know I am not a Catholic, but please intervene on my behalf. You and I seem to be connected somehow, please be my patron saint now. Please, Michael, you who stand with your foot holding down the demons that torment us, please subdue the evil that is breaking forth into my life now. Please, Jesus, please, anyone who will listen, help me make it through this day. I don't even know what to ask for. Please, just help me.*

Oh, my God, someone please help me. Not even a week has gone by since Jack's confession, and Liberty is down. *I can't bear anything else.* She didn't come to me this morning when I came out with sweet-feed, which was unusual. Lately, she has been following me around the paddock like a big dog, but this morning she was nowhere to be seen. I have been so enamored with her that I have been watching her play every time I get the chance. No other horse has ever held my love or my attention so well. I love the way Liberty moves, and I love the way Liberty looks, and I love the fact that Liberty loves me back. All my life, I have been waiting for such a creature.

When she didn't come to me this morning, I came out looking for her in the meadow and found her caught here, with her legs under the fence. *Oh, God, I am terrified.* It is cold, very cold, for the first week of January. It is one of the coldest on record. Although she was fine when I checked the horses last night, I have no idea how long she has been lying here freezing. *It looks like she slipped in the mud by the haystack, caught her legs under the fence, and has been lying here cold and wet most of the night. The ground around her is covered with manure. There is no telling how long she's been trying to get up.*

I pull her legs out from under the fence and drag her around, facing in the other direction. She cannot stand. I realize I am panicking and I am exhausted to the point that I can hardly stand, myself. *It has been too many days since I have slept. I've got to get Edward to school first, then I can go get Jack from the camp. Maybe together we can get her up.* I run back to the house and tell the kids what is happening, grab a sleeping bag and carry it back to try to warm her while Edward gets ready for school. Conner comes out to try to help, but he and I can't get her up, either.

I drop Edward at school, and rush to get Jack. Together we struggle, trying to get Liberty up, covering her with another sleeping bag, feeding her warm mash, massaging her legs, turning her over to the other side. The vet has told us on the phone that he will give us something that should help, and Jack drives to the clinic to pick up a hypodermic of Banamine while I stay with her. He brings it back, but giving it to her doesn't seem to work. *Nothing is working. Why my horse? Why mine? No one else in this family loves their horse as much as I do. It wouldn't matter to them as much as it does to me. What in the world did I do to deserve this, on top of everything else?* Eventually, our neighbors Don and Sara get home and help us to get her standing. Together, we get her into a stall, but of course, Jack has to be gone by the time Edward gets home, so I drop him back off at the camp, and there I am, left trying to care for the little horse and the children alone.

I go out to check on her the next morning, and Liberty is down again. Again, after taking Edward to school, I go and get Jack, and together we are able to get her up. We blanket her with a blanket I picked up at the Co-Op. *Come on, you can do this. You have to figure something out. It is too cold for her to stay on the ground, but you cannot spend the day with her today. There are just too many other things you have to do before the day is over.*   Someone from First Church, someone I thought was a friend, has called Jack's supervisor at the camp and made sure he was fired before he had the chance to find another job. Jack has not yet been charged with any crime, much less found guilty, but it makes no difference. He has to move out, too, before dark. Struggling to balance wounded children, dying dog, sick horse, trying to work, and moving my husband once again, we get Jack's stuff together and get him to a hotel to spend the night. *No matter how angry I am with him today, I'm not going to let Jack freeze, any more than I would let Liberty freeze. We have to do something.* We have only enough money to pay for a few nights. I am in despair, but none of our friends will take him in, and it is too cold for him to sleep in the car.

Late at night, I send out an e-mail. I spend what seems like forever trying to decide exactly how to word it. Because there is an active investigation going on, I am not at liberty to tell people what Jack has confessed to. At the same time, not to disclose anything at all would only serve to isolate our family. I want to be sensitive to Edward's need for privacy, and I cannot control what Jack is telling people, but somehow I have to balance all that against my need for my friends to know what is going on. I desperately need their support. Finally, what I decide on is this:

Dear Friends and Family,

I think it was Andy Rooney who once said something to the effect that he was beyond New Years' Resolutions. He had gone on to Revolutions: He was revolting against the way he was.

This has been that type of New Year's for our family. At about eight p.m. on New Year's Eve, Jack told me that he wanted to be, and had been trying desperately to be, a good husband and father, but that he was gay. By the time it was all over, it turned out that he had done some things for which he is likely to be arrested. I, of course, played by the rules even though I didn't like the game, and made all the appropriate referrals. At this point, we have met with police and investigators and are doing all the things that must be done.

The man I have fallen more in love with each and every day for the past two years is, in large part, a stranger to me. He moved out on Friday. In all likelihood, I will lose the farm since I cannot maintain the payments without his income and it looks like some amount of jail, at least, is likely. I will let you all know of my new address when and if we move. The kids are quite confused, and don't want things to change. I am heartbroken, and devastated. Jack is relieved that his fear of being caught is coming to an end.

Please pray for us. For healing, for peace, and for grace.

Thank you. Sophia

Friends e-mailed back:

"Being gay is not the crime... lying is." *Oh, Betsy, I wish I could tell you. The real crime is molesting our children.*

"Your strength in keeping the whole process together and by the book is amazing, too. But I have seen that strength before and I know what an amazing person you are even as you mourn. It brought back memories of another crisis we weathered together and I remember how much I admired your courage then and how much I still do now..." *I appreciate that, FTS, but I really don't feel strong at all. You cannot imagine what this is costing me.*

"You will be in my heart all day darlin' and prayers are going up for you all over the place." *Yes, please, pray. Pray hard.*

"I know the feeling of being in such pain that you don't think you can get through another hour. Another minute. I have been there, when what I thought was my marriage turned out to be not what was real at all, and I had no idea how to find out what was real. I have walked through the fire. It is possible to be re-born. Not just putting it in the past, but really, to heal and become a new person. God is big. I just wanted to be another voice in your world reminding you of that." *I was sure that if I told you, Kathy, you would understand. But is God big enough for this?*

"I just wanted you to know that, though at the moment I'm running at full-steam, you all are never very far from my mind." *Thank you, Sweetie.*

"I am so sorry. Please know of my prayers for you and Jack and the boys. Thank you for trusting me. I am feeling very sad also for your family. I will share my confidence that God IS working, we just don't know how or in what way. I love you." *Please, Mary, if you figure it out, please let me know.*

Over the next few days, I watch as our tiny savings are depleted trying to keep Jack from freezing and rushing back and forth to the vet. Heartbroken, yet internally raging against him, I keep hearing Laura's voice. "You've got to learn to lo-o-ove George Wallace." I keep praying, *Okay, Laura, that's what you said I'm supposed to do, but what is the loving thing? And even if I can figure out what it is, how do I do it? How can I possibly continue to love this man? And how can I not?* Knowing that there will no longer be any money coming in from Jack's salary, now that he has lost his job, I am terrified to have the vet come out to look at Liberty. *There is no way you can pay him. You'll just have to call him again and ask him what to do next.* We keep talking to the vet on the phone, and doctoring little Liberty as well as we can. Each morning, when I get up, she is down. The ground is too cold for her to stay there, even blanketed, so each day, we struggle to get her, and keep her, up.

Everyone has signed off on the safety plan. Doc, the Department investigator, Jack and I all signed the contract Doc has dictated to ensure the boys' safety. Jack is sure he will quickly complete the requirements and be allowed to reunite with the family, even though I have told him since the very first night that as far as I am concerned, it will be at least a year before I am willing to even *consider* letting him rejoin the family. I told him then and still believe that a more likely timetable is two to five years before I would ever believe it was safe for him to return home. Still, he is sure that he will be the exception to the rule.

On the second Sunday in January, Jack and I go together to the early service, so that I can take the children to the later service they are used to. Though the safety plan calls for Jack to have no contact of any kind with our minor children, and no unsupervised contact with anyone under the age of 21, Doc still thinks it would be appropriate for him to continue going to church as long as someone stays with him. Several loving volunteers have offered to do just that. At this point, Doc thinks that Jack's development may have been arrested* at the age of twelve, when his father caught him with his neighbor. His actual fondling of children seems to have been restricted to children in his own family. There is no reason at this point to think that the children at church are at risk, and God knows we both need the support.

After the service, the senior pastor pulls me away from Jack and into another room, and once we are alone says, "In cases like these, one person gets the church and its support and the other does not. I'm sorry, but that's just the way it is." I am stunned at the implication of what she is telling me. *That certainly is not my understanding of Grace, which is that either all of us receive it or none of us do.* It doesn't matter what Jack has done to tear our family apart, no matter how angry I am with him, I still believe deep in my heart what I am thinking as she tells me he does not have a place here. *Even the dogs get the crumbs under the table. Every repentant sinner has a place at the table of God.*

After church, other people come up to me as well, and almost every day I get calls. "If he comes back, my family and I will leave." "If you insist on coming, you will tear the church apart. It cannot take anything else." "If you come back, you will be putting your needs above the needs of the congregation." "If people find out we are harboring a pedophile," (you'd have thought we were asking the church to let him live in the basement rather than for a repentant sinner to come to worship) "they will withdraw their funding and people will take their children out of the after-school program."

There have been a few voices of support, but there are not many. Martha and Hoyt, Bonnie, and Earline have said to us, "Come and sit with us at church, and we will shield you on either side." Tommy and Lauren, Dale, and Sandy have been fierce in our defense. Harmon has called. Jean, Bruce, and Dottie have sent cards. Don helped Jack get temporary housing and Mattielyn has helped me negotiate the legal chaos, but most of my old friends are staying far away. I don't hear from them at all. *It is probably just as well. You are so hurt and angry at the church's response to the catastrophe that has hit your family, that you can hardly be civil when one of them does call.*

I hope it is because they are trying to be loyal to me that they are shunning Jack, but all it does is place me in the position of having to choose between my commitment to my husband and family, and my commitment to my church and friends. *I seem to be married to the one man in the history of First Church who is not welcome at the table except in theory. I would never divorce Jack if he were physically ill instead of mentally so. I know that eventually it will be clear to me what I need to do, but so far I don't know yet if this marriage is irredeemable or not. How can they?* I have also discovered that I am the mother of two wonderful young men who, even though they feel hurt and angry and betrayed, both by their stepfather's actions and by the church's response to our crisis, continue to believe that what the church has taught them is true. They, too, continue to believe that even Jack has a place at the table of God. And with the disdain of hypocrisy that only the young can do justice to, they keep telling me, "It's not right. If Jack can't go to First Church, we won't either."

I can't believe how much I miss him. It's not fair. None of this is fair. I didn't do anything wrong except believe that he loved me. Oh, God, I wish I could talk to him. How dare my body betray me like this? I was used to not being touched, after all those years of being alone. Now, all I want is for him to put his arms around me the way he used to and to tell me it is going to be alright. But I can't stand for him to touch me, now that I know that while he was holding me what he really wanted was to be touching my children. It wasn't my fault, but I'm the one who is paying for it. It's not fair.

Today we can't get Liberty up at all. I am panicked, desperate, despairing. With no money to call the vet to come out, and no trailer that we can find to rent, we get the neighbors to help slide her into the back of the pickup truck and we take her to the clinic. Jack is driving the truck, with me in the back sobbing, cradling the filly's head in my arms. We explain to the vet that we have no money and beg for charity. He says, "It's okay. We'll figure something out." He is starting her on an IV when we leave. On the way home, we are out of cell phone range, but by the time we get home, the vet has left us a message that little Liberty had died. He says he doesn't know why, there is no reason he can see, but it doesn't matter. She is dead. *I want to die, too. Please, Jesus, let me die, too.*

I have to go to work. "How's your horse today?" someone asks. "She died." *Oh, God, she died.*

Tonight the First Church senior pastor called, responding to a directive from the church council to call both Jack and me. She catches the full brunt of my despair. *It was someone from First Church who called Jack's boss to make sure he was fired; it is because he lost his job that we have no money; it is because we had no money to pay the vet that I put off taking Liberty in for too long; and it is more than likely because I delayed getting help that she has died.* I am erupting with grief. The pastor said she was told by the council to call me and to call Jack as well, and she asks for his number. What she has no way of knowing is that I have his cell phone in my own pocket at the time. His phone never rings.

Wednesday night, two weeks to the day after his confession, Jack goes to choir practice. The choir has been his small group, his support group ever since we married. He calls me afterwards, distraught. Quoting my friends to me, he tells me a group of them came up to him after choir practice and told him he was not welcome to come back. I believe what he is telling me, because without his speaking their names, I know who said each thing. I had already heard the quotes, word for word, before.

I have been told over and over by people I believed to be my friends that we are not welcome, as a family, to come back to church together. I am being forced to choose between my commitment to my family and my love of my church, and I am painfully aware of what they do not realize: if we leave First Church, I stand to lose much more than just my friends of thirty years. I will even lose my identity as a pastor, since my status is tied to my appointment to a local church. If I resign because we cannot worship together, Jack's betrayal will have endangered not only our marriage, our home, my children, my horse, and my job; it will have cost me the very sense of identity and calling I have been faithful to since I was seven years old. Other than my children and my life, I won't have much left to lose.

My struggle is hard enough just trying to discern what the faithful thing to do about my marriage is, without being condemned for my choice. *I said, after all, for better or worse; till death do us part. This is definitely the "worse" part, but Doc is still saying it could just be a case of arrested development. Maybe I should wait until Jack is farther along in therapy to decide what to do. The members of my old Al-Anon group repeatedly said don't make any major decisions for a year. It is way too early to be sure what the right thing to do is. It is one thing to be betrayed by a man I have known, at this point, for only five years, but to be betrayed by friends of twenty-seven years is unbearable. I can't bear this pain any longer. I am being condemned by those I love the most, for doing the best I can.*

Somehow, I keep going to work, feeding the children, caring for the animals, doing Jack's farm chores as well as my own. Since I work for the Department of Children's Services, I have to take Edward, who is still a minor, for an interview with the police and the Children's Services' Special Investigator* in another city. At least temporarily, that gives me some semblance of protection from my co-workers finding out about the investigation. After the Department Special Investigator leaves, the police lieutenant sighs, "Children's Services sure can mess up a good investigation."

I keep taking my children for doctor's appointments, psychologist's appointments, and psychiatrist's appointments. I am still driving on the weekends to see Ben, who is still in a treatment facility four hours away. I just keep doing all the things that need to be done, even though I have no idea how I am doing them. I am exhausted: physically, emotionally, spiritually. Each day, I get up and pray to know what the next thing is I need to do and to have the strength to do it. I pray it all day long. *Please, just tell me what the next thing I need to do is. Please, if I can figure out what the right thing to do is, give me the courage to choose it. Please, if I am brave enough to choose it, then give me the strength to carry it out.*

The boys have decided that no matter what First Church says, they want us to try to stick together as a family, including Jack. I can't argue with them. Over the past few weeks I have done a lot of research on sex offenders and have learned that taking away offenders' support systems only *increases* the chances that they will hurt someone else. Offenders with stable relationships and social supports are less likely to repeat their offenses than those without. It puts "loving your enemy" in a whole new light. My cutting off contact with Jack could only make it worse for society at large. Jill Levenson, Ph.D. put the dilemma eloquently:

> *Disrupting offenders' stability and social bonds is unlikely to be in the public's best interest if it exacerbates the psychosocial stressors that can contribute to reoffending… Sex offenders rouse little public sympathy, but exiling them may ultimately increase their danger.* [3]

So, we will weather this storm together as a family if we can, and if we cannot do that at the church where we have been, we will go together somewhere else. The boys have no idea what this choice will cost me, but still it is a choice all of us make together. *If any one of us does not have a place at the table, then none of us do.* Wife and children, hurt and angry, have still decided to stand in solidarity with husband and father. In spite of what he has done to our family, we have decided that if Jack is not welcome at First Church, then we will not go there without him. We are determined to love the sinner faithfully in spite of the sin.

Laura's voice still resounds in my head, as it has many times daily for weeks. "If you're going to love anyone, you've got to learn to lo-o-ove George Wallace." (When Laura said it with that Tuskegee accent of hers, love always had three syllables.) But as time has gone on, the message has evolved. While at first my personal George Wallace was the child molester I discovered I was married to, as the weeks have gone by I understand the message differently. *Okay, Laura, you want me to love George Wallace? Well, George Wallace has become for me these people you loved – members of our church – yours and mine – standing in the doorway of the church we both love, refusing to let your brother Jack come in. What do I do now? Although I may be frequently angry, even furious, with the man to whom I am married, even on those days I know he is just like you, a beloved child of God. You knew what it was like to be one of those kept out of restaurants, churches, restrooms, schools. You told me we are called to love everyone, but how do I love them, when they won't let him in?* The challenge has become for me to continue to love those who are asking me to choose, to love those who are telling me Jack does not have a place at their table, and that if the boys and I insist on coming to church with him, then we do not either.

The task is a daunting one, because I love this congregation with all my heart. I came here right out of college, when John was not yet three weeks old. I have grown up here, raised all my children here, and have volunteered as one of the appointed pastors for fifteen years. I have led worship here, taught confirmation classes year after year, married and buried members of the congregation, loved them with all my heart. That love for them now gives them the power to wound me more deeply than I would ever have imagined. I struggle to continue to love the church when individual members of the congregation have come to embody my own personal George Wallace. It is one thing to try to love the repentant sinner to whom I am married, but I struggle daily with the task of loving those who self-righteously violate my innermost basic belief – that everyone, even Jack – has a place at the table of God. *And if he does, then of course, so do they.* The task of loving the church that is betraying my faith in it has become more monumental than the task of loving the man who has betrayed my faith in him. And every Sunday, when it is time for worship and I know we cannot go together to the place I love, I weep.

CHAPTER SIX

Cutting the Ties that Bind

I keep looking frantically for a new place to live. Jack has not been able to find a job, and there is no way I can continue making payments on the farm by myself. Weekends and afternoons and days off are consumed with going to look at properties and houses, but none of them is The Refuge. Every time I drive home knowing I will eventually have to leave the place I love, I cry. If the kids are in the car I cry silently, with tears streaming down my face, hoping desperately they will not notice. If I am alone, I sob aloud and sometimes scream out my plea for mercy. *Please, God, if you are really there, have mercy on me. Please, Jesus, hear my cry. I cannot bear any more. I don't even know what to ask for. Please, help me.*

On the fourth of February, Jack's psychological evaluation is completed, and the safety plan is amended to let him move back out onto the farm. Both Doc and the Special Investigator for the Department sign off on it. Jack stays in a portable building down by the barn, about a quarter mile away from the house. It is driving me crazy having him out there, trying to make sure he and Edward don't cross paths, but at least it is free. Some nights I go out there to take him supper after the kids have gone to bed, and we talk until he falls asleep. Now that he's no longer acting out the abuse he says his father perpetrated against him, he has terrible nightmares and flashbacks. He wakes up shaking and sobbing. *I know that he is suffering, God. Please, help me be compassionate. Please help me be patient, and not so angry about the fact that if he had dealt with all this stuff years ago, we wouldn't be in this position now.*

The second week of February is the last chance for Conner to take his graduation exam again. Even though he has a special education diploma, in my state even special education kids have to pass the eighth-grade equivalency exam to get a regular diploma. Normally, they can continue taking it as long as they need to, but because the state has changed exams, this is his last chance at the old exam. He passed one part of it about a year and a half ago, and he has done nothing except study and take the remaining part over and over again ever since. He isn't a child who gives up easily. But all of the adults involved in his care – psychologist, psychiatrist, mother, tutor, friends – all of us agree that no matter how much he wants a real diploma, it is unrealistic to expect him to start over with the new set of tests.

His tutor, Sherry, has continued working with him for free ever since he completed his coursework. She says she has never known anyone more determined or harder-working. She and I take him out to dinner the night before the exam. Making sure he gets a good night's sleep and breakfast is all I can do. After I take him into the school building, I sob like I've gone crazy when I get back out to the car. His former teachers and the special education guidance staff have arranged for someone to read him the exam, question for question, and to sit with him while he takes it. They are giving him the best chance he has ever had, because even using the tape recorder, as the learning disabled kids are allowed to do, is over his head. Time after time, he has tried to work the recorder, but has gotten lost on the tape. For today's test, they got permission for an aide who was once in his classroom to sit with him and read the test aloud. The guidance staff said they would make sure he got breaks, snacks, and soft drinks in addition to the ones he has brought. They said they would keep encouraging him so he won't give up. When he finally comes out to the car, he says he thinks he has passed it. But then, he has thought that every single time before, four times a year, for six years. And this was his last chance.

We are still trying to stay together as a family, at First Church. Either Jack goes with friends to the early service, and the boys and I to the later one, or when we can arrange to go together, Jack and I go together to the first service and the boys go with friends to the second. It is not working very well. People continue to call. Friends continue to threaten to leave if he stays. We're not even six weeks into the new year, and it is already clear that if our family continues to insist on going to church together, albeit at different services, it will be divisive to the First Church congregation.

Ok, you have to do something. The last thing you want to do is to hurt the church you love. You may believe that no one person has the right to tell any other person that they are not welcome at the table to which God has invited them, but you have also traditionally respected the combined wisdom of this group. If everyone has a right to vote, you have to admit to yourself that more of them are telling you he is not welcome than are saying he is.

The meetings that are being held to address problems with both past and current pastors are upsetting people as much as they are healing, in the short run, at least. Jack has volunteered to be in the hot seat so people can tell him how hurt and angry they are with him, but two different leaders in the congregation have told us, "No." Even though what he did has left people feeling their trust in him has been betrayed, we have been forbidden from addressing these issues at the meetings. We've been told they will only detract from the issues at hand. That is on top of my having been told that I *must* not bring up my own experience with the former pastor, since the congregation has already moved on to addressing issues with the current one. The congregation's liaisons with the mediators told me they don't want the schedule delayed any more than it already has been.

That means that after exposing my shame and humiliation at my misplaced trust, I am not to be allowed the same outlet for healing that the rest of the congregation has been offered. I did not want my friend who spoke up about her experience to be left standing alone, but now I feel as though I am. The congregation, which was already torn and wounded even before the healing process began, is still losing members left and right. I have known for weeks that there are a number of reasons I probably need to resign, but I can't until after Valentine's Day, because I have a wedding to do for my friend, Wilma, late that afternoon.

February 14, 2004 is going to be a wild day. Early in the day, the very first one of my foster children is to be married. I am not performing that ceremony, because for that service my role will be as mother-of-the-bride. Lucy came to live with me twenty-four years and one month ago, and though she was eventually returned to her family, she has come and gone from my home ever since. Whenever she needs a place to live, she comes. Whenever she has a place she wants to go, she leaves. The most recent time she lived with me was last summer, when she lived in a portable building behind the house at The Refuge. It was living up to its name.

For Lucy's wedding, I have been able to arrange the perfect gift – a reunion with her birth son, who was given up for adoption a dozen years ago, when he was six years old. The lad is now eighteen years old and has never been adopted. For all these years, Lucy has never stopped searching for him and for his brother. After trying to work it out for years, I have finally been able to locate Lucy's older son, and to obtain permission from his social worker for him to meet his mother. I met with my foster grandson first, a couple of days ago, to make sure he wanted to meet his mom. He was too young to understand why she put him into state's custody at the time, and I had no idea what he had been told about it. I couldn't be sure that he would want to meet her without checking with him first.

Though I hadn't seen a recent picture of him, I couldn't miss him coming down the hall. He looks just like his parents. Even before he heard the story, he told me he couldn't wait to meet his mother. I told him anyway, because I wanted him to know. I didn't have to ask Lucy, because she has been actively looking for her son for years. She has no idea what is in store for her. I have made arrangements for them to be reunited at breakfast on the day of the wedding. All I have told my daughter is that I want to take the engaged couple for what will be the best breakfast they have ever had. I take them to her son's dorm.

We walk in and I tell the receptionist we are there to see the boy. My daughter grabs her fiancé and starts shouting, "What did she say? What did she say?"

I respond as casually as I possibly can, "Come on, breakfast is this way," and start walking down the hall, following the directions the receptionist has given me.

My daughter starts yelling her son's name, loud enough to wake up the entire dorm. When he steps out into the hall, they are mirror images embracing one another. The food at his dormitory wasn't that great, but who could taste it through the salt of all those tears?

Later in the morning, Lucy is married, and at the wedding I run into an old acquaintance, the pastor who is performing the wedding. It turns out that Jim is now the pastor of All Saints Community of Faith. The congregation is largely made up of gay men who were rejected by their prior faith communities because they came out. Several of them were pastors before being shunned by their congregations. *I am a straight pastor who is a member of a family that is not welcome to worship together at our church home because I am married to a man who has committed despicable acts – criminal acts – against children. Because we insist that he, too, has a place at the table with us, we are, all of us, outcasts; it has the potential to be a great match.* The congregation meets for worship on Sunday evenings, and has communion weekly. Jim says he would be glad for my family, even Jack, to join them if that is ever possible. When that reception is over, I race across the state to officiate at the wedding of Wilma, from whom we got the horses, and her fiancé Bill. Bill and Wilma found each other late in life; both weddings are signs of hope. It is a marvelous day.

In the evening, my Valentine's Day pastoral duties completed, I sit down at my computer and write First Church a letter of resignation as associate pastor. I remember with sadness the number of times I have walked across the room to stand next to one person or another on purpose, welcoming them to the circle when no one else wanted to hold their hand. I don't name the sins I know were committed by members of the congregation, people who were made welcome in spite of their humanity. I am saddened that although we have always welcomed those who made *other* congregations uncomfortable (depending on the decade: conscientious objectors, people of color, gays and lesbians, transgendered individuals) we are unwilling to welcome the one who makes *us* uncomfortable. Though the congregation might not have believed what they were saying, I believe what I told them through and through. They might not choose to include the man who has betrayed my family, but my children and I do. *Everyone has a place at the table, apparently, except the man my children call Dad. Every family has a place there except mine.*

I drive to the church, even though it is late at night, and leave the letter at the church office for the council meeting to take place the next week. I do so with the full knowledge of what this will mean for me, both personally and professionally. With this act, I lose not only my connection to the congregation that has been my family for thirty years, but also I lose my identity as a pastor. Weeping, I leave the keys that I have had for almost thirty years.

I have also written an open letter to the church, which will be read aloud at the meeting by my beloved friends, Hoyt and Martha.

To the Council and Members of First Church:

Last night, I shared with Hoyt and Martha my decision to resign as associate pastor, effective with this meeting. Martha suggested that if I wished to make a statement to the church, that she and Hoyt would stand with me. I have asked them, instead, to read this letter to you on my behalf.

Since the heartbreaking revelations of New Year's Eve, some of you have been absolutely wonderful, and I want you to know how much I appreciate your expressions of kindness and concern. But others have made it clear that when we say, "everyone has a place at this table" we are speaking of separate but equal dining facilities, with the people who make us uncomfortable eating elsewhere, or at least at a different time.

For our part, the boys and I have decided to stand in solidarity with Jack. Our family motto has always been, "you can go to treatment, or you can go to jail, but when you get out, you come back here, because you don't get another family." We have unanimously decided that if it applies to any of us, it applies to all of us. Jack is already in treatment, and he may go to jail, but as long as he chooses to remain with us, he is a member of our family, and we have chosen him. There has been a safety plan in effect since New Year's Day, which was written by our psychologist and approved by the Department of Children's Services. Eleven days ago, as a result of Jack's psychological evaluation, all parties agreed to amend it to allow him to move back home. At this point, no charges have been filed, and it has not yet been decided if any will be, so we do not know what will happen next. But whatever happens, we will face it as a family together.

I believe to the core of my being what I have said before you many times, that everyone, whether sinner or saint, whether perpetrator or victim, has a place at God's table. At my house, we are living that every day. I pray that someday, you will be able to live it, too.

With all my love, Sophia

Some time later, in response to my resignation, I get a letter from the chair of the church council saying that I am welcome to return, but no mention at all is made of the man to whom I am still married. I read the letter over and over again looking for some word of Grace for Jack, but I can't find one. The council wants me to know that *I* am family there, but the silence regarding Jack is deafening.

Sophia,

The First Church Council observed a moment of silent prayer before I read your letter of resignation as First Church associate pastor and expressed your appreciation and honor for having been in ministry with First Church. Hoyt and Martha presented your statement/letter concerning your decision to resign. Hearing your letters was a painful process for the Council as we know it was for you in making such a decision. The openness and depth of the discussion and concerns expressed by the Council for you, your ministry, and your family expressed the love in which you are held by First Church…

The Council also offers an open invitation for you to speak to us regarding your decision or any other concerns that you would like to share. First Church continues to affirm and to live out as best we can God's invitation: Everyone has a place at this table. In the same spirit of your family's motto "You can go to treatment, or you can go to jail, but when you get out, you come back here, because you don't get another family," First Church wants you to know and feel that you are family here…

Please know that our thoughts, prayers, and concerns are with you and your family during this difficult time. We pray for healing and wholeness for you and the family and for healing in your relationship with First Church.

Shalom, Chair of the Council, Kellogg's First Church

The very same person who wrote the letter on behalf of the council had already called me before I received it. When he called, he recommended: "Follow my example from when something like this happened to me, and go to church somewhere they do not know you." He did not elaborate. I did not ask. I read his letter fully aware of the knowledge that he sent copies of it to everyone on the council, making sure each person on it knew he went through the motions of following their directions, while only I know of his call. The contrast between his public response and his private one is overwhelming. It makes his letter a mixed message at best.

Another old friend in the congregation keeps calling, saying our family should not come back until enough time has been allowed for the "Safe Sanctuary Committee" which has formed to do its work. *I know committees, and I know this church and how we operate. It will be over a year before it finishes.* It has never been enough for the church that the safety plan calls for Jack to abide by all the state's rules for sex offenders, even though he has still not been charged, much less convicted. *No one has even bothered to ask what the state regulations are. The existing rules, as set up by the courts, have been designed to protect Edward and all the other children at church, but not a single person on the committee, which is talking ABOUT us, has talked TO either of us.* Instead, they want time to come up with rules of their own.

Not willing to absent ourselves from church altogether while the committee takes its time, the boys and I become a part of the All Saints Community whose pastor performed my daughter's wedding on Valentine's Day. It is somewhere we can go where Jack can worship with us if the safety plan is ever amended to allow it. The requirement for that happening is that the therapists for all parties involved, Jack, our minor sons, and myself would have to agree that contact between Edward and Jack is therapeutically appropriate, and on their recommendation, the court must agree. We don't have any way of knowing if that will ever happen.

I have been so traumatized by the events leading up to our leaving First Church that the week after we go to All Saints the first time I have a terrible nightmare. *In the dream, Doug, who is one of the members of the congregation, comes up to me after worship and tells me that we are not welcome there. He tells me that as a straight family, we do not meet the criteria for being members of All Saints.* I wake up sobbing, at having been rejected yet again. The next Sunday, I ask Doug if that is really how he feels about us being there. Do we make the others in the congregation uncomfortable by our presence? He assures me that we do not, and then he volunteers to become the "youth group leader" – I think just to make me feel better. My guys will constitute the entire youth group, which the congregation supports, just for them. They wrap us in their care in more ways than one.

In the meantime, Jack keeps looking desperately for a job, any job, which will fit the requirements of the safety plan and still allow him to help support his family. In response to my repeated suggestions that this would be a good time for him to go back to being an architect, since there are not usually children in office buildings and we desperately need the money, Jack finally confesses yet another part of the story. The real reason he has not been supporting himself by doing what he was trained to do is *not* because he is altruistic and has been trying to do good deeds. The real reason is that some years ago, a firm where he was working bought health club memberships for everyone on the staff, and Jack was caught voyeuristically watching the other members of the firm in the locker rooms. Word spread rapidly, and he had become a liability. Soon, word spread to other firms, as well, and before long he could not find anyone in town who would hire him. *Will we never get to the end of his lies?*

An organization in town is going to open a new facility similar to the old Reduce! Reuse! Recycle! store. They are taking applicants for the job of manager. Jack applies for the position and interviews for it, but does not get the job. While that in and of itself may have been bad news, it gives me an idea. In the fall, before Jack's confession, I had incorporated a non-profit to raise funds for the huge adoptive house of my dreams. My hope was to find a way to provide housing for sibling groups and young people transitioning out of state custody. After New Year's, I had given up on the idea when I realized that Jack and I would never parent children again. *Okay, I may never mother more children myself, but maybe I can at least raise money to make it possible for others to do so. If instead of giving up on my dream of providing a home for additional children I revise it, maybe I can still make adoptive homes possible for special-needs children. I do not have to house them all under my own roof.*

Reduce! Reuse! Recycle! went out of business last year. Jack and I could start a similar venture ourselves, that would raise funds to help remove the physical barriers that keep children in foster care. A store like it could accept donations of reusable building materials that would be sold to raise funds for adoptive families. The money and materials raised could be used in any number of ways, depending on what each child needed. A family wanting to adopt a child in a wheelchair might need their home made handicap accessible. A family willing to adopt a sibling group might need the addition of a bedroom or a bathroom. *I wouldn't have to parent additional children myself if I could make it possible for other families to adopt hard-to-place kids. I could still get them out of the system that way.*

I call Jack and suggest the idea. It would be a way for him to have a job and help support our family while raising money to help other children, without ever having contact with children himself. I've been reading the non-profit application for months, with my old idea in mind, so I have some thoughts about what might work. With the consent of a preliminary board, I apply for 501(c)3 status for the corporation, while Jack starts trying to raise money so we can start.

I think my ceaseless search to find a place where the boys and I can afford to live has finally borne fruit. After hundreds of hours of searching, this is a house I can feel good about and still afford. It is much farther from town, but it is closer to Bridgett's, the boys love it, and it could be fenced for the remaining horses. It needs things like doors and light fixtures, but I have a barn full that I have been collecting for years. It would be tolerable. It's not The Refuge, but it could work. I pre-qualify for the loan and we make an offer on the house, waiting to see what will happen.

The reply comes back that the owner of the house is in a complicated mess with his current mortgage, and that our offer will have to be approved by his mortgage company. There are multiple forms to complete and negotiations to participate in. The realtor had insisted we sign a form which guaranteed him the commission before he would even show us the house, and as the process goes on he proves to be impossible to deal with. We often catch him in lies; I feel trapped. This is the first place that has given me hope that I could leave The Refuge without hating where I live every day. It drags on and on.

I still struggle every day trying to discern what the loving thing to do is for my entire family. While on the one hand there are days I want nothing more than to divorce Jack and quit having to deal with him altogether, on the other hand there are days I miss terribly the man I thought I knew. Not only that, but almost daily I have to listen to my children asking when the only dad they know will be allowed to be a part of their lives again. They are constantly asking things like, "Can Jack come to my birthday party if Doc comes with us?" or "Would it be okay for him to just do this with us, or that?" "Could we all go to church together if we just don't talk to him?" "Could we send him a gift or write him a letter?" Conner especially is having a hard time with the fact that as far as he is concerned, if I could get rid of Jack, then there is nothing to keep me from getting rid of him. He is a child who takes everything literally, and if our family's claiming rule is to apply to any of us, it has to apply to Jack as well. In his thought processes, there are no exceptions for any reason.

Still many times every day, I keep praying. *Please, just show me what the next thing I need to do is. Please, give me the courage to choose it. Please, give me the strength to see it through.* I am crying almost all the time when no one else is watching. Daily, I go to work and have to face another eight hours of screening child abuse calls, waiting for someone I work with to get another report on the man to whom I am married, waiting for them to do the history check and find the report I have written. Listening to my co-workers joke and laugh aloud whenever a report comes in about a family in which a woman has remained with an abuser, joking about why she stayed with him, is unbearable. *There is no way they will ever understand just how complicated it is. They can't imagine how children cling to the idea of the only father they have, no matter how badly he has abused them.*

In March, I get a call from the IRS. Although it normally takes about fifteen months to receive 501(c)3 status, my application does not have any glaring errors, and they are granting my request only five weeks after I applied. *I can't believe what I'm hearing.* The caller says that through all the schedules and forms, I have only gotten one date wrong on one form, where I put the date of the application instead of the date of the last day of the first fiscal year. All he wants me to do is change the date, initial and date the change, and fax it back to him, and I will be done. Once he receives it, he will send me back my non-profit authorization letter. I am so excited that I must ask the man half a dozen times if he is sure that is the only mistake. Finally, he wants to know why I keep asking. I explain that I did not have the money to hire an attorney, so I completed the application myself. Just the instructions were hundreds of pages long. Once he understands why I am so excited, he laughs and says I must be pretty smart.

The handful of people I have convinced to be the non-profit's initial board have already met and authorized hiring Jack once $10,000 is raised. So far, he has raised about $3,000, and we are anticipating another $500 coming in a grant from one of the churches. We still have almost $6,500 to raise before we can hire him. I send my mother and stepfather (to whom she has been married for over twenty-five years now) an e-mail:

Dearest Parents,

I just can't do it. I have met with the realtor three times to sign the papers to list the house, and every time I get to that point, I just start crying uncontrollably. I just can't do it. I think I can, but then when it comes right down to it, I can't.

So I've been trying to come up with another plan, and would like to ask the two of you to consider something else. You offered to help me make the payments on the farm long enough to sell it. Would you be willing to try something else to help me try to save it? Would you be willing to lend us – or me – the money all at once, instead of a little at a time? We could use that money to make a tax-deductible donation to the non-profit, to get it started. That way, we could go ahead and sign a contract on a building and Jack could start work immediately. If we do that, then instead of having to sell the farm, Jack could start a full-time job, which would enable us to keep the farm.

If it works, we could not only go back to making the farm payments, but we ought to be able to make payments to you to pay you back for this loan, and finally for the car, too. If it doesn't work, God only knows when I would ever be able to pay you back. We'd have to surrender the farm to the previous owner, and move. But then, at this rate, we'll have to do that soon enough, anyway.

What can I say? You put my brother and sister through college, and then they have basically been successful ever since. Me? I was too proud to let you put me through college, and I have been struggling to survive financially ever since. Maybe if I would just eat my pride and ask for what I need, my whole life could turn around. So please, consider this possibility. It is taking a chance on us, I know. But please, I am begging you for this chance.

With all my love, no matter what you decide. Sophia

In a great act of generosity, and in spite of the fact that my parents are both retired teachers living on a limited income, they grant my request. They make me a personal loan of the money, which we then donate to the non-profit, fulfilling the board's requirement that $10,000 be raised before we start. We are finally ready to begin.

Over the next few days, Jack and I look at several properties that are possibilities for housing the store. One of them is in a wonderful location, and is a fascinating, quirky building that would be great for what we have in mind. We make an offer on it, but it is refused. Then, the rental agent for another property offers us a deal, and the board approves the location. Almost all of the initial inventory comes from the materials I have been saving for my dream house. My heart is breaking every time I tell Jack he can take something else from the barn, as the reality of the end of my dream comes crashing down. My building materials are supplemented with fixtures from a store in town that is converting one of its showrooms into office space. They donate all the lights and plumbing fixtures from their former showroom to us. We rent a truck, and carry those materials to the new location, as well.

Since we have no money to pay employees, Jack wants to use court-ordered community service workers, as he did at Reduce! Reuse! Recycle! I am very concerned about his being in a position of authority over anyone he might be in a position to abuse, and he has already proven his inability to act appropriately with young people over whom he has power. The risk of his taking advantage of young probationers is way too high for my comfort. I insist that any CSW's who are assigned to the store must be a minimum of thirty-five years old. Jack reluctantly agrees to my demand. He tells Jane, who places CSW's for the state, about my requirement concerning their ages, and she agrees. At last we have a building, stuff, and someone to work there. With that tiny beginning, on the fifteenth of March the store opens for business.

Jack is still required by the safety plan to have no contact with Edward, who is still a minor. Keeping them apart has been a logistical nightmare for me. Even with Jack sleeping in the portable building down by the barn and only being allowed access to the house while Edward is at school, coordinating their movements to make sure they do not pass each other, even accidentally, is exhausting me emotionally. Lack of sleep is exhausting me physically. I am constantly on the verge of tears.

Now that we have another possibility for a place Jack can stay that will not further deplete our virtually nonexistent monetary resources, we immediately move him into the offices at the store. For the first time in months, it feels like there is a little respite from my distress.

Work for me is becoming even more unbearable. As a state employee in good standing, I am theoretically eligible for a transfer to a comparable position in another department, but it requires getting my name on the "transfer registry." Time after time since January first, I have sent in my application to try to get on the registry. I have e-mailed my materials. I sent another copy by inter-office mail. I even sent a copy by registered mail. I keep calling, asking about my application, but nothing. *I'm never going to make it. The longer this drags on, the more miserable I am. I have to get out of Intake before I fall apart.* I have started having panic attacks at work several times a week, during which I am in so much pain I go into the bathroom and collapse, unable to breathe, trying desperately to regain control in order to go back out to my desk and pretend that everything is fine. I live in constant fear of the day someone will come across the report and office gossip will spread the word about the agony of my private life throughout the place I work. Sarah and Rolanda are the only two of my co-workers I trust enough to know what is happening at home. They hold me up, supporting me, befriending me though it all. *If it weren't for them, I don't know what I would do.* My supervisor continues to listen to my distress and to walk me through the investigation, as we talk frequently about what is happening, and the supervisor from Special Investigations is helpful, too. But on and on it drags, unending.

While I am always hoping we will be able to stay at The Refuge, I know that if the deal on the house I made the offer on comes through, I will have to take advantage of it. That process drags on and on as well. Day after day, we get one delay or another from the realtor. It seems there is an endless supply of reasons he has not done what he has assured us he will do. Each day he delays, our financial situation grows more desperate. Jack isn't making enough to pay even the store's rent, much less to pay his salary, so I am paying both the store's rent and our house payment out of my salary, falling further and further behind every day. *I can't keep this up. No matter what I do, I can't afford to do any one of the things I am trying to do on my own, much less cover them all.* I am growing more wretched by the day.

In the meantime, Jack has been worshipping and singing in the choir at another church, which gave him a list of rules about what he needs to do to attend worship there. Tonight, he called and let me know that he went to choir practice not knowing it had been cancelled, and instead of waiting in the car which is where he was supposed to wait, he went into the building to wait in the choir room. While he was playing the piano, a child came into the choir room looking for someone, and Jack took him back to the adults responsible for him. *Who knows whether it was an honest mistake or not? It was still a violation of his agreement with their church council to be in the building alone.* As a result, he has been asked not to come back there, and once again he is without a church home.

I am frustrated and angry with Jack for not following the letter of the law, and start going back to Al-Anon. I had gone to the group for a long time, years ago, when one of my kids was in treatment and for several years afterwards. That time, I had been in such distress I talked at almost every single meeting I went to for my first two years. This time, I resolve to keep my mouth shut, to listen, and to see what I can learn. This time, I am going to deal with my feelings about Jack. My favorite part of the meeting is at the beginning when we read the twelve steps. This time around, my version goes: "I admitted I was powerless over Jack, that my life has become unmanageable." Every time I say it, I feel a great relief. Listening to the women talk during the Tuesday night "after-the-meeting" meetings at *The Grille* helps me believe that anything – even surviving this – is actually possible, if I can just persist.

A friend of ours has been sentenced to six months in jail for an act of civil disobedience, and a worship service is being held for him before he leaves. Although the service is not being held at First Church, many of the First Church members are there. I weep as much for my own loss as I do for Don. After the service, two members of the First Church congregation come up to me, expressing their surprise that I've been gone from church. When I try to explain, one of them says, "I don't think most people realized that it was a package deal." *They could've asked, when we all disappeared.* I am struck by the way that so few people followed up when we left. My letter was written to the both council and congregation, but I suspect the congregation never received it.

By the time April rolls around, I have given up trying to get on the transfer registry, and have started applying for every job I can think of. It doesn't matter what it is. Sundays, I read the paper and send a résumé and a cover letter to every job I even vaguely qualify for. For reasons I have not yet figured out, it has been a completely fruitless job search. Almost nothing I send out even gets a response. Once, when I sent a résumé to someone I know, at a place I had worked before and for a job I was way overqualified for, I got back a form letter that said they had many applicants more qualified than I was. No matter what I try, I just don't seem to be able to get out of the child abuse Intake Unit.

Jack's story continues to expand. Today, Gabe told me a part I hadn't heard before. As a child with Hemophilia and HIV, he was constantly afraid of being injured. This was a fact that Jack used to his advantage. Gabe is telling me now that whenever he did not want to participate in whatever sexual activity Jack wanted him to do, Jack would not let him leave until he had done it. Saying no was not an option. Jack, who stands almost a foot taller than Gabriel still, must have been huge by comparison when Gabe was just a boy. He would use his size to block the doorway, refusing to let Gabe leave the room until he had performed whatever sex act Jack wanted. Though Gabe says Jack never actually hurt him, he didn't have to. Just the unspoken threat was enough to coerce Gabe to comply. Gabriel learned as a child that he was helpless to defend himself, and after that, Jack was able to rationalize that since Gabriel eventually gave up resisting, he must have been consenting. It is a dynamic they share in common with many victims and abusers. Once Gabriel learned that he was powerless to stop Jack, Jack was able to continue to abuse him even after he reached adulthood. Jack does not appreciate the idea that if you don't believe your "no" will be respected, your "yes" has no meaning at all.

I am revolted that Jack threatened Gabe's need for safety to get what he wanted from him, while he took advantage of my desire for safety to get what he wanted from me. It is disgusting, and inexcusable. It seems he is willing to use people in any way convenient, in order to get whatever he wants. I made a commitment not to file for divorce as long as he followed the rules of the safety plan, and to give it at least a year, but I don't have any confidence this will ever get better.

Every day, I feel worse. Week after week, when I go in to see our psychologist, I say that I can't understand how I am still functioning. *I am the embodiment of the expression "the walking wounded." I AM a walking wound. I don't understand how I continue to do the things I have to. I have no energy. I have no hope. I have no idea how I am still going to work or feeding the kids. I have no idea how I can still be kind to my husband when I believe this is all his fault.*

Many days, I try to discern whether or not Jack was truly abused by his own father, or whether he is faking it because he thinks that will justify his actions. Either is possible, since my understanding is that between a third and a half of sex offenders were themselves abused as children. I have no objectivity in this regard; I just can't tell. *He could, of course, be lying. But I don't think he's that good of an actor, and I don't think he was faking the nightmares. Even if he is telling the truth, it may explain his actions, but it still does not excuse them. Regardless of whether or not he was victimized by his own father, it has still been Jack's choice to do what he has done. He clearly knew it was wrong, or he would not have hidden what he was doing all these years. He chose not to tell. He chose not to get help.* Doc and I discuss antidepressants, but I know that they would do nothing to change my circumstances, and it is the reality of my circumstances that is wearing me out. *It is hopeless. They won't help this time. You don't just feel badly. Things really are bad.*

One afternoon, the boys and I go to a friend's house. Ingrid has been one of my best friends for years. She was also one of those who said they did not want Jack to come back to First Church or to the choir there. Of all the friends who cast Jack aside in January, Ingrid is the only one who tells me now, "If Jack needs a place to stay, he can come sleep on my couch. I was really mad at him, because of what he did to you and to the boys. But if he needs a place to live, he can come here." Jack is all right for now, but it means the world to me that she makes the offer. *Thank you, Ingrid.*

Then, one day, when I am praying to Mary, in front of her stained glass window in the sanctuary at All Saints, I finally get the call that Conner has passed the test to get his regular diploma.

Thank you, Mary. Thank you, Goddess, for a glimmer of hope in what has become for me a desperate situation. Shortly after that, as closing of the deal on the house I made the offer on is finally approaching, I get the word that the process has dragged on for so long that my credit rating, which was good enough to qualify for the loan when we first made the offer, is now shot; I no longer qualify for any loan at all. No matter how exhausted I am, the search for somewhere the boys and I can live has to begin again. *Come on, now, you can do this. Don't you dare give up now. You know what you have to do. The next right thing. Just do one thing at a time, just like you always have.*

Jack seems to have radar that picks up my discouragement and desire to give up. He sends me another letter:

> *… As you know, change has always been a struggle for me and this period of change is no exception. What is exceptional is the way you continue to model for me the all-encompassing love of God. I continue to see in you new dimensions of love which I had not expected to experience. The selflessness, patience, willingness to hang in there, no matter what, inspires me to work harder to try the new things I need to try in order to make it through this trying time.*
>
> *I'm beginning to discern a difference between the sort of feelings that motivated me in my previous relationships and the ones that motivate me now. There is less guilt and more desire to experience the joy from doing the right thing. There is less fear of rejection and more fear of failure to achieve what I need to do in order to support you and the children.*
>
> *Please continue to hang in there with me. I want to arrive at the point where I can return your love in kind.*
>
> *I love you. Jack*

After countless more hours on the Internet and weeks of driving and looking, I finally find a picture of another place I think I can learn to love. Even farther from town than the last one, and much farther away than where we currently live, it is at least a farm with a barn. I call and give Jack the address. He goes and looks at it, then after work, I do. One more time, we make an offer, and I begin to hope. It is weeks later before we get a response. One more time, my hopes fall crashing to the ground. *I have no idea when our current mortgage holder will lose patience with how far I am behind. I have no idea where I will take my children if we have to move.*

CHAPTER SEVEN

Manna for the Day

In May, Jack goes to talk with our mortgage holders to beg them to rent The Refuge to me temporarily, with a moratorium on the payments until I can get caught up. He calls me afterwards, thrilled that they have agreed. For the first time in months, I quit crying for a few days, believing I can stay in the place I love. But then, when I go to discuss terms with them, they say they are sorry, but they really can't afford to do it after all. They say that they had been drinking the night Jack went by, and it was the alcohol talking instead of good sense. They say they cannot possibly do what they agreed to.

They insist we place an advertisement in the paper to sell the farm. *You know you can't put your own number in the paper. You can't even talk about it. Every time you even think about leaving, you burst into tears.* We run our landlord's number for people to call, and list the amount we still owe as the asking price. After the advertisement runs a couple of weeks, they have received only two calls, and we discover that the amount we contracted to pay for the farm far exceeds its current property value. After talking to several mortgage companies, I realize there is no chance we can get even what we owe out of the property. Making enough money to move is out of the question. Finally, one day the husband and wife from whom we bought The Refuge come out to see the place. I am not there at the time, but Jack tells me they came by.

Jack said the two of them walked around and got a look at the things we have done, the chicken coop, the pond, the fenced paddock, and the stall. They had an opportunity to remember what the property was like. *You're running out of time here, and you know it.* Weeping, I drive to their house and leave them a letter telling them how much I have loved living in our small valley. I don't knock when I leave it; I just stick it in the door. I cannot bear to talk to them about it. I am crying too hard to talk. I just want to say thank you, while I still can. The letter reads in part:

I am sorry I missed you today. I just wanted to thank you for making it possible for us to live at The Refuge for the past two years. We have always referred to it between ourselves as "God's Country" or Gaia, the ancient word for Mother Earth... When Jack lost his job in January and I realized I could not possibly make the payments with only my income, I started crying, and I haven't stopped yet. I cannot tell you how much I love the native beauty of this land, the delicate beauty of each wildflower, and the cheerful gurgle of the creek that has kept us company day and night these past two years. It feels as though my heart is breaking...

So, thank you for your kindness these past two years. Thank you for making it possible for me to hope, and to dream, and to sleep at night with the creek outside my window...

With all my gratitude and best wishes, Sophia

When the wife reads the letter, she remembers how much she, too, loved living where we live now, and how sad she was when they relocated to another county. And somehow, she is moved to give me another chance. She and her husband talk about it, and figure out exactly how much they have to have to let us stay. And then, by a miracle, they decide to let me rent the place. Sarah, one of the only two co-workers of mine who knows what is going on, gives me a mitzvah* of $500 to pay towards what it will take to get them to let us stay. I don't know what that is. She explains to me that a mitzvah is an undeserved gift to be passed on, an act of human kindness. Someone has once given this gift to her, and she is passing it on to me, on the condition that some day I will pass it on to someone else who needs it. *It is manna* for the day today.*

The day that epitomizes the entire year so far is in May, as well. On this day, in the mail, I receive the notification letter that I won Ben's last treatment appeal. After all the time spent fighting them, the state has finally been ordered to pay for the treatment that all Ben's doctors agree he needs. I didn't have the money for an attorney to represent him, so I had represented myself against the state's attorney at the hearing. I am still rejoicing with relief when literally, twenty minutes later, I get a phone call and find out I am being sued for over $16,000 because our private insurance has not paid his bill from when he had to be hospitalized following an out-of-state suicide attempt. Adoption assistance has already let me know that they do not consider themselves responsible for his emergency room bill, even though they had approved his treatment at the out-of-state facility where he was when he tried to kill himself. Their rule is that in-state facilities *must* be used first, even in this case when Ben was not in the state at the time he needed to go to the closest emergency room. As one of my professors described my life years ago, upon reading a paper I had written for her Religious Autobiography class, sometimes it seems like my life isn't just one thing after another, it's one *damned* thing after another. For people who rule with their hearts, that is often so. The high of victory followed by the low of defeat sums up the entire year in less than half an hour.

While we are talking today, Jack says that he meant well when we first married, and that in the beginning it was me he was attracted to, but that things started to fall apart for him the first time he saw one of the boys in his underwear. After that, he says, while he was with me he would be fantasizing about them. I am revolted. I am furious, too. He says he does not stalk children, that he just likes children and "it is not [his] fault they trigger [him]," but I know that is garbage. He has methodically sought out children who were vulnerable and needy and has then taken advantage of them. I don't believe for a minute that he didn't think he would do that with my children, too. I think that is *exactly* why he married me – so that it *could* happen. Many times we had talked about the fact that he seemed distracted when we were together, but I had no idea that it was because he was obsessing about my children. He sure didn't tell me about it. I keep going over things in my mind, looking for clues I might have missed. I hate myself for having been so blind and for endangering the boys, but I still cannot figure out what would have given him away any sooner. As Doc said, he is just a very good liar.

Frequently, Jack expresses his eagerness to "work through all this" or to "get all this behind [him] and to come back home again." For my part, the more time that goes by, the *less* likely I think it is that will ever happen. I made a commitment to myself to give it a year, but I do not believe a lifetime would be enough.

When Jack wants to know "how can [he] make it up to [us]," I usually think the most helpful thing he could do would be to leave us alone so we could get on with our own lives. He isn't helping us in any other way. Even Sundays, the day he is supposed to come out to the farm and help with things I cannot do myself, he just uses us. Every week, we have to vacate the farm early Sunday morning and stay away all day so he can "help out" around the place, but all he does is eat the food I have worked hard to pay for and to cook for the boys, watch TV, and do his own laundry. He plays with the dogs and the horses (which is what I'd like to be doing since it is my day off, too) but does not do any of the things on the list of chores I leave each Sunday explaining what I need help with. Things stay on the list week after week, and every time we come home and nothing is done, I get more angry about it. Still, the court order currently in effect gives him the right to be on the property – which he still jointly owns – on Sundays, in order to "maintain the property." If he *really* wanted to make it up to us, he would be making my burden lighter instead of just using us, expecting me to pay for and cook his food, and making my life more complicated.

On June 1, the mortgage holders of The Refuge finalize the terms to rent me the property and we sign a new contract. The mitzvah Sarah gave me, combined with a gift from my dear friends Martha and Hoyt, makes it possible for us to stay on, just a little longer, in the place I love. Only God knows how long the reprieve will last, but for now, at least, it is a reprieve. After signing the contract, I go home, sit on the deck, and listen to the creek. *Thank you, Jesus, thank you, Goddess. Thank you for every single day I get to stay here.* For the first time in all the months since Jack's New Year's Eve confession, instead of despair, my tears are of joy.

In early July, my friend Deborah is going to be married, and the boys and I decide to go to Florida for the wedding. Deborah and her fiancé, Douglas, send me money for gas, so we all pile into the car and head south, making the long drive down to the coast. I desperately need the break. Jack has promised to go by the house while we are gone to care for the dogs and horses, but I can't be too sure about anything he says these days. All I know is that I need to go so badly that it is worth the gamble.

While there, I get a call that sends me reeling. A worker from a state agency for Family Services calls on my cell phone to say she has been assigned to Edward's case. When I tell her I know nothing about her assignment, she assumes I am lying. I do, after all, work for the Department, and I did sign the safety plan, back in January. The worker keeps telling me that her intervention is required by the safety plan, and she argues that obviously, I must know; instead, what I *do* know is that there is *nothing* about her in the safety plan at all. She says she is to come to our home weekly to make sure Jack is not there. I argue with the worker that if they want to check to see if Jack is not in the home, they should check to see if he is where he *is* supposed to be, instead of further victimizing the family. The worker tells me that if I refuse services, charges will be brought against me for failing to protect Edward, and that I could lose custody of him.

Nothing I can say convinces the worker that a stranger in the home could be disastrous for Conner. *She doesn't know Conner; she doesn't know how threatened he is by any change in his routine. She has no idea how many years it takes to gain his trust. She can't imagine how terrified he is of strangers. She not only doesn't know how it will affect him, she doesn't even care. All she cares about is that if I don't do what she is telling me I have to, she will charge me with failure to protect Edward.* What I know is that not only will an intruder be threatening to *both* Conner and Edward, but our lives are already so complicated by weekly trips to psychologist, psychiatrists, tutors, the general practitioner, the nephrologist, work, and school, that I cannot bear the thought of trying to juggle yet one more thing. The worker insists. If I refuse services, she tells me I could lose custody of the very children I have fought so hard to protect. *But, if I accept services, Conner could spiral out of control.* It is just the scenario I feared most the night of Jack's New Year's Eve confession.

When I get back to work after Douglas and Deborah's wedding, I find out that unfortunately no one bothered to let Doc or me know that the safety plan that he dictated on New Year's Day, and on which the Department signed off shortly afterwards, has been changed. Even though the Children's Services case has been closed for months, a Department supervisor who reviewed the case up the ladder is now insisting that the plan be amended to protect the Department from any further liability. Just as the Family Services worker told me, the requirement the supervisor insists upon adding is that since Children's Services closed the case, a Family Services worker has to be assigned. Sure enough, that worker's job is to police the home, checking weekly to make sure Jack, who has been moved out of the house and into the store since March, is no longer there. The supervisor has chosen this route because my employer has no jurisdiction to require someone to see if Jack is where he is supposed to be instead. They are, after all, Children's Services, not adult services.

Over the next several weeks I fight back against the Department, trying desperately to protect my children from further harm. Doc recommends that I let the worker come to the house once only, and I agree. On the day before the appointment, a storm intervenes, and a tree falls in the road, blocking the worker's approach to the house. The tree is covered with poison ivy, and the worker declines to climb over it. While the worker and I talk in her car, which is parked in the road, Edward anxiously rides his bicycle back and forth while Conner paces furiously. Each of them was so traumatized by his time in the foster care system, that they assume anyone from that system is their enemy. This invasion of their home, their safe place, by this woman they do not know leaves them feeling even more violated than the abuse Jack perpetrated. At least they knew that Jack had no intention of removing them from their home.

An avalanche of e-mails and phone calls follows. Later in the week, Edward tells Doc and me that if the Family Services worker comes back again, he intends to run away. On the day of the next appointment I cancel it, informing the worker that I am refusing services until and unless the court orders me to accept them. When I get home, I discover that Conner is so anxious he has continued to escalate until I got there, not knowing I have already cancelled the appointment. By the time I can get him to Doc's office, he is so distraught he kicks out the windshield of the car in the office parking lot before I can even get him into the building. Knowing we have no money to replace it, our friend Robert hires Conner to work for him over the weekend. He pays Conner far more than he earns, giving him the ability to pay for the windshield himself.

In spite of the children's terror, nothing I can say changes the opinion of the Department supervisor who is insisting on Family Services. She is resolute in her decision. I go to work and argue with the Special Investigator's supervisor that the boys have been safe all these months. There is no reason to change the safety plan that has kept them so, at this late date, long after the case has officially been closed. The Special Investigations supervisor tells me that the Department is just trying to cover its own liability by passing the responsibility off to another agency. What it does to the children is of little importance compared to protecting the agency. This sentiment is echoed almost word for word by the Department's attorney when I go to meet with him.

I offer to go ahead and divorce Jack, even though I have no way to pay the legal fees. By this time, he has been staying at the store and we have been living apart for more than enough time to file the papers. Still, on July 16, I get back an e-mail from the supervisor of Special Investigations, stating that she has talked to the Department supervisor, who says that even divorce would not be sufficient, because "a divorce does not guarantee that there would be no contact" between Jack and the boys.

I continue to fight against my employer to defend my children from further abuse by the Department that is supposed to be protecting them. Sure enough, just as the Family Services worker threatened, charges are brought against me, alleging that my youngest son, Edward, is neglected and dependent upon Department intervention to protect him. The state files a petition requesting that the judge order me to accept the services Doc has already told me are not in my children's best interest. They also request an order of protection, prohibiting contact between my husband and my children.

When I read that part of the petition, I am frustrated beyond words. *I can't believe they want anything else. Why didn't they just tell me that to begin with? If anyone from the Department had ever told me such an order was needed, I would have gladly filed for one months ago.* Their argument at this point is that without a court order, there is nothing the Department can do to make our family follow the safety plan. While technically that is true, we have already been following the safety plan to the letter for six months without any exterior enforcement at all, even after the case was closed. We have voluntarily moved Jack off the property and into the store, even though the Department itself signed off on permission for him to return to living on the farm. In spite of all that, all these months later, the Department is still interfering in my children's lives. I go to the courthouse and obtain the order of protection, trying somehow to appease the Department supervisor who does not trust my integrity to continue following the safety plan our doctor dictated on New Year's Day. Still, that is insufficient to make her happy.

Every day, I continue to fight against my employer. The judge appoints me an attorney, as I cannot afford one and am in danger of losing my children, and the children are appointed a *Guardian ad litem** as well. When their attorney comes to the house, the children hardly speak to her, but her presence does not threaten them as much as that of the Family Services worker. They know enough about court to understand that this is their attorney, who will represent them. Doc and I have spent quite a bit of time explaining the concept that their *Guardian ad litem* will represent their best interest against the Department they are so threatened by, and against the Family Services worker they are afraid will remove them from their home.

When the attorney asks how they feel about the Family Services worker, Conner mutters, "I don't go into her home and go through her stuff, and I don't want her coming into my house and going through my stuff to see if Jack is still here."

Edward is able to verbalize, "When she comes, it brings back up what happened. It makes me upset to think about it, so even if she doesn't ask me about it, just her being here makes me mad." They don't say a lot, but they say enough to help their *Guardian* understand.

When we go to court, our doctor comes along, too. Doc explains to the judge that it is not in my children's best interest to have yet another person involved. Multiple services are already in place. There is every reason to believe the boys will tell if their stepfather violates the safety plan. Mine is the last case heard, and I am already exhausted even before we begin. When the judge rules, he starts out by saying, "Family Services is a good service," and my heart sinks. *Okay, if he tells you that you have to accept these services, then you will.* Then he goes on, adding, "but not in this case." He rules that the charges against me are not true, that Edward is not neglected or dependent on the state for protection, and is not in need of Department intervention in order to be safe. The original safety plan is allowed to stand. I promise the judge that if Jack violates the safety plan in any way, I will let him know. For the first time in seven months, the family is safe from further harassment by the state.

It is within days of the court hearing that I have an appointment to meet with the new Commissioner of my Department, not to talk about my own children, but to talk about issues regarding the Department itself. The Intake Unit is still in the start-up phase and has not yet gone statewide, but there are many things going on which concern me. I took the job despite my misgivings about the Department because I hoped that the new Intake Unit would make things better for the children of the state, but the things I see day after day trouble me.

After the meeting, the Commissioner has me speak with someone else to give her more details, names, and issues. I tell the woman about supervisors who are gone for hours at a time, making it impossible for their teams to find them, and leaving no one to screen their team's child abuse calls. I tell her about supervisors who look up employees they don't like in the perpetrator database, hoping to find a justification for firing them. I tell her of absences and manipulated time sheets. I tell her about church bulletins mass photocopied week after week at taxpayer expense. I tell her of Intake workers being driven to tears by cruel supervisors, and of other workers who try to talk callers out of making child abuse reports time after time. I tell her of how our efforts as supervisors to address these issues are thwarted by management farther up the line. I tell her of my concern that children will die as a result of our incompetence, and how when I discuss these things with my supervisor, she tells me, "The Department of Children's Services doesn't kill children. Other people kill and abuse their children." It sounds like a parody of "Guns don't kill people. People kill people," but every time my supervisor says it, she seems to be serious. I am assured no one will ever know the information came from me.

In the midst of all the chaos of my life, this week has brought me a glimpse of Grace. Through the fog of my despair, I see one from time to time, and this week it has been Bonnie who made Grace real to me. Bonnie is especially important to me because when she found out about what Jack had done, she was one of the few friends who did not put me in the position of having to choose. She was one of those who offered from the onset of this disaster to sit with Jack and me at church. It was an offer that had given me reason to believe in Grace at a time when I desperately needed it. This week, she has embodied Grace yet again.

A few days ago, Bonnie's husband died, and today folks from First Church will be gathering at her house. I want to go, even though it will be the first time I have seen most of the folks there since Valentine's Day. I know it will be agony to see those who rejected Jack and me, but I really want to go for Bonnie, who has always been there for me. When I called to ask her if she would be willing for me to come, Bonnie made a point of inviting Jack to join us, too. When I expressed my concern that others might not approve of his being there, her reply was, "I can do anything I want to do in my own house."

So, today I go to Bonnie's house as my old friends of almost thirty years gather. It is excruciatingly painful to see the way the members of the church who have avoided me gather around her. *Okay now, you can do this. This may be hard, but Bonnie's love for Jack and for you, too, is a sign of Grace, and you have been starving for a sign. She knows, if no one else here does, that your children lost their father no less than hers. She understands that, in a different way, you lost your husband, too.*

There are few others who speak to Jack and me today. He spends most of the afternoon standing in a corner, looking like a trapped animal, but he, too loves Bonnie and is grateful for her support. Since I left, First Church has a new senior pastor, who is here. A number of old members have told me it is better at church since she came. They have said she is reaching out to former members, but I have not heard from her. I have been praying since she came. *Please, let her coming change the prevailing attitude of the church. Please, let her make some overture towards our entire family on behalf of the church to heal this breach.* She comes up to me and asks me who I am, saying she recognizes me from a picture at the church. When I tell her my name, she says, "The church safe sanctuary committee is still working on it," and turns and walks away. A couple of folks come up and say the church has not responded very well to our distress. *No kidding. The people gathered round Bonnie mostly ran from us. But Bonnie's love, and that of a few others, is once more manna for the day.*

On Sunday morning, I work up my courage and call my parents. I haven't talked to them in a while, because my mother doesn't deal well with bad news, and I haven't had any good news

to share in a long time. I don't have any today, either, but it has
been so long I call anyway. My mother sounds tense. When I ask
what's wrong, she says, "I hadn't heard from you in so long I had
written you off. I didn't know if you were alive or dead."

I ask, "Mother, if you were worried about me, why didn't you
call to see if I was alright?"

She answers, "Well, I didn't call because I was afraid it might
be bad news."

"Oh," I reply as gently as I can, "so you didn't call me for the
same reason I didn't call you."

Last week, I was home from work because Edward was sick.
Today when I went back, I found e-mail instructions on my
computer to report to Internal Affairs, and not to tell anyone that
is where I am going. Though I can't be sure, I suspect it has
something to do with my reading the record of Edward's
investigation, which the Family Services worker was furious about.

Throughout the entire investigation, I have relied on Policy 14.13
A.2.a., which says that information regarding investigations can be
released to the parent or custodial guardian, and I have read the
record. At first, I would just sit at my desk, dazed, and look at the
report I had typed into the computer, reading it over and over again,
trying to make myself believe it was real. Then, as the investigation
went on, I on several occasions discussed what I found there, either
with my supervisor or with the supervisor of Special Investigations,
so both of them knew I was reading it. I made no attempt to hide
the fact, because I believed it was within the limits of Department
policy, and neither supervisor told me anything to the contrary. The
Family Services worker did not seem to agree with my interpretation.
She knew I was reading it because when I told her I did not know
she had been assigned, she accused me in the written record of lying.
I wrote asking her to retract it; she refused.

I can only reason that: since within days of winning in court
against the Department and meeting with the Commissioner I
have been reported to Internal Affairs for something, and since
the Family Services worker was infuriated that I had read her
entries, my reading the record must be to blame. Sure enough, in
spite of the policy, IA accuses me of *stealing* the information in the
record. When I give them the citation, they look it up and read it.

Then they tell me the policy says information "could" be released, not that it "would" be, and reiterate that I have stolen the information I read. I am horrified. Neither my supervisor nor the Special Investigations supervisor has ever told me I should not be doing it, and as far as I knew, it was within policy, but Internal Affairs is accusing me of being a thief. Not only that, but although it is written in the record that the Special Investigations supervisor knew I was reading it, they tell me my supervisor has denied to them that she knew anything about it. I have no way of knowing if that is because I met with her supervisor and the Commissioner, but at any rate, I am out on a limb, alone.

The IA representative goes on to tell me that the written information in the record itself is *never* released to parents or guardians, and I know that at least that part of what he is telling me is not true. There have been occasions when I have testified in court against the state on Ben's behalf, when the attorney has supplied me with the entire written record before I testified. I don't have any way of knowing what other incorrect information the IA representative might be telling me, but I do know one thing: if I am fired, I will lose my rights to continue the insurance benefits my children so desperately need. If I resign instead, I have the option of continuing their health insurance through COBRA for an additional eighteen months. Even though the COBRA premium payments are enormous and I have no idea how I can pay for them, with any luck, eighteen months will be long enough for me to find another job with benefits.

I *cannot* take the risk of being fired and losing the boys' health insurance coverage. In addition to the multitude of psychiatric diagnoses I knew my sons had when they'd been adopted into the family, Edward has another diagnosis, Polycystic Kidney Disease. It is a progressive disease, which is fatal, and the only known treatment is a kidney transplant. For years, I have paid enormous premiums to keep his health insurance in place, because we have no way of knowing when his kidneys will finally fail completely and the transplant will be needed.

With that in mind, it doesn't make any difference whether the Family Services worker made the report to IA, or whether it was someone in my own unit who turned me in as a result of my blowing the whistle to the Commissioner. *It doesn't matter why.* If *you are fired, you will lose the kids' health insurance, and since Edward will eventually need a kidney transplant, you cannot take a chance on it. They are not likely to fire you if you have already turned in your resignation. That's what you'll have to do. But then, how will you feed your children next week? Next month?* I leave the IA office in shock, go back to my desk, and fill out a resignation form giving thirty days notice. From the moment I hand it to my supervisor, I have thirty days to find a new job and a new way to support my children. *I may have been the one who read the record, but if it hadn't been for Jack's predatory actions, there never would have been a record to read. Every single disaster that has hit me lately eventually leads back to Jack.*

By this time, I am so stressed out at work that my panic attacks are happening almost daily. After turning in my resignation, knowing I am finally leaving with or without a job waiting elsewhere, my coworkers say they haven't seen me this happy in months. A surgery Conner has needed for several years has been planned for the summer, so I immediately make the calls to make sure it is scheduled before my notice runs out. That makes it possible for me to take the last ten days of my notice as sick leave, in order to stay home with him while he recovers. During those ten days, I read in the paper that a child has died due to one of the very problems in Intake I had reported to the Commissioner. *Thank goodness I wasn't there. At least this way there is no doubt at all in my mind that it was not my fault.*

One of my greatest fears during all these months has been that an Intake employee would discover my file and tell everyone I work with what it contains. It has hung over me like the sword of Damocles. It has been horrible enough that I have had to deal with my family's anguish and our shame over what happened to us. It is bad enough that I struggle daily with trying to discern the faithful thing, without everyone I work with making my private life a topic of office gossip. When I told the IA investigator that, he said that if anyone had ever said anything to me about the report I filed, I would have been in violation of policy myself if I failed to report that person to IA. What I thought at the time was *he must be a fool. If everyone in the Department who discussed cases got fired, the Department would have no employees left.* But my shame has hung over me long enough. At the very end, as I am leaving, I tell two other supervisors what happened so they will at least have heard it from me first, in case another report comes in, and then finally, I am free.

My middle adopted son, Ben, has been in and out of one treatment program or another for a number of years, ever since an aggravated assault charge landed him under the jurisdiction of the juvenile court in the county where we used to live. The judge's direction that he must complete a treatment program before he can come home seems, two years after the fact, as far away as when the boy first went into treatment. He seems determined not to complete anything.

Treatment programs for children are classified by the level of restriction the children experience. Level 1* refers to a setting such as a foster home, which has no restrictions other than one might experience at their own home. Level 2* facilities have several trained staff available around the clock, such as those in a group home or therapeutic foster home. Level 3* has trained staff awake in shifts twenty-four hours a day and a setup or location that makes it unlikely the child will be successful at running away. Wilderness programs fall into this category, as do some locked facilities with on-site schools. Level 4* facilities are locked wards such as those found in psychiatric hospitals, frequently with cameras monitoring the children at all times.

Ben has been in a number of different facilities over the years. At most facilities, he has been so violent and resistant to treatment that when his time ran out or his violence became too overwhelming, he was moved to another facility. This last time around, over two years ago, he started out in a wilderness program but was moved to a locked Level 3 unit in another state after he broke the nose of one of the women on the staff. It was determined he was a danger to the employees of the wilderness program, and he ended up out of state because there was no Level 3 facility in our own state that was willing to risk admitting him.

In the locked unit, as in the wilderness program, Ben refused to participate in any school activity, so that at seventeen he still has only two half-credits in academic subjects and five and a half more in electives, making him still a freshman. His two brothers are exceedingly frustrated with his lack of cooperation and consider it a punishment to have to go see him, since he adamantly refuses to do what it takes to get passes to come home. In the entire two years, he has received a pass to come home only once, for Christmas, after which one of the staff members told me that he had not actually earned the pass, but had just been given it because they thought it would be good for his self-concept. Immediately after he received the pass and saw everyone at home, he reverted to his previous behaviors, which were what got him locked up to begin with.

Within days of my notice expiring at Intake, it is released over the news wires that the state's health insurance plan, which covers the kids who have adoption assistance, is going down the tubes. Less than two hours after the news release, I receive a call from the treatment facility where Ben is currently being treated. They are calling to tell me Ben has to be out of there by September 15. I remind their administrator that I cannot just pick him up and bring him home because he is under court order to "complete a program" before he returns home.

The administrator tells me that is not a problem for him, and sends me in the mail a cover letter for Ben's treatment record. Even though the record documents how over the previous two years Ben has not met a single treatment goal, the administrator believes his letter will prove to the judge that Ben has "completed the program." He does his best to make it sound like Ben is ready to come home. Although Ben had been in a violent altercation with staff only the week before, the letter includes phrases like:

> *He has made some progress. Specifically, Ben has decreased aggression toward others and has significantly reduced and possibly eliminated self-injurious behaviors. His school attendance and participation has also improved as he is now engaging in some of his work, rather than sleeping in all of his classes... Our treatment team feels that Ben has received maximum therapeutic benefit from this program and therefore recommend his discharge... It is unrealistic to expect that Ben will be able to earn his PEER, PLEDGE, and HONORS level at this time.*

No amount of trying to convince the administrator that adoption assistance would continue to pay, even once the insurance ran out, makes any difference. I have the Director of Adoptions, our psychologist, Ben's psychiatrist, and the Department psychiatrist all review Ben's information. All agree that it is not safe for the rest of us for him to come home. I have very little time to figure something out.

CHAPTER EIGHT

The Heron

The only person, it seems, who thinks it safe for Ben to come home is the administrator of the out-of-state Level 3 where he has been for the past two years. This is the same man who said Ben was ready to come home the day it looked like his insurance was going to run out, and who sent me the letter saying Ben had achieved "maximum therapeutic benefit" from the program. On the 14th of September, I receive from this same administrator the packet of information I have been waiting for because I needed it to apply for another placement for Ben. He has sent it too late for me to find a place before Ben's projected discharge, which is tomorrow.

When I read the packet, I can see why he delayed sending it. It is full of documented violence the facility has failed to inform me about. The most disturbing thing is the description of an incident in which Ben has "thrown a kitten into a river while on an outing." This action has been attributed to "thinking errors" which "have been addressed." Ben's explanation that: "It was an accident. I didn't mean to throw it in the river. I meant to throw it on the rocks," is not exactly comforting. Ben's local doctors and I are extremely concerned that his behavior has deteriorated to the new low of killing small animals. It is one more bit of evidence that none of us are likely to be safe if he comes home. Even this makes me mad at Jack. If he had been the man he presented himself to be and consequently enticed me to believe he was, he would be living at home now. Then, if I did have to bring Ben home, Jack, who still stands four inches taller than Ben and probably weighs eighty pounds more, would at least make us feel safer. His presence might even help temper Ben's violent tendencies, since he tends only to attack people smaller than he is. But Jack is not here, and I have to protect Ben's brothers the only way I can – by refusing to let Ben come home.

After talking to Doc and Ben's *Guardian ad litem,* I write to the facility administrator on the 15th to let him know that I will not be picking Ben up that day, and fax a copy to his office so he will receive it the same day. That administrator has also told me repeatedly that the insurance company has been making him spend an hour each week in case consultation just to certify approval for Ben's treatment one week at a time. It proves to be to no avail to suggest to him that the administrative law judge who ruled on the appeal said that no certification was necessary, and that the judge has offered to be in a conference call with him and with the state's insurance company to tell them that,. *It is hopeless.* The administrator insists that Ben was miraculously healed the day the insurance took a dive, and is ready to come home. At one point, I even ask him, "Would you want to take Ben to your house?"

His reply? "Not on most days." No kidding. Me, either.

Having left Intake without having landed another job, I immediately begin working at the store in Jack's place. This serves two purposes. It keeps Jack away from any children who might come into the store by chance, and it makes it possible for him to do pickups and deliveries – a service we desperately need. Implementing the transition is difficult. Because of Jack's reputation with many of his old customers as "The Reduce! Reuse! Recycle! Guy," for them he *is* the store. Any time he is there, those customers only want to talk to him; and once he starts talking he does not want to leave to do the things he needs to. Often, they refuse to deal with me if he is not there. Finally, we agree that the only way for the transition to work is for him to be completely out of the store during the hours I am there. He can come in for pickups and deliveries. Otherwise, he is to leave the running of the store to me.

Though our agreement is that he will stay away from the building during the hours it is open, he constantly violates that agreement. He always has some reason he cannot leave before I get there, or has to come back during the day. It is distressing to me, and hard for me to take over when customers are constantly asking for him any time they see his truck. I get great relief from continuing to go to Al-Anon meetings, and weekly admitting that I am powerless over Jack, and my life has become unmanageable. Between the meetings, weekly therapy, and church, somehow I continue to function, even when I can't see any reason to.

All the local professionals who read Ben's treatment record from the Level 3 facility agree that what he really needs is not to be stepped down to a lower level of care and sent home, but stepped up to a Level 4 facility. No matter what the cover letter says, they unanimously agree that if he has been unable or unwilling to meet a single treatment goal in over three years, then what he needs is not less structure, but more. Since he has previously been turned down by every single Level 3 facility in our state, which was how he ended up in another, we send his information packet to a new Level 4 that has opened recently enough that they have not previously turned him down. The intake team at the Level 4 concurs that placement in their facility would be appropriate, and they put Ben on the waiting list for a private-pay bed (which includes everyone not in state custody) in their facility.

In the meantime, I continue to refuse to pick him up, even though the administrator at the facility where he is has reported me to Children's Services offices in both their state and my own. He claims that I have abandoned Ben, and tries to get the Children's Services Department in either state to come and get him. Needless to say, neither state wants to be responsible for him, especially after they receive the volumes of documentation about why he is on the waiting list for another placement, and why his doctors do not believe it is safe for the rest of the family for him to come home.

Jack has been asked, again, to leave a church. In this case, as in the case previously, he voluntarily told the pastoral staff everything that happened. Even though he has still not been charged with any crime, this new church, too, asked him not to come back. This time, what the church wants is a period to determine what the rules will be for his attending worship there, rules in addition to the requirements the state has already placed on him. Once more, my faith in my own denomination is being challenged, because once again, the denomination of which I am a part has refused a place at the table to the man to whom I am still, for better or for worse, married.

When I receive the October newsletter from First Church, it contains an article boasting how *everyone* has a place at the table there. The article is written by the same council chair who publicly wrote me saying I (but not Jack) was welcome to return, but who privately called and told me I should go somewhere they did not know me, even though I had done nothing wrong. *You have to stop reading this newsletter. It is not good for you.* It is more than I can bear. I call the church office and ask to be taken off the mailing list, explaining that technically, with my resignation, I no longer have any relationship to the congregation. Crying every time I get the newsletter and being reminded that we are not welcome as a family to return is too painful. Getting the news about the people I love is not worth the anguish of the reminder of my loss. Ten months after our crisis began, the congregation I love has finally been able to drive our entire family away without ever having to take a public stand on Jack's "unwelcome" status.

It is also in October that Jack takes his first lie detector test – a twice-yearly requirement of all the members of the court-ordered sex offenders' groups. Each time he has told his story for the preceding ten months, it has gotten bigger – not in relation to my own kids, but in relation to other children and adults he has known ever since he was a child himself. Finally, he admits that he has lied to me about almost everything he has said to me since he has known me. It is no wonder I believed he was my perfect match, because what he says now is that he would always tell me whatever it was that he thought I wanted to hear. The hesitation and pause that characterized almost all his answers were not a result of ADHD, as he had claimed, but were actually a result of his efforts to coordinate the lie he was *about* to tell with all the lies he had told before. *What he never understood was that all I had ever really wanted to hear was the truth.*

The day he takes the lie detector test, we meet for lunch afterwards. He is sobbing with relief that he passed. There is nothing, other than what he had already confessed to, that is within the statute of limitations. When asked what all the tears were about, he says, "It is because passing the test means I am finally, after all the years of lies, and the ten more months of partial truths, telling the truth." What I am thinking, I do not say. *I wish they had asked him if he was gay or straight. At least then, he would have to admit it to himself.* He has changed his mind about this issue every day for the past nine and a half months. Sometimes, he has even changed his mind several times in the same day.

Not only is Jack constantly waffling about his sexuality, but also in order to pass the lie detector test, he has had to reveal quite a bit of additional information. He keeps talking, because his probation officer will check to find out if he has told me these things: he has been involved in sexual activities with animals. Of the two hundred children he initially confessed to having "inappropriate thoughts" about during "outwardly appropriate interactions," it turns out he actually did fondle over a hundred and eighty of them, in a ratio of about ten boys to every one girl. Most of this sexual battery occurred while he himself was still a minor, life-guarding at his church's swimming pool. He would roughhouse with the smaller children, throwing them up in the air and then fondling them when he caught them on their way down. He would time going into the locker room to try to catch a look at them undressed.

He also admitted sexual contact with multiple eighteen-year-old community service workers at the old Reduce! Reuse! Recycle! store. He admitted that since he is not supposed to be masturbating to fantasies of minors or former victims, he has been "getting around that" in his mind by "aging" them in his imagination to consenting adults. But the biggest thing he seems to have been holding out on is that while it was Edward that he was attempting to molest, Ben (who fortunately was not at home during this time) was the one he has been fantasizing about, ever since shortly after our marriage. It seems he didn't want to tell anyone because he was holding out hope that as soon as Ben was eighteen, then he would be allowed contact with him. I know I agreed to wait and be patient to see what he is like when he is through with therapy, but right now I never want him to touch me again.

I keep thinking about the ways that Jack's "truth" has evolved over the past ten months. Initially, he looked relatively good for a child molester, and his story was easier to believe. The doctor who did his psychological evaluation told me he thought Jack's development was fixated at age twelve, when his father caught him with their neighbor, and the preliminary diagnosis of arrested development at least gave me some reason to hold out some hope. My own doctor knew I would beat myself up mercilessly if I did not do absolutely everything within my power to save the marriage, and encouraged me not to act hastily because I might regret it later. My Al-Anon group's standard recommendation was that no one make any major changes for a year, and I put the two together. "Arrested development" plus "give it time" became, in my mind, "Give it time because if this is a case of arrested development then there may be hope." My pairing the two together was an unfortunate juxtaposition. I had been in love with Jack and had desperately wanted there to be hope. For all I know, the doctors, whose job is to help people and to cure them if it is possible, may have needed or wanted for there to be hope, too. Maybe they see so many child molesters whose cases are hopeless that Jack's looking so good in the beginning may have given *them* reason to hope, too, that this might be one they could help.

If the lie detector test had just been given earlier in the year, we all might have responded to Jack differently. His is not a case of arrested development, no matter what he led us to believe. Jack is not really even technically a pedophile, except in the word's most general sense. Though the word is commonly used to refer to adults who prey on anyone under the age of consent, as a medical diagnosis the term "pedophile" refers only to an adult who is sexually attracted to children who have not yet reached puberty (two-year-olds, for instance, or prepubescent girls). Jack, on the other hand, is specifically sexually attracted to a very narrow group: those who are recently-pubescent males. Because Jack's sexual preference is adolescents, technically he is an "ephebophile*." Criminally sexual actions which are acted out on pubescent youngsters of the same sex are known as "pederasty*." And it is because his attraction is to children who have just hit puberty that he has been about to lie to himself about their ages, and to lie to everyone around him as well. Their little tufts of pubic hair were all it took for him to be able to claim that the children he was abusing were actually consenting young adults. He has lied to us about the extent of his activities with children, claiming to only have had "inappropriate thoughts" about interactions with them while in truth he had been fondling them since he was in high school. He has lied to everyone, including himself, about the pervasive nature of his sexual attraction to children and to males. *I may believe that with God all things are possible, but it looks like there has never been a reason to hope. Jack just made sure no one knew.*

Today is another one of those days I feel like I want to kill Jack. I once told the investigating lieutenant that occasionally I have days like that, and he looked alarmed. He didn't need to be.

It's not that I would actually do anything to hurt Jack, but sometimes he frustrates me beyond belief. Ever since New Year's, I have been trying to work out a deal with the Department and the police that will best serve Edward. What happens to Jack is much less important to me than how it affects my son, and Doc keeps telling me that what is in the best interest of Edward's recovery is that whatever happens to Jack *must* not be dependent on anything that happened between them. Since Jack had just started trying to desensitize Edward so that later he could abuse him further, Edward does not think that what Jack actually did to him was all that bad. In fact, he thinks that the worst thing Jack did to him was lie.

Jack had told Edward the same thing he told Gabriel when he abused him, "This is what fathers and sons do." Though neither Edward nor Gabe liked what he was doing, both of them, without another father to whom they could compare Jack, believed him. And according to Jack, that was what his father did to him. Now that Edward knows it is not what fathers are *supposed* to do with their sons, he believes the worst thing Jack did to him was to tell him that lie. And Edward, who is a frequent liar, does not think Jack should have to go to jail for his offense. For all these months, we've been trying to keep Jack out of jail *not* because he does not belong there, but because Doc says it will be worse for Edward if he goes. In that case, we will start having to deal with the fact that Edward thinks the sentence is unfair. The child, who up until now has *not* felt guilty, will almost certainly start to feel that way if he thinks Jack is being unfairly punished. And he doesn't need to be further victimized on Jack's behalf.

So today, after spending almost ten months trying to work a deal everyone can agree to, we finally do. Everyone agrees that Jack will not be charged with the abuse of Edward, on the condition that he does not violate the safety plan in any way. He will not have a criminal record as long as he does nothing else he can be charged with. The district attorney agrees. The Sheriff's Department agrees. Children's Services agrees. Everyone who needs to agrees with the plan.

Within hours of the agreement's finalization, Jack calls and tells me he has decided he wants to plead guilty to a felony in order to be assigned a probation officer. *Great. The sun has not even set on the long hoped-for day of victory on Edward's behalf before Jack thwarts months of negotiations. That's wonderful.* I remind Jack that I am not willing to be married to a felon. If he makes this choice, it will mean the end of our marriage. Furious with me, he relents. He will abide by the agreement. Or so he says.

My life continues to be an unbearable series of ups and downs. Within seven days, we have a party to celebrate Conner's finally receiving his high school diploma, at the age of twenty-two, followed by the most traumatic series of events since Jack's New Year's Eve confession. Conner's party is on a Thursday night. The next day, unbeknownst to me, Jack receives a call from someone who says they want to donate windows and doors to the store. They say they are moving, so the donation has to be picked up on Monday at four p.m., and that a mentally-handicapped fifteen-year-old male will be there to let Jack in to get them. On Monday, Jack neglects to tell me that a minor is to be at the pickup, nor does he ask anyone to go with him to get the donation. He does call me later to tell me he could not find the address, but that is all.

The following night, Tuesday, as I am waiting for the Al-Anon meeting to start, Jack calls me. I don't answer the phone, but after he hangs up I check the messages. His offenders group has just gotten out. It turns out, the pickup from the day before was a setup. There are stings going on for perpetrators around town, and his was the call to see if he would go somewhere where there would be an unsupervised child under the age of eighteen. Although there was no child there, because he went, he was in violation of the safety plan. He is calling me because the therapist running his group wants to see if he will actually tell me.

My agreement with Jack has been from the onset that I would not file for divorce as long as there was no felony conviction and he did not violate the safety plan in any way. I have been willing to wait and be patient until he completes the therapy group before making any decision about our marriage, only on these two conditions. This is a clear violation, a clear sign that he is willing to have contact with minors rather than do what the plan and his therapist require in order to keep them safe. It is the last straw.

I am relatively sure he would never have told me about it, had he not been confronted by his group, and the fact that there was no actual child who had been at risk does not make any difference to me at all. His intent is all that matters to me. Since I have absolutely no money to pay for an attorney, the next day, Wednesday, my friend Julie helps download the fill-in-the-blank forms to file for divorce. I fill them out, print them, and have Jack sign them. Because the financial commitment for The Refuge was based on our joint salaries, Jack has agreed that our only financial settlement will be that he will honor his commitment by continuing to pay a portion of his salary directly to our mortgage holders, decreasing the percentage each year. He is still legally liable on the loan, but I do not expect he will ever make good on his part of the settlement. He certainly hasn't made good on any other commitment he has ever made to me. We go to my friend Shirley to get her to notarize the documents. *She was one of the witnesses to our marriage. It is only fitting she should be the witness to its end.*

On Thursday, a week after Conner's party, I file the papers with the county clerk. Although Jack goes with me to file them, he still does not seem to comprehend that for me it is all over. Even as I am handing the notarized originals to the clerk, Jack is asking her how long it will be before I can request that the divorce be finalized. *He still wants to know how long he has to get me to change my mind. He just doesn't get it. He does not even realize I am not going to.*

Still desperately broke, I had no money for Ananda's meds this month, and when I get home from the clerk's office, he is having seizures again. *It is my fault, for not being able to figure something out, to somehow be able to make it all work. Surely, I should be able to come up with something, some plan that will cover everything.* Finally, I beg the vet for meds and promise I will pay for them when I can. It buys me a little time, and over the next few weeks Ananda's seizures ease, and the growths, that had started reappearing, slowly disappear.

The day after the divorce papers are filed, I receive yet another call from the administrator at the treatment facility that has been treating Ben. Since they have been unable to convince or manipulate me into picking him up, they intend to bring him across the state line next Thursday. Their plan is to drop him off at the juvenile court and leave him there. At this point, he has been on the waiting list for a private-pay bed at the Level 4 facility for two months, but still remains at number twelve on the list. He had actually moved up to number eleven once, but when the Level

3 administrator tried to get either state to take custody of him, he was taken off the list. It was only when I called to ask where he was on the list that they put him back on it, but he had to start again at the bottom. I have no other way to provide for his care, and am still being told by his doctors that it is not safe for us to bring him home. He is also still under the juvenile court judge's requirement to "complete a therapeutic program," which he still has not done. I start negotiations to put him into state custody in order to get him into a state bed. I hate to do it, but while there are no private-pay beds available, there are beds available at the Level 4 reserved for kids in state custody. There is no other choice that I can figure out.

I spend most of the next few days either on the phone with Ben's *Guardian ad litem* trying to work out the logistics, or still trying to get hold of the juvenile judge in the county where we now live to let him know that Jack has violated the safety plan. I agreed to let him know if that happened, and am trying to be faithful to that agreement, but everything I try only causes me more frustration. The juvenile court clerk refuses to give the judge the message because she says she cannot find any record of the agreement in the file. The clerk of the office that processed the order of protection says they cannot let him know because it is a matter before the court. Neither of those comments makes any sense to me, but I cannot get past either secretary to speak with him directly, and neither secretary can give me any help with how to do what I agreed to do.

Finally, I call the lieutenant who investigated the case. He suggests that since I can't get through to the judge, I try to convince Jack to turn himself in. "Please, Jack, at least go and talk with the officer," I beg on Wednesday. Eventually, Jack agrees to go talk to him the next morning. On Thursday, the day Ben is to be put into state custody so he can be transferred to the Level 4, we can't find Conner's Basset hound, Buddha, when it is time for me to go to court. Eventually I can't wait any longer, and we have to leave without putting the dog in the house. Once in town, I spend the morning in court with Ben's attorney. When I come out of the building, having finally done what I have always resolved never to do – return one of my children to state custody – I turn my phone on, and there is a message. I play the message back, and it is from Jack. He had, as he promised, gone that morning to talk to the police officer in charge of the case to report that he violated the safety plan.

We knew that the violation was likely to result in Jack's arrest, since the condition of his not being charged with the original offense was that he comply with every condition of the safety plan. Even though there was no actual child at the sting, he had still been willing to violate the plan by going somewhere he believed there would be an unsupervised, underage child. Sure enough, he has been arrested. *The good news in this for Edward is that Jack has been arrested not for what he did to Edward, but for his willingness to endanger others.* Jack's message is to let me know that he is now a resident of the county jail, and to let me know where he left the truck so I can go get it.

Jack also asks a favor of me, one I am unwilling to grant. For the past few months that Jack has been living in the offices at the store, there has been no running water. It was cut off after the leasing agent discovered there was a leak somewhere under the concrete floor and was unwilling to have it fixed. Jack has been "borrowing" water from an outdoor faucet at an adjacent building ever since. In his message, he let me know that he was so nervous about going to talk to the police that he was sick and relieved himself that morning in not one, but three different restrooms in the offices. He wants me to "borrow" water myself (he's sure they won't mind) and to flush the three toilets for him. He has left for me not just a figurative mess to clean up, but his literal excrement to clean up after. I am absolutely livid. *He is so totally lacking in respect for me that even though he knew when he left this morning that he would not likely be back, he still left this disgusting job for me to do. His only purpose in maintaining a relationship with me is to be able to use me. No matter what his words say, his actions show time after time that he doesn't care anything about my feelings at all.* Hoping that he will soon be released and will be able to take care of this task himself, I shut the doors to the offices and refuse to do what he has asked. I will not do this disgusting thing for him. He can do it himself when he gets out.

We go home, and still cannot find Buddha. We search for hours. Finally, one of our neighbors finds his body on the train tracks. He had been hit, probably before we even left that morning.

Within a period of a few hours, we lost husband and father, son and brother, and the dog who was Conner's dearest companion.

Jack has sleep apnea. I go to the jail after supper on the night of his arrest to take him his C-Pap machine, and I also take his prescription for it with me. They tell me they are not accepting anything for inmates just then, and I have to come back two hours later. The jail is an hour away from The Refuge. I sit in the car and weep; there is no point in going home only to turn right around and come back again. I have been given a list of the things Jack can have in jail, so I go to an all-night store to get them. When my two hours are up, I go back in. They give back to me some of the things on the list. I ask why.

"These have to be in individual packages."

"But the list says it will only be accepted in bulk form."

"The list has been changed."

"I don't understand what is wrong with the pens. They are black pens in clear tubes just like the list says."

"These are gel pens. We only accept ink pens here."

"But he has to have the C-Pap. He can die without it. The list says he can have anything he has a prescription for, and I've given you his prescription for it."

"Well, we can give it to him, but he can't use it. There are no outlets in the cells."

I feel like I am the criminal. He's the one in jail, but I am the one who is embarrassed and ashamed.

The children are already in bed when I get home. I take one of Jack's old denim work shirts off the hanger where it still hangs in the closet I used to share with him. I carry it over to the bed and carefully arrange it about where it would have been if he were in it, on his side of the bed. I rest my head upon its empty chest, wrap the armless sleeves around myself, and cry myself to sleep.

In the days following Jack's arrest, the boys are finally able to put words to the anger that has been festering in them since January. Edward is furious that Jack has been willing to endanger another child. The anger he could never feel on his own behalf erupts in justified righteous indignation for the safety of others. Conner, too, begins to express his anger, and his growing awareness of his own ambivalence frees me to finally express to them some of the feelings I have been having all along. At long last, I have an opening that allows me to begin to explain to Conner that marriages are not like adoptions. It is possible for one person to do things that make it impossible for a marriage to continue. Doc and I talk to him about how the relationship between members of a family is a safety issue: just like Ben cannot come home because it is not safe for him to do so, neither can Jack. In fact, now that Jack has demonstrated his willingness to endanger other children, he may never be able to come home again. Finally, the door begins to crack open in Conner's thinking, making it possible to discuss the possibility of my divorcing Jack without threatening Conner's sense of safety.

The other thing I have noticed with Jack in jail is an overwhelming sense of relief. For eleven months, being around Jack has been like being with a counseling client twenty-four hours a day. I have tried to be just as kind to him as I would be to any of the others of God's children, but it has been wearing me out. I made the mistake of telling him in the beginning that I just wanted to know the truth, and he has been using me ever since like the toilet he left his filth in at the store. He just keeps filling me up with things I do not want to hear, and there has been no end in sight. I haven't wanted to discourage his telling the truth after all these years, because at least if he's talking to me I've known where I stood. I've wanted to do the right thing, but hearing about his sexual attraction to every living thing on the planet but me sure hasn't been good for me. Having him locked up is a relief. I have been exhausted just from listening to him.

The next week, there is a telephone hearing for yet another insurance appeal. This time, Ben's treatment is being denied and I have appealed because the insurance company is insisting that since we have transferred him to another facility, then he must have completed treatment at his prior facility. On that basis, they are attempting to justify that they are released from the prior court order. For some reason, we have a new judge who is unfamiliar with Ben and what is going on. In anguish, I describe what has been happening to him. When it is all over, I am sure that I have lost the appeal.

I decide to go ahead and file the quitclaim deed Jack signed and had notarized back in January. I am not sure why, but this has been even harder for me to do than it was to file for divorce. I read one last time its sad contents: "For and in consideration of the sum of Ten Dollars ($10.00) cash in hand paid, I hereby sell, assign and quitclaim to Sophia Ruah all my interest in the following land: 40 acres, more or less, with house, barn, and improvements. Send Tax Bills in Name and Address of New Owner." I have put off filing it for eleven months now, because it is distressing for me when I think about the end of what I had believed was our mutual dream, but by this point it is clear that it is the right thing to do.

I have been faithful to my commitment to Jack for almost a year. Eleven months have passed since his confession. My agreement with him, which was that I would not file for divorce as long as he did not violate the safety plan, is no longer binding me. He is now arrested and in jail for a felony, a sex crime, which means that for the rest of his life, he will never again be able to live in a house where there are minor children. I am likely to have children and grandchildren in and out of my house for the rest of my life. It is over. Jack's dream was not the same as mine, anyway. He stole my dream; he corrupted it, taking my vision of a way to help abused children, and turning it in his own mind into a vehicle for abuse he intended to perpetrate himself. It is enough.

Driving to the courthouse to file the quitclaim, I am sobbing, when I see my friend, the heron. Sometimes, on especially hard days, I see her standing in the creek outside my bedroom window. It is almost as though she comes to keep me company from time to time. Today, as I am driving down our road, she does something she has never done before. She flies along the driveway, then stops in a tree. When I catch up with her, she flies a little farther, then waits again. She flies with me almost the whole eight tenths of a mile down our road, before she flies away. *Is your coming to me today a sign? What is it that you are trying to tell me? It feels like you are just keeping me company, not saying I should be doing it, or landing in the road in front of me to say stop. Just keeping me company, telling me I am not alone in my despair.* It is the last day I see her for the next nine months.

On the day of Jack's arraignment in criminal court, I am sitting in the back of the courtroom when the juvenile court judge comes in. I go over and sit next to him, apologizing for not being able to notify him in person of Jack's violation of the safety plan. I tell him of my attempts.

"Did you put it in writing?" he asks.

"No," I reply, puzzled.

"There's nothing I can do unless it is submitted to me in writing," he explains.

This whole process is so frustrating for me that I think I am about to burst into tears. It is hard to believe that no one I spoke to bothered to mention this fact. I would have been glad to write it out if I had only known that was what I needed to do. Neither secretary told me. As this drags on, it is more and more clear to me why the rich and powerful get more justice than the poor and powerless, who cannot afford attorneys to negotiate the system for them. At least the judge knows I tried to honor my promise to him. At this point, that's all I can do.

COBRA is the interim insurance plan that is available to state employees for a limited amount of time after they separate from state employment. As such, it is regulated very strictly, and my first payment has been looming over me for quite some time. By the time the first of December rolls around, I still have no money to make the initial COBRA insurance payment, which is due. I beg every friend I can think of for a loan, without success, and have no idea what I am going to do. The paperwork I have received says that if the payments are not made on time, coverage will be cancelled, and I am desperate to keep that from happening. Conner's meds alone are over $2,000 a month, and I have no way of knowing when Edward's kidneys will finally fail and he will need the transplant which is the only treatment for his disease. I am frantic. I beg. I plead. I try to find anyone, anywhere, who will make me a loan, but in the end, the deadline comes and goes, and I have nothing. The store is getting further and further in the hole and is not even paying its own rent, much less paying me.

With no idea how I will be able to continue to provide for Conner's medications, Doc and I are finally able to convince him to agree to let me apply for disability for him. It is an idea we have approached him with many times over the years, but he simply wants no part of it. He wants a job, and he does not want to be disabled. He has stonewalled us time after time. But this time, faced with the possibility of no way to get the medications that keep him alive, he finally consents. I fill out the applications, and the waiting begins.

Friday afternoon, Gabriel comes into the store. "Mom! Mom!" He is forever yelling my name before he even gets through the door. Today he is both excited and sad that Jack has been arrested. "It's not fair that Dad got arrested for what he did to Edward. Why didn't anyone arrest him for what he did to me? What he did to me was worse, and it lasted for years longer. Isn't there any way we can have him charged with what he did to me, too?" I tell him I don't know. What the police officers told me was that it has been too long since Gabriel was a minor. I tell him that I don't think it is fair, either. It is difficult for me to believe that there is a statute of limitations on the rape of a child, especially since while Gabe was a child he had never been able to tell anyone who would do anything about it. He is right – it isn't fair that now when he is ready to speak up, the courts won't let him. I give him the officers' contact information, but when he calls them, they tell him the same thing they told me. There is no justice for Gabriel because he is over eighteen. He gets no justice because he is no longer a child.

Throughout December, the store's landlord keeps calling, wanting money, but there is absolutely nothing I can do. I had been subsidizing the store with my income from the state, and now that is gone. *I am doing the best I can. I can't even keep up at home. There is no way I can pay anything on the store's bills.* Each time he calls, he has less patience. Time and again I offer to vacate the premises, since that was our agreement at the onset – they would give us a chance, and if we did not make enough money to pay them, then when they ran out of patience they would write off what we owed them as a charitable donation. All we would have to do was leave the building clean and "broom-swept." I know the day is approaching. I continue to pour over Sunday newspaper classifieds, looking desperately for any job I qualify to have, and send off résumés to anything that is even a remote possibility. I have sent, by this time, probably hundreds with hardly any response. It seems I cannot find myself another job no matter what I do.

On my birthday, a day that could have been a terribly sad day for me, the guys from All Saints take Conner, Edward, and me out to eat. Their taking our family in is the best thing that has happened to me all year, and many times after church one or another of them has paid for our dinner when I could not. Tonight, Bill, Charles, Doug, Jim, John, Mickey, Steve, Tony, Vaughn, and Vince all take us out to a wonderful restaurant to which I have never been before. I get shrimp scampi, one of my favorites. I am more grateful for the friendship of these kind men than I can adequately say.

Jack's family knows that we are in dire straits this Christmas. I weep with gratitude when his aunt sends a check, and when his sister sends us a certificate for a ham dinner. I receive in the mail a small package from his brother and sister-in-law. I open it and burst into tears. *There is no way they could have known.* Each year for my whole adult life, my favorite birthday gift has been to receive Christmas ornaments from my friends. When I put them on the tree, I remember those I love and those who have loved me. This year, the ornament I receive from Jack's brother and his wife is the only one I get. *Oh, thank you. Thank you. You have no idea how much this means to me. I will always remember the kindness of your entire family during this terrible time whenever I hang this gift. Thank you.*

I receive from Jack this Christmas gift, a poem he sends me through the mail:

My Daily Prayer

My sweet, my dearest wife, my love,
I pray each day to God above:
Take care, O Lord, to watch, protect,
The ones I've placed within Your debt.

Our sons – Edward, Ben, and Conn –
Watch over them while I am gone;
The donkeys, horses, dogs, all fuzzy,
They're more than pets and ripe for hugging.
The land we share and asked Your blessing,
Guard from it all second-guessing.
The times are hard, there's not enough
To go around. Oh, God, it's rough!

You're left alone to hold together
The fragments, not being sure of whether
These are right, the proper choices,
Listening to divergent voices.
"Sell it! Keep it! Give it back!
Look, it's clear! Oh, no, it's black!"
"Mama, do this. What I need..."
It's more than you can do, indeed.

My heart goes to you, straining out
Of my weak chest, so full of doubt.
"Why did it happen? What's the point?"
My soul is broken, out of joint.

My dear beloved, understand,
I struggle still to be the man
You asked to marry, sacred trust,
From God, who through it all is just.

Just so you'll know, Jack

I take him packaged cookies and hard candy, the only gift he is allowed to have. I can send him a card, but only through the mail. When I take the cookies and candy to the jail, it is Sunday morning visitation. I guess the guards are being as nice as they can stand to be, but the process is humiliating for visitors. Even without the need for a search, since these are not contact visits, it is a miserable experience. They don't take reservations, so you have to go hours early to get in line to sign in. There are only a few booths with phones, so only half a dozen people can visit at a time. Often, one or more of the recording devices attached to the phones don't work, so they won't let anyone use those booths, and even fewer visits can take place simultaneously.

Sometimes, people wait all morning and don't get in to take a turn, but the jailers don't continue with the same list in the afternoon, so visitors have to come back in to line up again and sign in again at one. On really bad days, it is possible to wait all day and never get in. Visits are for a maximum of one hour, and since it is so hard to hear, sentences must frequently be repeated or just guessed at. To talk loud enough for the machines to record the conversation and for the other person to hear, you end up practically shouting, so there is not even the illusion of privacy.

Then what little time we do have, Jack spends raging about how much he hates the therapist who was the leader of his therapy group, and how he is sure he is not *really* a pedophile, because "[he] just likes to be around children, and it isn't [his] fault some of them trigger [him]." He wants a new psych evaluation. On and on he rages. It is a familiar refrain. Jack really doesn't throw anything away – not even tired, old, worn-out excuses that haven't worked in a very long time. I hate coming here.

Jack is always saying how he can't wait till he gets out because all he wants to do is hug me. He seems to have no appreciation at all for the fact that touching him is the *last* thing I want to do. I am so revolted by his actions and his feelings about my children that it takes enormous effort just to visit and to be kind to him. He seems to have absolutely no idea of how he affects people.

For months, I have been trying to get a writer from our local paper to do an article on the store, thinking that would help us since I cannot afford any publicity. She has been putting it off for quite some time, waiting to see if we are really worth doing an article on, but she has finally received enough positive comments about us from readers that she has decided to give us a try. She comes to the store to meet with me, and I tell her the entire story, about Jack, about the kids, about everything. *The last thing I want is for her to do an article and then hear about all the chaos from someone else, making her sorry she ever wrote about us at all.* She is kind beyond words, and says she will do an article anyway, as soon as she can work it in. Shortly after our interview, just a day or two before Christmas, I receive the notice that the store is being evicted.

CHAPTER NINE

The Cruelest Blow of All

On the day before Christmas Eve, Ben has a pass to come home from his new Level 4 treatment facility, but when I get up in the morning, we are completely snowed in. Trees are down, and I cannot get out of the hollow in which we live. I call the boys' grandparents, to see if I can borrow a four-wheel-drive car, and Skip offers to come pick us up to go get Ben. We walk down our road and climb over downed trees to get to where he has parked. The road is terrible, and the trip takes hours longer than usual. We are nowhere close to making it back in time for our appointment with Doc tonight. *Oh, no. This is not good. Since the doctors' offices are going to be closed on Monday for the holiday, Conner will miss two appointments with Doc in a row. That has always put him in danger of hospitalization.* Still, it cannot be helped. I try calling Doc from the road, thinking maybe Conner can at least talk to him on the phone, but I cannot get through, even to leave a message. Try as I might, I cannot will the car to go any faster.

By the next morning, the downed trees have been cut into firewood by our neighbors, and we are able to creep along in our own car down the road to the Interstate. We celebrate Christmas Eve together with all three boys and their grandparents for the first time in three years. All of us go to church with Skip and Mary Jo, and then to their house, where Ben is able to see family members he has not seen since he went into the wilderness program just over two years ago. On Christmas morning, we go to All Saints to celebrate Communion, and then go again to the boys' grandparents' house for dinner and to celebrate with them one more time. Afterwards, we take Ben back to his treatment program. It is a marvelous pass.

Each day for the next few days, I feel worse. By the last day before the first anniversary of the New Year's Eve on which my life pivoted, my emotional resources are completely depleted. *I have to have a break. I have absolutely nothing left to give these children.* Each day of the preceding week, all I have been able to think about is what I was doing that time last year. *That was the last normal Christmas Eve I will ever have, and I remember wrapping the presents with him… That was the last normal Christmas morning I will ever have, and I remember sitting in this very room as the children unwrapped their gifts, except he was here… That was the last Christmas service I will ever have worshipped in the church that I loved, and I remember what we read, and what we sang, and who was there. I remember inviting Saddam in his spider-hole; even he had a place at the table where Jack does not… I miss First Church so much that I think my heart will break.* The people at our new church are kind and adopted the boys for Christmas so it would not be so bleak. They provided Christmas dinner, even, as well as Christmas gifts. But it is not my home, and I so long for home.

The plans are for the boys to go once again with Skip and Mary Jo to the cabin over the New Year's holiday, and I desperately need the break. *I cannot remember ever being this desperate. I keep living two years at once, the current one, and the one I am reliving in my mind from a year ago. I have to do something, because I know that the next two days will likely be even worse.* The boys are talking and excited and are really getting on my nerves when I make a big mistake, the biggest. When Conner asks, I admit that I really want them to go. "Yes," I say. *Yes, Conner, I really do want you to leave for the weekend. I really, truly, desperately need the time to grieve alone.*

Suddenly, all the abandonment issues of adopted children hit the fan. On the way to Doc's it is already winter-dark, the boys are being loud and obnoxious, and I am overwhelmed by their behavior and my grief. I put both of them on time out. Conner is furious about it, and is seething. He was already angry because at the store today Edward hit him where it hurts and then ran away, laughing and taunting his older brother in front of the community service workers that he could not catch him. Conner adamantly refuses to go with his younger brother to their grandparents'. I know I cannot possibly take care even of myself over the weekend, much less Conner, so I tell him he has to go. He balks. By the time we get to our doctor's office, he explodes. Doc tries to calm him down, but Conner still insists he will not go with his brother, in fact he will not go anywhere except home, with me.

Conner's psychiatrist cut back on his meds a few weeks ago because he seemed to be doing well, and he just does not have the resources to cope with the frustration he is feeling. I try to explain to Doc that I cannot take him home with me. *Please understand, I just can't. You've got to talk him into going with Edward. I can't even remember what you just told me to say to him. Please, help me.* I am collapsing internally, and Conner erupts. Like a volcano once it is released, his fury seethes over to others, not just his brother. The eruption is terrifying, and he runs from the office out into the waiting room, where his threatening behavior and knocking over of chairs frightens two other patients who are also in the building. The police are called. Eventually, he does take more meds and calms down enough that he can go home, but it is too late. The damage has already been done.

Somehow, I survive the weekend with him, God alone knows how. That Monday, Jack's and my divorce is final. On Tuesday I discover that there is no such thing as a day so bad that Children's Services cannot make it worse, when I receive notification that I am being sued for child support for Ben, now that he has been put back into state custody. On Wednesday, I receive the finalized divorce decree in the mail. And on Thursday, when I meet with Doc, his first words are, "Do you want to go first, or do you want me to go first?" Although I do want to talk about being sued, I tell Doc he can go first. The next few sentences are more than I can bear.

Doc says Conner frightened other patients the night of his outburst, when I was exhausted and in despair and dared to admit I needed a break. The other doctors in the practice do not want Conner to come back. I hear Doc's voice saying that because Conner is the one who is most dependent on him, he believes it is in Connor's best interest that all the members of the family transfer together to another doctor. He would be glad to try to help us find a new doctor, but we cannot stay in treatment with him. As a result of Conner's outburst, the entire family has just been fired as patients of the practice.

Through the fog that has taken over my mind, Doc's voice comes, promising to try to negotiate with the practice to get us enough time to make the transition, but he cannot guarantee it. The bottom line is that Conner, who is the most fragile member of the family, is the one who exploded, and Doc believes he would be even more damaged if he knew that he had to change treatment providers while the rest of the family got to continue with the doctor we have all been seeing together. Just like the stand the family took with the church a year before, it is all of us or none. Because the one child has to leave, so do we all. And as Conner's mother, after almost twenty years of Doc's being my greatest support, so do I.

I cannot respond. All I can do is get up, shake his hand, thank him for keeping me alive all these years, and stagger to the car. It is the cruelest blow of all.

I had started seeing Doc when I was so suicidal that I would tell myself multiple times daily, *all I have to do is just not kill myself until I talk to him again. All I have to do is not kill myself until Thursday.* My goal had been to stay alive long enough to get my children out and on their own, and it had been a major issue when the last three children were adopted, to commit to staying alive long enough to get just three more children grown. There were even days over the previous twenty-five years when I was in such deep despair I figured out exactly how many more days that was, until the last one turned eighteen, until the last one graduated from high school. Each of the children, as I had added him or her to the family, had extended the timeframe. Each one was a chance I was taking on being able to help that child before I wore out. I never knew how long I was going to last.

Although my despair had lifted for the two years of the fairytale marriage, it had returned on the night of Jack's New Year's Eve confession. One of my worst triggers has always been the fear that I could not provide for my children, that I would be powerless to keep them safe and, like my stepbrother and stepsister, they would be taken away from me and even worse would happen to them then. The events following Jack's abuse of Edward have brought back a depression as severe as any I have ever experienced. His actions have triggered every fear I am especially vulnerable to. I was responsible for exposing my children to a man who abused them. I have been unable to find a way to financially provide for them in the aftermath. I have placed them at risk for being taken away from me. I have thought a million times since then, *this is all my fault. I am bad and I deserve to die.* It has been Doc's voice, all these years that has said, "No." Whenever my mind has reverted to its default setting of self-destruct, his has been the voice I listened for: "It wasn't your fault." "There are some people who would stop abuse if they knew." "No one can ever make you go back to not knowing you can ask for help." "You are safe now." "Your children are safe now." "You can protect yourself and your children." "It's okay if you think about it." "It's okay if you *don't* think about it." "You don't have to make it all make sense today." "You don't have to kill yourself today." "You don't have to do *anything* today." Doc kept my children sane, it is true, but mostly, he kept *me* sane, and for almost twenty years had made it possible for me to parent a string of children no one else wanted. I would never have made it without him.

Now, even that support is being yanked out from underneath my feet. I have no power, even to negotiate. I have no power to beg or plead. *This decision that affects my children, my life, my ability to survive is being made by other people based on one child's collapse in response to my own despair. It is my own fault, and there is nothing I can do about it. Nothing at all.*

After I leave, I realize I do not know if I am supposed to bring the children in tonight for their regularly scheduled appointment. I call back. Doc says yes, for now they can come back, until the whole practice meets as a group to decide the timeline. *I have to talk to the boys before we go tonight and explain what happened, because it will be too risky to tell Conner at Doc's office. Conner will have to have time to process the information somewhere other than in the office that has just rejected him.* With my heart breaking, I drive home and talk the boys through what our doctor has said. When they find out what the response of the practice was, Conner says he will not go there again, that he is so upset he is afraid he will hurt someone if he gets mad. I beg him, "Please, go with me tonight. Our relationship with Doc is too important to me for it to end it this way." He takes his bedtime meds before we go, to help him cope. For this night only, a friendly church nearby lends our doctor and family a room in which to meet.

The next week, I get a call from Ben's counselor at the Level 4. Since I had to put him into state custody to get him admitted, and because his state social worker then insisted he only needed Level 2 care (Ben told him he didn't want to remain in the facility but preferred to be placed in therapeutic foster care), in spite of the fact that everyone else involved in his case agrees that Ben needs to be placed in a Level 4, our insurance is decertifying him one more time for continued treatment. The fact that he was returned to my custody after his admission makes no difference. We still don't have a ruling back on the November appeal, so there is no current ruling in place that can be used to force Ben's insurance to pay for the treatment he needs. The counselor says the staff needs to work out his discharge plan, because they have to send him home. *They have got to be kidding. He has only had one successful pass home after over two years away. No one in this family has any reason to trust that he will not resort to violence again.* I am in shock. All I can say is that I cannot agree to take him back until his doctors and *Guardian ad litem* agree.

Over the next several days, I make dozens of frantic phone calls, and several visits to the adoption assistance office. Finally, encouraged by Ben's *Guardian ad litem*, adoption assistance agrees to pay for what his doctors characterize as a "reasonable transition" period – a minimum of three additional successful home passes. The transition period will be paid for through the end of the January, so each week for the next three weeks I see Doc on Thursday mornings, drive three hours each way to pick up Ben, and then take all three boys to Doc's office for family therapy that night. On Sundays, I drive Ben back to the Level 4, pick up the other two boys in the evening when I get back to town, and head to church.

While all that is going on, Jack keeps raging by phone and mail about how his difficulties are all the result of a misdiagnosis. Completely out of patience, I write him at the jail:

> *… You may not remember this, but when you confessed to the police in January, what you told us at the time was that you had never touched those 200 kids inappropriately. You numbered them as victims, but then told us you only had "inappropriate thoughts" when you did things like hold them in your lap, pat them on the back, etc… You couldn't be prosecuted because your behaviors had not been inappropriate – only your thoughts… You never disclosed the other information until just before your lie detector test… And now you are angry because you were being treated for what you had disclosed, instead of what you had done… Your therapist can only help you with what you tell him… I am sorry that you have chosen to blame him for your own failure to disclose, but that is something I cannot help you with.*

During the same period of time, the store is having its "Lost Our Lease" sale. *Okay, I give up. I am falling apart. The kids are falling apart. My whole life, it seems, bit-by-bit is falling apart. On the last weekend of the sale, I will run an ad in the paper that says, "Free Stuff." I just cannot bear the thought of all the materials that I have collected here ending up in the dump, and that is where the landlord says they will go if I do not get them out of the building.* Then, the promised article in the paper finally runs. The store is on TV, and the article is more than I could ever have hoped for. The response is phenomenal.

For the first three days after the article runs, the store does more business each day than it has done in any month prior to that. One of those days, a uniformed police officer comes into the store. *Oh, no. There have never been any customers in the store before, and now that there are, I am going to be ticketed for having too many cars in the parking lot.* Then the officer, whose name is Chuck, comes up and tells me he needs to talk to me in private, and I begin to panic. *He could have given me a ticket with everyone standing there. Is it something about Jack? Is it about the kids? Is someone hurt? Is everyone safe?*

We go off to one side, and the kind officer says, "We saw your article in the paper, and this sounds like a good cause. The police officers have a warehouse, and we were wondering if you would like to use our basement." Relief washes over me. *Perhaps it is a sign. Perhaps I am not supposed to give up, after all.* I agree to meet him after work, to see the space. *It is a wonderful space. Maybe it will work.*

Days later, as the sale is still going on, another gentleman comes over to talk to me after he has looked around. He saw the article in the paper, too. He is from Habitat for Humanity, he says, and he doesn't want me to give up, either. If I can find a place to go, he will lend me their tractor-trailer in which to move. He says he thinks he can help me, if I will let him.

In the days that follow, the store makes enough money to pay part of what is owed me in back salary, and to pay moving expenses. Money is put down on the new space. Insurance on the new building is obtained. I just keep putting one foot in front of the other, taking care of kids, taking care of the business, taking care of the farm, and all the time my heart is breaking. I just keep praying. *Please, God, tell me what I need to do today. Please, Goddess, give me the wisdom to choose it. Please, anyone who will listen, give me the strength to carry it out. Please, just tell me what I need to do next.*

Finally, our doctor's practice meets to make its decision regarding our family. After the meeting, Doc tells me they have agreed with him that it is in Conner's best interest for the entire family to receive services from the same provider. Unfortunately, instead of that meaning that Conner will get to stay, it means that since the practice wants Conner to leave, their decision affects the entire family. He says they have agreed to give us fourteen months to find and transfer to a new doctor, since fourteen months is the amount of time Conner cannot qualify for state insurance because he is COBRA eligible, even though I cannot afford the COBRA payments. They have agreed to give us this time only because Doc has been seeing Connor for free ever since his adoption assistance ran out, and we have no insurance or income to pay another provider. We have fourteen months to terminate with our doctor of eighteen years.

I have been talking to Doc for so long about everything concerning the kids and everything concerning my life, that I can hardly bear the thought of losing his support. *I always thought I'd keep seeing him until the last of the kids left home, but I still have two more at home, and now I only have fourteen months left. I can't face starting over again with someone new. Fourteen months is too little time to go from seeing him three times a week to none at all. I can't begin to imagine how to start getting ready.*

Finally, the plan I arrive at is this: although I will continue for the time being participating in family sessions with the boys, I will start weaning myself off my dependence on Doc, just at the time I am the most fragile, most desperate, and most in need of his support. I will immediately stop going into the building with the boys on Thursday nights, when I take them for their individual sessions. On Thursday mornings, when I have individual therapy, I will go once a week for four more times, then every other week for four times, every three weeks for four times, and then once a month for four times. For the last four months, I will not talk to Doc at all except in the Monday night family sessions. That works out to exactly fourteen months. Edward does not want to transfer to another doctor, either, and I am just too worn out to try to make him, so his therapy will terminate when our time is up.

We're never going to make it. We only have fourteen months to try to find a new doctor Conner can trust enough to keep him alive.

I have no illusions at all that I can maintain Conner at home without Doc's constant interventions, and I am still, even after all these years, so suicidal from time to time that I know I will not likely live long without his support myself. Even knowing that I am more likely than not to commit suicide without weekly therapy, it is still too overwhelming to think about starting therapy again with anyone new. I just do not have the energy it would take to invest in learning to trust someone else. As it is, my depression is so severe that I hardly have energy to breathe. I am utterly incapable of even thinking about asking for help. I am a void of despair so vacuous that nothing can fill me; there is absolutely nothing left to me with which I can reach out. *I will not last long like this.* I begin trying in earnest to discern how to provide for my children in the event of my death. I begin, quite purposefully, making plans for their future care.

CHAPTER TEN

When Life Makes Death Look Good

Valentine's Day, 2005, I have nothing to celebrate. Jack is in jail. The divorce is final; the quitclaim filed. I can see no other way out than my own death. But after Valentine's is over, I notice that Sunday mornings are not quite as difficult for me. I stop crying every time it is time for church at First Church. I no longer spend every Sunday morning thinking about what we were doing there the year before, and the twenty-seven years before that. *Last year, beginning with the Sunday after Valentine's, we were at All Saints. The congregation at All Saints has become my family. All Saints is becoming my home.*

Over and over, the members of the little church have gone out of their way to make us feel welcome. Their differences from the congregation at First Church are many, the most touching of which is the way they minister to our entire family. In particular, I am moved by their offers to give me time for myself. While occasionally members at First Church would say things like, "Let me know if you need anything," the folks at All Saints seem to sense how impossible it is to think of things and then to ask for them, when one is so deep in despair. Instead, they offer specifically, "Why don't you bring the boys over at ten o'clock on Saturday morning, and we will feed them lunch and then take them to a movie so you can have some time to yourself." Their ministry to us is like taking food to someone after a death in the family. They don't just make vague offers. They actually act concretely. They don't expect me to ask for help when I'm so depressed I have to keep reminding myself just to breathe. They just go ahead and do things that are kind. They have closed ranks to make sure the boys are never alone with the one man in the congregation from whom they might be in danger. They don't joke behind my back about my being a martyr because I don't come up with things for them to do. They just go ahead and help. They are teaching me how to care for others at the same time they are making it possible for me graciously to receive.

Without any insurance at all for Conner, we have been begging for samples of medications from his various doctors. *Anything, just to keep him stable. Anything, just to keep him alive.* Then, much to my surprise, I receive yet another letter from COBRA. Although I did not meet the deadline to make the payment to keep it going, it turns out there is a grace period of forty-five days in which you can have it reinstated. I have two more weeks to figure it out, somehow, someway. I am down to two days before the final deadline I have been given by COBRA, when I receive in the mail the forms I need to file for a quick income tax refund. The amount I receive back, plus what I was able to pay myself as a result of the article in the paper about the store, are together enough to pay COBRA what I owe by the deadline and have it reinstated. It costs over $5,000 to do it, but once again, for a month at least, the boys are insured.

For his part, during the same period of time Ben comes home. When his Children's Services worker had told him he was decertified for treatment and was going to be moved somewhere within two months, he decided, as he put it, that he could do ANYTHING for two months. For that amount of time, he followed rules, did his schoolwork, and raced through the level system. In response, the juvenile court judge agreed that Ben had done well enough at the Level 4 facility to meet the requirement he had put in place years ago that Ben must "complete a program" before he can come home, and he has been able to have a total of four successful passes. While his doctors insist his discharge from the Level 4 is premature, it is still done. Ben comes home with no wraparound services*, because adoption assistance requires that we choose between wraparound services from the Level 4, and continuing with our long-time family doctors. They are not willing to provide different services for the different children, regardless of their needs. Being forced into the choice, and knowing that wraparound services would last four months at the most, we decided to remain in treatment with our current providers.

The Level 4 had taken Ben off all his medications when he got there, but before he came back home they had already started him back on one of them "as a cushion." *It is not enough.* Ben is home less than two weeks before he admits that his Bipolar Disorder* is out of control and he is rapidly cycling from homicidal mania to suicidal depression – sometimes multiple times daily. He also admits that he has been bulimic for years, and that his urge to self-mutilate has progressed even further. The next day, before I can get him to our doctor's offices I receive five calls that he is being disruptive at school, and that night, in Doc's parking lot, he runs away.

We spend what seems like forever in the parking lot, talking to Doc and the police officer who responded to our call. On the way home, I receive a message from Jack that the public defender and the district attorney have finally come to an agreement, and he is going to be released on time served and two years probation. The next morning, I get a call from someone at the police department covering where we now live. He says I need to go to the juvenile court that retains jurisdiction over Ben to file a runaway petition on him, so I do. In the meantime, Ben has shown up at his school (not to go to class, but to see his new friends and hang out) wearing clothes that were not his own, blue hair, and earrings. The police were called and began looking for him. When he saw them, he ran away. He was missing overnight, but was caught the next morning after he broke into his school, vandalized it, and spent the night there. Although he denies having done it, they caught him on videotape. With no other way I can think of to keep him safe if he will not stay at home, I put him back into state custody.

In my spare time from dealing with Ben, Conner and I are moving the store, using the Habitat trailer. Conner and I do almost nothing for the next two months except fill the trailer up at one store, and then unload it at the other one. Over and over, the prior rental agent's attorney contacts me. They are suing us for the back rent, even though that was not our verbal agreement. Though we were verbally assured that since we were a non-profit they would not sue us but would just write off any arrearage as a non-profit donation, they have decided not to honor the agreement. The written contract says they can sue; therefore they are doing just that.

Gabriel came into the store today, as usual yelling for me before he even made it through the door of the warehouse, "Mom! Mom!" His news is tragic. Jack's abuse has affected Gabe's sexuality in some very sad ways, one of which is his predilection to act out sexually with multiple partners. He has been charged with having intercourse with a younger relative. She is seventeen years old, and he has full-blown AIDS. That makes his action the equivalent of attempted murder. He says he didn't do it. All I know is that *if* he did, he was only doing what Jack taught him. Like so many things in our lives these days, the tragedy happening to Gabriel now can be traced back to Jack.

Over the weekend, Jack's family is having a family reunion, and Jack's sister invites me to come. All the women gather in one of the hotel rooms. "What are we going to do about Jack?" one of the women asks. I am overwhelmed with relief. I thought he was only my problem. They have been his family longer. He is their problem, too.

His sister talks about Jack's accusations regarding their father. "He says Dad put his fingers in his rectum," she says. The other women laugh.

"Your dad was a doctor. He stuck his fingers up *everybody's* butt," one responds.

"He also says Dad exposed him to male nudity."

"Of course he did," another woman answers. "Your dad was the team doctor for the high school. He took Jack with him into the locker room after every single game."

None of us knows what really happened, but they seem open in discussing possibilities. Sex, in their family, is not exactly the elephant in the living room Jack made it out to be. Like my own sister and brother, Jack's siblings don't remember things the same way Jack does. They have not, however, turned their dad into a saint. They may not remember him doing anything to them, but they are open to the possibility that when they were not around, something different may have happened to Jack.

"I know Jack says he did, but do *you* think your dad abused him?" someone asks Jack's sister.

"No, I don't," she replies. "I can't be sure, of course, but I don't think so."

As I get further and further behind on everything, I continue making plans for the boys in the event of my death. *Conner will go live with friends, Edward with his half-sister. Ben is in the care of the state, if one can call it that. I don't think they are taking very good care of him, but he sure is loving it.* For almost a month he has not even been registered at school, he admits having access to and using drugs, and he has gotten tattooed. *Well, at least technically, he is not my responsibility.*

Late at night on the fifth of March, we finally get everything out of the old store, and everything we can into the trailer for the last load to be moved. The building is broom-swept, the dumpster is full, and there is nothing else Conner and I can do there until it is emptied again. Over the next few weeks, we just keep going back over to the old location and continue loading the dumpster full each time it is freshly emptied. Between trips, we are trying to have a grand opening for the new store and get everything put away. I talk to one person who tells me to let go and let God be in control, and then the very next person tells me to be faithful to my vision and hold on. Edward, who has been having a hard year with all the chaos, is failing every class he is taking except one. And then, there is the upcoming child support hearing.

It seems unjust that I am being sued for child support, when I have done so much for these kids over the years, starting with taking them when no one else wanted them. I am appalled when I discover that the adoption assistance contract, which guarantees payment for whatever the boys need that is related to their pre-existing conditions and cannot be provided at home – up to and including 365 days a year of psychiatric hospitalization – does not include paying for their being placed back into custody if that is what they need. The experience of witnessing another parent in the courtroom being handcuffed and arrested, even though he is currently caught up on his child support, just because he was behind previous to this court date, is terrifying. *I am sure I will be arrested next.*

When the judge enters the figures into the computer and tells me the amount of child support I am expected to pay, I burst into tears. I ask her, "I just want to make sure I understand that you are telling me that the amount I have to pay for child support, plus the $1,097 a month I have to pay for the boys' health insurance which is required by the adoption assistance contract, is more than the adoption subsidy altogether, and those amounts plus my rent and car payment are more than my total income. And that does not include gas or food or electricity or anything else."

The judge replies, "Didn't you know they were special-needs when you adopted them?" When I answer in the affirmative, she asks, "Well, what did you expect?"

What I am actually thinking is, *Well, I sure didn't expect THIS*. What I say is, "My understanding when I adopted them was that the Department was supposed to pay for whatever they needed, and if Ben needs to be in Department custody, it should be covered."

She says, "No, it is not. The contract does not cover child support." I leave the courtroom weeping, and a young lawyer follows me out, offering to file an appeal for me.

I tell him, "I have no money – I cannot pay you."

He replies, "I don't mind. I will do it for free, because they made me mad."

Even though child support cannot be released by bankruptcy, I am overwhelmed and go to talk to an attorney about filing for it, just to cover the back rent from the store and Ben's old psychiatric hospital bill, which our insurance is still refusing to pay. Both of them are suing me personally. At least bankruptcy would provide some relief. *I am so angry I can hardly function. If it hadn't been for Jack, I'd still be living in the little house I could afford on my own, or at least if we were living on the farm we'd have two incomes. I never would have been in this fix at all if it hadn't been for his lies. But then, I am the one who believed them, so what kind of a fool am I? How much of this really is my fault? And how much of it is his?*

Jack has written me several bizarre letters from jail, and has left several strange phone messages. He was especially incensed that when the time came for Conner and me to clean up the last of the things at the store, I had expressed my revulsion about the messes he had left in the offices where he was living. I had completely avoided them during the time I was working the store because they were so disgusting. I was furious about his leaving them that way, and had refused to clean them up, hoping he would get out of jail and take care of it himself. He wrote me a letter railing on about how I had saved this task till the end just as an excuse to beat him up about it later. I am so angry at his virulent response that I have not made any contact with him since. I have been trying to discern how in the world to respond in a loving way, even though I don't particularly feel that way most days. On his birthday, which he is celebrating in jail, I write him the following letter:

Dear Jack,

I have had a number of responses to your last phone conversation and letter. None of them were very kind, and I have tried hard to remain kind to you, in spite of everything. Even when I have been angry, I have tried not to attack you, personally, only what you have done. So please understand that this letter took a while because it is the calmed down, toned down, trying-to-be-nice response.

1. I suspect that you are off your meds, because your response was not in proportion to what I said. I did not mean, insinuate, imply, or infer that you needed to be thrown in with the general population and either beaten or killed. What I did mean, and still do mean, is that you need to stop lying to yourself about your problem. You are a pedophile, and you are an addict. What that means is that your disease tells you that you do not have a problem. And, Jack, you have a serious problem. It is my experience of you that you are not an innocent victim who, as you put it "just likes to talk to kids, and then some of them trigger me" but rather, you are someone who does set out to put yourself in situations where you have access to children. Your attraction to children, until I found out the depth of your pathology, was one of the things that attracted me to you. You even liked my kids, who are often unlikable, at best. Think about the activities you have chosen. You chose to be a bell choir director, you chose to be involved with children's Sunday school, and you chose to be a step and foster parent. You say you only abuse children you know well, but that is not entirely true. You have admitted inappropriate activities, especially fondling, with any number of kids. While it may be true that you only had sex with Gabriel, you certainly were involved in sexual activities with many others. No matter what you think, grooming kids so that you can have sex with them later (if you're lucky) really makes you a fairly typical pedophile. If you are "not like all those others" perhaps it is only in the depth of the lies you tell yourself about what you do.

2. Think back to the last day before your incarceration. Think back to your phone message to me telling me you had been arrested. You told me you had not flushed the toilets that morning due to your bowel problems, and told me I should go get water from a neighboring building where you said there was a sympathetic tenant who would not mind if I got some. Surely you, of all people, can understand my revulsion and my putting this task off as long as possible. Surely you, of all people, can understand my being so overwhelmed at all the other things I had to do that I put this one in the back of my head and wished it would go away, or at least that it could wait until your sentencing hearing, when maybe some miracle would occur and you would get out and you could take care of it yourself. Surely you, of all people, can understand my avoiding dealing with something I did not want to do. So, like you have done with your past, I shut the door on it and walked past it every morning and pretended it was not there. I did not save it, as you accused, so that I would have something to beat you up with at the end. I avoided it because it made me furious that you had left it for me to do, and because it made me want to vomit.

3. I was astonished when your sister told me that you had told her you thought we might get married again after your release. I can assure you, Jack, that while I have tried to remain a friend to you, we will never be married again. I know you have a hard time processing information you hear, so let me write it out for you: our agreement was that I would wait as long as you did not violate the safety plan and as long as you were not convicted of a felony. As far as I can tell, the only part of that you heard was that I did not want a sign in my yard. It goes much deeper than that. As a convicted sex offender, it is a felony for you to ever live with children – other than your own biological children – ever again, for the rest of your life. That provision has even stopped sex offenders from living with their own biological children if their wives have other children (their stepchildren) as well. I will always, more than likely, have children and grandchildren living with me, or at least in and out of my home – for the rest of my life. In addition, you cannot live or work within a thousand feet of a school or facility that provides childcare, for the rest of your life. The Refuge borders a church camp, where childcare in the form of camp is provided all summer and many weekends. The property is less than one thousand feet wide. There is nowhere on our property where you could live, ever again, for the rest of your life. Even if there was, I would never place myself in the position of having to spend the rest of my life worrying about moving anytime that any one of my neighbors might decide to start a daycare, since the law also applies to felons who have a prior residence and job in place, and then have had to move when a daycare was started within the one-thousand-foot limit. You have chosen this path, but I do not choose to live it with you. I will be your friend as long as you want. Ruth was Naomi's friend, not her wife, when she said she would go wherever Naomi went. I will remain your friend. I will never be your wife again.

And that should be, in the long run, good news. It is time for you to discover who you are. I think that no matter how you are feeling right now, with the fear of rape and death overwhelming your senses from incarceration, it is more likely than not that you are, in addition to being a pedophile, gay. Once you get out, the gay men's chorus would be a good place for you to find fellowship and check it out. You are free to discover yourself, Jack. You are free to find out who you are and what you will do, separate and apart from your parents' expectations, or your church's, or your family's. Your brother and sister seem to have taken your initial disclosure about being gay very well. I believe they will support you in your exploration. I know I will. That love and support and freedom are my gift to you for your birthday. You are free, Jack. You are free to be who you are, to discover who you are, without guilt, without pressure to conform to any expectations. You are not married. No one has any claim on you, or any expectations. You do not have any commitments. You are free.

Happy Birthday, Jack. You are Free. Sophia

The next day, Jack leaves me a phone message, thanking me for the letter. I had worried about its being cruel, but his message is to thank me. "I woke up this morning, for the first time in my life, free to admit to myself that I am a gay man. Thank you for setting me free. Thank you for the birthday gift." *Finally. It's about time. Maybe now each of us can get on with our own lives.*

Edward's horse has gone lame overnight, for no reason I can find, and I have no way to pay the vet. Sable is not just limping, but is dragging one of her legs in such a way that I am afraid it might be broken, and I do not think Edward can handle losing anything else. *I can call the farrier*. He deals with horses all the time, and he is cheaper to get to come out than the vet. He can at least tell us if the leg is broken.*

I make the mistake of deciding to watch the farrier work with Sable through the bars of the gate, but "It is," as we say in our family, "not a very good idea." She spins to get away from him, and smashes into the gate. Though at the time I am standing a few inches away from the gate, the play in the chain is more than the distance from the gate to my head. The top bar hits me just above the eye socket, and knocks me flat on the ground. By the time I can get up, my head is bleeding like a faucet. I stagger to the house, telling the farrier to stay with the horse, and get Edward to ride with me to the closest doctor's office, in case I pass out on the way. I hold a towel to my head while I am driving; the wound is bleeding like crazy. At the clinic, they are able to get the wound cleaned out and to get me stitched up without my having to drive all the way to the emergency room in town. The black eye that results is most impressive. On Sunday, the entire right side of my face matches the purple on the altar. The guys at church are full of jokes about how some people will do *anything* to be liturgically accurate.

Over the weekend, one of the lighting galleries delivers to the store a truckload of some of the most spectacular lighting fixtures I have ever seen. *Although each of these has been damaged in one way or another, they are by far the most beautiful things we have in the store.* Then, since Jack's truck has died, Officer Chuck, the kind man who offered me the space in the police officers' basement, picks up a load of donated paint for us. He follows that by going over to the old store and using his truck to finish carrying the last of the trash over to the dumpster. *Finally, finally, other than being sued, that chapter in my life is over.*

After church on the second Sunday night in March, the congregation of All Saints is driving to supper to celebrate Edward's upcoming birthday. I am alone in my car, since the boys are riding with their youth group leader in another car. Though my children are out of eyesight, another car full of church members is behind me and they see what is happening. I am driving along a four-lane road when a semi crosses the center lane and begins driving straight towards me. It is the strangest experience. I don't change lanes to get away from it, I don't panic, I am not afraid at all. I just keep driving, with the strangest sensation of curiosity. *Oh, so this is how it will end*, I think to myself. *I always thought I would kill myself, but I'm going to get hit by a truck.* My next thought was of regret. *I sure wish I had straightened the house up before we left for church. I just hate that someone else will have to clean up all that mess after I am gone.* I feel no fear, no panic, no instinct for survival, no urge to dodge. I am so overwhelmed and ready for my life to all be over, that I just continue driving calmly towards the semi. The friends behind me tell me later they were panicked, watching the semi headed towards me, but at just the last moment, it pulls back across the center line and misses me. I am so numb it hardly even matters to me, but my friends report they were praying for my safety at the same time I was readily anticipating the end.

Sable is fine now, but because I had to leave suddenly for stitches in my head the day the farrier came, I have not yet paid him for that visit. I go to his house to drop off the check, and while I am there, meet his wife. It turns out they are building a larger home in order to adopt more special-needs children, in addition to the three they already have. Their family exactly fits the definition of the type of family the IRS has approved to be helped by the non-profit. *While we aren't making enough money to help them financially with their building project, when the time comes that they can use the types of materials we have in stock at the store, we can provide them with whatever we have that they need. Had it not been for Edward's horse going lame and the accident that led to my going to their house, I would never have known.*

Once again, I am furious with Jack. First, he gave away the underwear I had to buy for him when he first went into the jail, since he had none of the only type that is allowed. That in and of itself wouldn't have been so bad, had it not been for the fact that then he wanted me to replace it. He was not at all happy when I told him I would replace one pair once only, after which he would be on his own. Either he kept up with his things, or he would have to find someone else to supply them. Since that episode three months ago, he has been begging for cigarettes, which I will not buy him. I appreciate the fact that he has started smoking again since he has been in jail, but it is not a habit I am willing to enable, especially after his father, mother, and sister all died of three different types of cancer. And that's to say nothing of the arrogance of his asking me to pay for cigarettes when I can hardly afford to buy groceries for the kids.

After thinking about it for a long time, I decided I would buy him the only kinds of "comfort food" that he was able to receive, and spent part of the little money I had buying him the maximum allowance of coffee, hot chocolate, and sweetener, along with envelopes and stamps. I decided I would spend the money to buy it for him all at once because gas is so expensive it would be cheaper to do that than to make repeated trips to the city where he is in jail. Within weeks, he asked for more. When I expressed my surprise, especially about the stamps, since he certainly wasn't using them to write to me, he let me know he was selling the stamps individually and the drinks by the cupful, at a fraction of what I had paid for them. He "thought" he was making "us" a profit. I would bet anything that he was using the money to buy cigarettes. It is a mistake I will never make again.

Edward has traditionally celebrated the weekend closest to his birthday with Skip and Mary Jo at their cabin on the lake. This year, by the time Edward's birthday rolls around, Ben has been placed by Children's Services in yet another institution. On the weekend that is supposed to be Edward's special time with his grandparents, Mary Jo invites Ben to come on a pass. She does not understand that Doc was so alarmed by some of Ben's comments at the last family session that Edward is under doctor's orders to have no contact with Ben at all, except in the doctor's office. That means that Edward can't even go to his own birthday weekend, because Ben is there. He is furious with his brother for messing things up for him yet one more time.

On the morning of Edward's sixteenth birthday, I have no money and no hope of how to get any, and am weeping with despair. *Please, Jesus, help me. I can't even pay for gas to take him to what is supposed to be his birthday party, much less to buy him dinner for his birthday once we get there.* I am already in town in the morning to pick up a donation for the store, and am just blindly doing each next thing on my list with no idea how it will work out. I try to stop crying long enough to go into the agency giving us the donation, when I see someone I know from First Church. Earline puts her arms around me and holds me while I cry. Before I leave, she slips something in my pocket and tells me not to look till I get home. *I hope it will be ten dollars, maybe twenty if I am lucky. Then I can buy gas and get Edward something to eat, too.* I sob when I get to the store to drop off the donation and look in my pocket, even though I am not yet home. It is a one-hundred-dollar bill, a tithe of Earline's tax return. *Once more, it is manna for today.*

On the day after Edward's birthday, the reporter who wrote the article about the store's "Lost Our Lease" sale in the paper comes to check out our new location. Liking what she sees, she decides to come back with a friend from a television news show, and do a feature for the show from our new location. No matter when it shows, it will make a difference. Anticipating their return, I get some friends to help, and we get a sign up at the new location to get ready. The reporter says she has another event she has to cover if the sun shines, but if it rains, they will be there on March 31. I pray for rain. I even get my friends to pray for rain. But on the day they hoped to come, the sun shines. *You've got to remember. Your timing is not God's timing. There is another plan, besides your own. I just wish to goodness I knew what it was.*

CHAPTER ELEVEN

Signs of Grace

On Maundy Thursday (or Holy Thursday, depending on your tradition), my friend Bonnie tells me that when she looks at me, I seem to be filled with what looks like golden butterflies. I hold on to that image with all my might. I feel so anguished, so suicidal, so hopeless and despairing, that the notion that I might be filled with something beautiful and good is something to treasure. I have no hope left, and keep trying to figure out what that image could possibly mean. I keep thinking about the scene out of *Star Wars* where Obi-Wan says, "If you strike me down I will become more powerful than you can ever imagine." *I keep going back and forth from the notion that maybe the image of something good within me means it is time for me to finally kill myself, because whatever is good in me will continue to do good after I am gone, to thinking maybe it means I am not all bad and should hold on. Maybe it means I don't deserve to die after all.*

The night between Good Friday and Holy Saturday is long and tortured. All night, it seems, I lay awake trying to make sense of what has happened to me, just as I have on many nights this year. As the morning approaches, I am filled with despair and the question slowly changes from "What good can possibly come from this" to "What lessons have I learned from this?" I come up with three answers. *The first thing I have learned is that if you dare to admit that you are at the end of your rope, someone will knock the chair that is keeping you alive out from under your feet. The second answer is that when someone you know unilaterally decides to end a relationship with you, the absolute most you can hope for is to develop an exit strategy that gives you the best chance at staying alive. And the last is that if what is in your best interest conflicts with the best interest of someone else's family, there is no one who is human, no one at all, who won't choose their own family. All three answers lead to the same conclusion: only God is left in the end.*

Then I get up, just as I do every day, and go to work. In the afternoon, I get to spend some time with one of the children – now grown – that I helped to parent. It is such a joy to be with her that Bridgett and I talk long into the night.

The next morning, Easter Sunday, I am awake long before the sun arises. I watch the darkness fade as dawn approaches. *Only God is left. Only God is left.* And as the Easter sun breaks the horizon, I finally let go of my desperate, death-grip hold on life and take a flying leap of faith into the waiting arms of God.

If, as my friends joke, my life really is like Job's, then this must end well. Job held on to life and refused to give up faith, and in the end his faith was rewarded. I keep thinking back to the strange things people said in the weeks before I was married, people who had no idea I was even contemplating such a step. Things like, "I don't know what this means. I just know I am supposed to tell you to walk by faith and not by sight." Or "I don't know what you're thinking about doing, but God has laid it on my heart that I should tell you to go for it." I have been clinging desperately to those words for three and a half years now. Act by Faith, not by Sight. Go for it.

I was given this vision of helping to house homeless children, and I have taken on this task of parenting the ones I already have. I keep wrestling with what it means to let go of control and yet still hold on to my vision and have faith. *How can I hold on to that vision when everything seems so bleak? Maybe, as Bridgett said last night, Job is the answer. Earlier in the week my mother told me I was getting older by the minute and if what I really wanted to do was write, I had better get started. Bridgett told me last night that my story was the feminization of Job. Today is Easter Sunday, Resurrection day. The day "the stone got rolled away and Jesus got loose." Do I get turned loose from my tomb of despair, too?* I sit down at my computer and begin to turn the letter I have started to Edward into these pages, an act of faith that the story will end well.

The following day, I receive in the mail a letter that says I won Ben's November insurance appeal, and that after all the months of waiting, the judge has once again ordered the insurance company to provide the care he needs. The good news is counterbalanced by our financial situation. We have no money for electricity, for groceries, much less for rent. The few days after Easter, I begin begging, calling churches and asking for help, pleading with pastors I have known; but it is the end of the month, and discretionary funds are depleted. No money comes. In the end, it is our tiny little All Saints Community of Faith, with so few resources of its own, that raises the money for our family's electric bill.

By the last week of the month, there is no money to pay the court-ordered child support or the COBRA insurance payment that is due.   My checking account is depleted and its little overdraft protection plan is already in the negative numbers.   Still, the memory of the parent in the courtroom being arrested and taken out in handcuffs on his way to jail, terrifies me.   *I know it is a bad idea, and that I shouldn't do it.*   On the day both payments are due I write checks to cover them and turn them in.   All I can do is pray that a miracle will happen to cover the checks and keep me from going to jail for not being able to pay for my children's necessities, and also now for writing bad checks out of fear.   *I'm never going to make it.   I have no ideas left.   I have no reason to hope.*   It is an act of desperation, but then, faith is often desperate.

April begins as March ended.   The first couple of days, I faithfully go to the store and continue unpacking, organizing, arranging, cleaning.   Each day, at least one person comes in – sometimes, only one – and buys something worth just enough to buy groceries to feed the kids that night, or to buy just enough gas to get home and back again the next morning, in which case I pull supper out of my dwindling supplies and try to keep the boys from knowing how desperate I am.   *Why can't I ever make enough that I don't have to worry about tomorrow?   What am I doing wrong?   Why is it always only just enough for today?*

I am so worried about the checks I have written that I can hardly function; I am immobilized by the fear that I will go to jail.   My own past, the one about which I went back to having nightmares after Jack confessed, leaves me terrified of being unable to escape.   The thought of tight places, even being in the hospital touched by people I do not know or attached to an IV from which I cannot escape, leaves me paralyzed with fear.   I have avoided the hospital, even at my most depressed, because I know that if I were not suicidal before I went in, I most certainly would be once I knew I could not escape.   Jail would be even worse.   On Monday, I continue praying for a miracle, but begin calling folks I know who have lived in housing projects, trying to find a loan shark.   I am not sure exactly how to find one, but I keep hoping someone I call will.

When that doesn't work, I call an old friend who co-signed a loan for me once before, to ask if he will do it again.   When I paid it off, he said my credit was good with him. He can't, he says, because he and his wife are currently living on loans themselves, but he tells me I was lifted up in prayer at First Church on Sunday. He says people know I am in trouble, and he encourages me to keep calling people asking for help. *If my old friends know I am in trouble, and no one has even called to see if I am alright, I can't very well call them and ask for a favor.* In desperation, I write my second husband, begging for a loan. I am on the brink of suicide, and once before when an employee of his committed suicide, he said he wished he had known the man was in trouble, because he would have helped him. After I drop the kids at Doc's, I mail the letter, praying desperately for relief.

The following morning, I awake to a telephone message that Ben has escaped from state custody, has run away, and is missing. Instead of being able to spend the day trying to find a way to cover the checks, the day is consumed by trying to figure out how to best care for him. *He may still be in what is loosely referred to as "the care of the state," but you know that the only way to make sure he is actually cared for is to continue to advocate on his behalf.* In response to the judge's ruling on my last appeal, the insurance company has called saying they have found a secure facility for him. I begin the process of trying to have him put back into my custody so I can place him there. Unexpectedly, after a day of unending phone calls, it actually seems it is going to work. The police have found him. A detention hearing is set for two thirty at which all parties have agreed he will be placed back into my custody and then transported to the secure facility. I am literally driving in my car on the way to court when I receive yet another call from the facility. The insurance company somehow found out Ben had been placed into state's custody, and is now refusing to pay and has decertified him once again for treatment benefits. After spending all day trying to work out a plan to keep Ben safe, I arrive at court only to have to have to tell all those waiting for me that it is not going to work out after all.

The state insists they will not transport him to the waiting facility even though there is a bed waiting for him, because if insurance will not pay for it, they will not pay for it, either. In the end, all parties involved (the *Guardian ad litem*, the state attorney, two representatives from the campus from which he has run, his social worker, and I) trek over to the Children's Services offices to regroup and decide what to do next. While in the waiting room, I discover that the local mobile crisis unit was required the day before to respond to yet another crisis with my son. On that occasion, even though he had admitted being suicidal and had refused to sign a safety plan, they still had not certified him for hospital admission.

If two doctors agree to sign commitment papers, they can overrule mobile crisis. Out of desperation to keep him from running away yet again before he can be transported somewhere safe, another plan is born. I call his psychiatrist and the family psychologist, and they both agree that based on what transpired the day before, he is probably committable. After the meeting, at which all parties agree to step him back up to a Level 3 secure facility such as the one that just accepted him, his social worker transports him to see his doctors. After talking to him, both of them find that he is, indeed, at risk of harming himself or others, and he is taken to the hospital for admission. *Even if they can only keep him a few days, at least he will be safe for those few days.* By the time I get home late at night, I am exhausted.

The following morning is Wednesday. The checks have surely bounced by now. Altogether, including the overdraft amount, it comes to nearly $2,000 that I need to break even and have any hope of covering the checks. I know even as I am driving in to work that I do not have enough gas in the tank to get home. *If no one comes into the store at all today, as sometimes happens, I have no ideas left about what to do.* All the way to the store I sob, begging God for mercy. *Like manna,* I keep praying, *please give me just enough for the day.*

My mother called yesterday. She's been out of town, and I dread calling her back. I still have no good news to share, and my mother has never dealt well with bad news. But after I sweep up the store and organize all I can bear to, I return the call.

My mother begins, "How are things going, or shouldn't I ask?"

"No," I answer my mother, "you shouldn't ask. I have no good news to tell you." When she offers to help, I say, "No, Mother. I cannot take any more money from you because I feel like a bottomless hole, and that it is hopeless."

When my mother replies, "You are right, Dear Girl, you are. Something has to change: where you live, your lifestyle, something," all I can say is that I know. It wouldn't do any good to tell her about the hundreds of unanswered résumés, sent out week after week, the hopeless efforts to find another place to live, my desperate attempts to raise money for the store.

The only thing I can think of to say is, "I know, Mother. I am doing the best I can."

When my mother says, "You should ask if it gets to be an emergency; and that if that time is now, you should say so," all I can do is weep. I cannot even answer. I hear my mother in the background, telling my dad they need to do something now.

My mother asks what I need, but I don't dare ask. "Whatever you can spare," I whisper. The wire, when it gets to the bank, is for $2,000 exactly. I can buy gas to go home. I have just enough money to pay the overdraft, cover the checks, and live on for a few more days until the article come out in the paper on Saturday. *Manna for the day. My mother doesn't even believe in it, but it is manna for the day.*

One more time, I've found out something else Jack lied about. When I insisted that any CSW's assigned to the store had to be at least thirty-five years old, he had relayed that to Jane. At the same time, he was supposed to tell her about his criminal activities with children; that had been our agreement. She told me today that the excuse he actually gave her was that the younger men were sometimes hotheaded, and he wanted to "protect" me in case I was ever at the store alone. She said he likely did not tell her what he had done because he would have known that she would *never* have agreed to place CSW's with him *at all* if she had known the truth. Some days it seems he has never told anyone *anything* that was the truth – unless it got him what he wanted.

On Thursday, the newspaper reporter comes with the television reporter and her cameraman, and the feature about the store is filmed. In the evening, at our doctors' offices, I see the ex-husband I wrote asking for a loan. He looks straight at me, but does not even speak to me. I nod at him, and flee in shame for having been vulnerable enough to ask. The next morning, I get a message to call the Social Security Administration regarding Conner's disability claim. In fear and trembling, terrified by the thought of any more bad news, I call. He has been approved. It won't be a great deal of money per month, but it will be something. More importantly, his meds will be covered, up to four prescriptions a month – and four is how many he takes to survive. This also means that if a new doctor can ever be found for him, there will be a way to pay for it. I start crying with relief on the phone, and the woman gently reminds me, "He may not come when we want Him to, honey, but He always comes right on time." It is an answer to many prayers. The checks will start in a few weeks. *Manna for the day.*

Encouraged, I call the insurance administration to ask about the check that I have been notified has bounced. They say they will run it through again. That Saturday, the article runs in the paper. A few new folks came in. The folks from church take the boys with them to the zoo, and I get a badly-needed morning off. Then, the next Thursday, the feature about the store runs on television, and a few more folks start coming in to the store. It is not as many as when we had the "Lost Our Lease" sale, but it is more than have come in since we moved.

On April 15, just minutes before midnight, I get a call that Ben has again been transported to the state psychiatric hospital, after climbing eighty feet up a tree and trying to bite through an electric wire to kill himself. The next day, exhausted and despairing, I drive once more to work without much hope that anything will help. I am overtaken by gratitude when a woman comes into the store and buys $2,200 worth of lights for a house she is building. It is enough to cover the amount overdue for the store's rent, and to pay me enough to take care of part of my own house rent that is overdue. *How come I can't make it happen, but You keep providing manna for the day, each day?*

Three days later, Conner can't walk. After beating around the bush a little, he finally tells me he has been in pain since before the boys went with the church to the zoo, and that it keeps getting worse. I rush him to our family practitioner, only to find out he has an infection in his spine. The doctor starts him on antibiotics, and schedules us to see the surgeon the next week. The next day, I get another one of those good news/bad news mail deliveries. The good news is that Conner's first disability check has arrived. That means that at long last, he should have medical insurance of his own. The bad news is that I also get a bill for the court costs from the last time I was there with Ben. I was so upset, apparently, that I missed the part about paying court costs. The letter says I can be jailed if I do not pay them. *Just what I need: one more thing to worry about.*

The day after the letters come, Conner is in so much pain that I take him straight to the Emergency Room after we see Doc. Sure enough, when they run his disability insurance, it is miraculously in place. He is admitted to the hospital, and is scheduled for surgery the next morning. I am up with him almost the entire night. There is the possibility that the infection in his spine is related to his spinal cord not being completely closed. When it is time to take him down to surgery, I get a call from the insurance office downstairs. Even though I have brought his conservatorship papers, they need, of all things, a copy of my tax return from the previous year to show that although he is twenty-three, he is still my dependent; and they cannot take him to surgery until they get it.

I call the tax accountant's office, but there is no answer. Desperate and on the off chance that it might still be there, I go out to the parking lot and start searching the car. Sure enough, a copy of the return is still in a stack of mail in the car. I take it in to the hospital's insurance office, and they approve his certification for surgery. About that time, I get a frantic call from anesthesia. Conner cannot sign the form giving them permission to anesthetize him. Since I am totally lost in the bowels of the hospital, they send someone to get me and lead me back to the correct office. I sign the form, and they take him away to surgery. I go back to his room and collapse.

A week later, Conner is discharged by the surgeon, which is good news. The bad news is that his blood work has come back. The increased dosage of one of his meds, which was changed after the episode of violence at New Year's, is affecting his cholesterol levels and his weight. He very reluctantly agrees to start an exercise program after being told he must by all three of his doctors: general practitioner, psychiatrist, and psychologist.

Because Conner does not trust people he does not know well and does not like going to unfamiliar places, we are severely limited in our choices. A small workout facility we find gives us an option. They are open twenty-four hours a day, so we can go when no one else is likely to be there. It is small, so it is not too threatening. And we still have a check we have been treasuring ever since Christmas – one hundred dollars from Wilma and Bill, for our family to spend on any Christmas gift we would like. Even though Conner is the only one who needs it, Edward and I both agree that we will spend it on a three-month trial membership at the little fitness club, to see if we can encourage him to do what he needs to in order to keep himself alive. We only need nine more dollars to pay the difference. *Thank you, God, for providing once more what my little family needs. One more time, You have provided what we needed, even before I knew we needed it, when I didn't see any way to make it happen. It seems we never get enough for tomorrow, but once again thanks to Your bounty, we have manna enough for the day.*

Chapter Twelve

Phoenix Tears

I am tormented that I have no money to pay Ben's child support. I am in constant fear of going to jail for being unable to do so. For weeks, I have been crying every time no one is looking: in the kitchen while cooking, in my bedroom, in the bathroom, in the car, between customers at the store. Wiping tears away when I hear anyone coming, I just keep trying to figure out how to make it all work. I have been over it hundreds of times, possibly thousands.

The practice says Conner has to leave. Doc says it would do more damage to Conner if he knew the other members of his family were able to continue to see his old doctor, so the practice has fired us all. Without Doc's support for Conner, I know I cannot maintain him at home, so another placement will have to be found for him; without Doc's support for myself, I know I will not last long without attempting or committing suicide, so a placement has to be found for Edward, as well. The only way I can think of to move them to other placements without their thinking it is their fault, which of course it is not, is to let the court go ahead and sentence me to jail for being unable to pay my child support, which of course I have no way of doing, anyway. Virtually all my friends know how terrified I am of being unable to escape. Jail would be the scenario for suicide that would be the most understandable to the people who know me. No matter how many times I go over it, my death seems the only way out. The only thing that makes sense is to take the boys to friends' homes when I get the summons for court, and then commit suicide before I am arrested.

But all the while I keep going over these things in my mind, my body keeps doing everything I need to do. Day after day, I go to work, feed the kids, get them to their doctors, pray that each day we will make just enough money for that day. *Just enough to eat. Just enough to buy gas. Manna for the day.* Then, unexpectedly, the lawsuit over the rent for the old store is finally settled. I have had to deal with it every two weeks for months, as the case has been continued time after time. I have written explanation after explanation about what happened, and what we were told when we rented the building. I have provided documentation of our 501(c)3 status, how much we have paid in rent, and what is still owing.   And then finally, I get a letter from the landlord's attorney. They have finally agreed to do what we were told on the front end they were willing to do. They are going to write off the overdue rent and late charges as a donation to the organization. *After all this time, it is over.*

Still trying to survive day to day, I write a letter to a retired Catholic priest, a Monsignor I knew years ago, asking him to pray for me. *He always seemed a little closer to God than most of us, and I am desperate. Daily, even moment-to-moment, I totter on the edge of suicide.* One morning, after an especially bad night, I take the letter and leave it in the chapel where I know he will be saying mass later in the day. That day, someone who cannot possibly know what I did comes into the store, and out of the blue says, "I will pray for you."

Jack has left me a message saying he has been offered a new deal. Although it is now several months after they told him they would release him on time served and two years probation, he still has not been released. The catch is that he can't get out of jail until he has a place to live and a job, and it is really hard to find those things from the inside of a cell. The new offer is that they will convert his two years probation to state time, transfer him to the state prison, and when he has served a third of it, the state will have to find a halfway house where he can go. The idea of his being in the state prison is nauseating. The chances of his surviving as a child molester are slim, and I do not think either the boys or I could easily handle it if he is killed while there. I beg him not to take the offer, and eventually, he agrees instead to keep trying to find a place to live and a job.

Still, I keep going through the preparations to kill myself when I receive the summons. Every day, I carry a little more of Jack's stuff to the store, collecting as much of his stuff in one place as I can. *This way, his sister will know where it is when the time comes, and no one else will have to separate my stuff from his.* I just keep trying to get ready to die.

I have been actively suicidal for long enough that some time ago Doc recommended I write letters to the boys for them to have after I am gone. He knows he cannot stop me if I am determined to end my own life, and they are his patients, too. The first one turned into a book of stories Conner had asked me to write for him as a graduation present. I finish it, have it bound, and give it to him as a gift. The second letter, the one for Edward, I have been working on turning into this book, trying to let him know that none of this was his fault. Every time I eat with someone, or see someone for what I believe might be the last time, I tell that person how much he or she has meant to me. *One by one, I am telling the people I love goodbye, whether they know it or not.*

On Thursday morning, the nineteenth of May, Conner has an appointment with our psychologist. When he gets up in the morning, he decides he does not want to ride all the way in to town, and that he will just talk to Doc on the phone. Knowing that he will not use the entire hour if he is on the phone, I get in the car and start in the direction of the office. I am able to arrive before the phone call is ended. I use the rest of the time to talk to our doctor myself.

"Last week, you asked me what I wanted to do," I start. "What I would really like to do is to tell you goodbye. I don't want the last thing I said to you to be some note I wrote in pain and left on your door." And I proceed to tell him how much he has meant to me, and to my children. I am able to tell him that I don't know when I will run out of time, I don't know if I will get a chance to say goodbye, so I want to do it in advance, just in case. *I feel terrible about the anguished, bitter notes I've left. Please know that they do not represent how I feel most of the time.*

Before the hour is over, I am not the only one in tears. For the first time in all these five months, I am able to believe that I was not fired as a patient just because I failed at stopping Connor's outburst, nor because I was unable to repeat the phrases he gave me to say. "No matter what happens at the end, remember this," I say. "Remember I said thank you." And I give Doc a copy of the book I wrote for Conner. The book describes how Doc slowly earned Conner's trust and became one of the most important people in his life. In the inscription, I thank Doc for the gift of words – words which brought order and calm to the cacophony of terror that reigned in my head before I met him. *It doesn't make any sense. Nothing has changed, but I feel better. It is as though Doc's tears have washed away my pain.*

Later in the day, I have my weekly lunch with my friend Jim, the pastor of All Saints. Then I drive over to Martha's to receive her comments on the manuscript of Conner's book. He has been giving copies of it as thank-you presents to all of his friends, and she is among them. Martha's response is enthusiastic. She tells me to double-space it and send it off to someone she knows. I drive home, dutifully double-space the document, and print off another copy. After we celebrate the high school graduation of one of Conner's biological brothers, I drive to the airport post office (the only one open that time of night) and mail it off. *Why not? What does it matter at this point if I lose my privacy? If I lose my life, I have nothing left to lose.*

The day after I met with Doc to tell him goodbye, several folks come into the store. Tracee comes first, buying stuff worth $40 – enough money to buy gas to get back and forth to the annual church retreat that the boys want badly to attend. Sherry comes in from public works asking about setting up a recycling drop-off in the back parking lot. If the police benevolence association is willing to go along with her proposal, which would supply the police with the proceeds from the recyclables in exchange for allowing public works to use the site, then the benefit for the store will be in the number of people who have exposure to the store's location. While the store would not get any money directly, it has the potential to make an enormous difference for us due to the free publicity and the number of people who would be on and off the property. After Sherry leaves, someone else comes in and buys something for $35, then another person buys $5 worth of stuff from the yard sale section. I can pay myself a tiny bit of what is owed me. *Manna for the day each day, it is manna for the day.*

After work on Friday, I drive two hours to be with my friend Wilma. Her mother just died, and only two weeks after the murder of her brother. After the funeral, I drive the two hours home, tend to the dogs and horses, and then drive two more hours to the state park where the church retreat is being held. By the time I arrive it is one in the morning. I collapse, exhausted, and sleep.

The retreat is in a beautiful location. The lodge has two large dorm rooms and two smaller bedrooms. It is in one of the small rooms that I awake on Saturday morning. Off and on throughout the day, the group eats and talks. One of the folks thought to plan an activity in which those of the group who want to do so make collages about their lives. In the bottom right hand corner of mine I put a picture of a house obscured by the trees and garden in front of it. On the picture, I put the word "dream." *My dream home. I can't quite see it, but the dream is still there. I don't even know what it would look like anymore. It is still just a dream. Maybe the manuscript of Conner's book will sell. Maybe we can make a few dollars off of it. Maybe we can survive a little longer. Maybe I can hold it together long enough to get the boys settled in new homes before I fall apart.*

There are only a few days left of school and I am growing more exhausted by the minute. Then the phone rings late one Monday night. It is my beloved son, John, who lives out of the country. My one birth child, he is in the states for three weeks for his high school class reunion. I weep to hear his voice. I have been so suicidal for so long that I feared I would never hear it again.

Jail continues to loom in the future as a very real possibility. I know I will have to commit suicide before I go to court, because I can't be sure I will be able to kill myself in jail. I don't like the scenario, but it still seems to be the only thing that makes sense as I try to juggle all the variables in the larger picture. I still cannot get past the idea of just giving up. *After twenty-five years of fighting with the state on behalf of all the children I have taken in, they have finally won. The threat of jail is simply more than I can handle. I have fought them until I just cannot fight anymore.*

All the time I am thinking, trying desperately to arrive at a different ending, folks come in and out of the store. I stop and talk to them, sell an item now and then, socialize, try to make sense of my life. Make a few phone calls trying to find a placement for one last child whose grandmother asked me to find an adoptive home for him. Think a little more. Show someone around the store. Think a little more.

One morning I read Conner the book I wrote for him, the book he has been showing to everyone, but has not yet read himself. I weep when I get to certain parts, choking back tears. *We have come so far, just for it all to be lost here so close to the end. Only a couple of years from his independence, I am exhausted, and can't make it any longer. I just can't think of a scenario that hasn't already been shot down, in which everything works out in the end. Conner can't keep seeing Doc, so I can't either. I am getting worse by the day, just trying to cut back to seeing him less frequently. I know I am not likely to last long. But still, Doc keeps telling me it is in Conner's best interest for me to be fired, too. No matter how I go over it, in the end, the only scenario I can imagine ends with my death.*

When I get home from work, the bill for child support is in the mail. To my astonishment, there is nothing listed as being in arrears. I can't figure it out. *Maybe someone who knows me paid it, thwarting my plans for suicide.* I break down and cry, not knowing whether to be grateful and relieved, or frustrated and angry that my careful planning has been delayed another month. I look at the figures again and again. *Arrears – 0.00. I don't know what it means.* Finally, I start reading over the letter, line by line, until I get to the small print under the graph that reads, "amounts in arrears for the current month are not included in the totals." *Nothing has changed. It is all just the same.*

A check is in the mail, too, from our homeowner's insurance company. Keeping the house insured is one of the requirements of my rental agreement. If I am *receiving* a check, it can only mean that my payment arrived too late, and that my homeowner's insurance has been cancelled. I could have used the check to pay the child support, but my checking account is already so overdrawn that there is no way I can cash it – it would only disappear into the overdrawn amount. *It looks like money, but it can't help me at this point. I am so far behind I can't get caught up.*

This is my first chance to see John in over two years. When he called the night he first came into town, we went over his schedule. The first two days would be spent with one grandmother, the next two with the other grandmother. The four days after that he was going to spend with aunts, an uncle, and cousins on the other end of the state. He said he would save the next Thursday for me, we could spend the entire day together, just the two of us, and that he would come on Wednesday to the store to see his brothers. He named the place where he wanted to have breakfast that Thursday morning, one of our old favorites. *What I do not – cannot – tell him is of my fear of going to jail, of the likelihood of my committing suicide if I do. I know, though he does not, that this might well be the last time I ever see him.*

On the day he is to come to the store to see his brothers and me, the day before the one he and I are to spend together, John calls me at work. He has just gotten in from visiting his cousins, aunts, and uncle. He is too tired to make the fifteen-minute drive to come see us, and I am stuck at the store and cannot leave. The breakfast the next morning that I have looked forward to is also cancelled. He has already made plans to eat lunch with my parents the next day. He wants to know if I would just meet him about an hour before they are to get there, so we could have an hour together. Then, we would have lunch with my folks. I am devastated. *It isn't that I don't want to eat with my parents. It is just that he has already had* days *with them, and tomorrow was to be our only time together on this whole trip.* He already told me that once his class reunion starts on Friday he will have no other time for me, except on the morning he is to fly out – maybe. This Thursday, he had told me, was for *me*, and I have so looked forward to it. I sit at my desk and sob, my body racked with sadness and disappointment. When I finally see him, he says, "It is just too painful to spend time with you. It is one thing to know, generically, that other people suffer. It is something else to see your mother suffer." It feels as though my heart has broken.

June 1 rolls around, and again I have no money to pay child support or COBRA insurance, which is always paid in advance for the next month's coverage. I call the insurance administration to find out if there is any grace period. They say there is a one-month grace period to pay what is due in order to reinstate it. Until the money is paid, however, we will have no insurance coverage whatsoever. The whole month struggles on this way, day-to-day. If I am lucky, someone comes in and buys just enough to feed the kids and buy gas for the day. If they don't, I take something out of our meager pantry, and we comb the car for loose change for gas. Come the end of the month, I can pay one month's payment, but it leaves us in exactly the same position for the month of July. I have a month to get caught up, or we will have no coverage at all.

One Saturday, Edward wants to go with his sister to visit a friend of her family's. I refuse to let him. He wants to know why. "Edward," I answer, "the only thing your mother ever asked of me was not to let you spend time with that person."

"That's not fair," he complains.

"Edward, it may not be fair, but I am going to honor what your mother asked of me. She believed you would not be safe with that person, and after she told me why she thought that, I don't think you would be, either."

Edward is furious that I am trying to protect him from someone he doesn't want to be protected from, when I failed to protect him from Jack. It does not help to try to explain to Edward that from the very first time I found out about Jack, I made sure Jack never had access to him again. His question is the same as mine. A million times this year I've asked myself why Jack did not set my radar off, and the only thing I can figure is that Jack's preference is boys. But whatever the reason is, I am determined to trust my gut response and his birth mother's instincts as well.

There is also a good thing that happens in June. After all my lamentations of anguish and distress, Doc changes his mind about firing me along with Conner. He says that while he still considers it to be in Conner's best interest that all the members of the family transfer together to another doctor, it is clear at this point that is not going to happen. In that case, Conner will be better off if I continue to see Doc and live, than if I kill myself. In desperation, I grasp at the straw he is offering me. *If Doc is willing to continue to see me, then maybe I can hold on a little longer. I already know how not to kill myself one week at a time.* Within days, my old friend, the heron, comes back.

I start going back to see Doc once every week, instead of once every three weeks, which is how far I have gotten on my schedule. The despair and desperation start to ease. Finally I am able to consider at least the possibility of staying alive, of picking up the fight where I left it off. I start to laugh again. *There is just something about knowing that I am not in it alone that makes it more bearable. No matter how many times Deborah calls from Florida, it is just not the same as having a doctor here in town. Perhaps survival is possible, after all.*

By July, I have neighbors moving into the space adjacent to where the store is located. One of the Olympic training teams is moving in, and I am delighted to have company. It sure does get lonely here from time to time. Most days, at least one customer buys something, usually just enough for the day. On other days, I go looking for Tracee, hoping to collect another twenty dollars towards the carpet and paint she is buying to get her house ready to sell.

On the fourth of July, I am blessed to have the most wonderful experience I have ever had with Ben. The group from church has gone downtown to watch the fireworks, and we are all propped up on a railing, waiting for the show to start, when Ben comes up and throws his arms around me. His group home is also at the fireworks, and his group leader has given him permission to watch them with me. For the entire show, he sits next to me with his arm around my shoulder, glowing with excitement. *This is probably the most normal mother-son interaction I have had with Ben in all the years since his adoption. I wonder if it is because it wasn't planned, it was spontaneous. He didn't have time to think about it before it happened; he didn't have time to make it in his mind into anything other than what it actually is.* His company is a joy to experience, and I am filled with delight.

I write the juvenile court judge begging her not to send me to jail because of my inability to pay his court-ordered child support:

Your Honor:

Since I do not have an attorney, and do not have any way to pay for one, I beg you to allow me to make my statement directly to the Court. I am writing you in regard to child support for one of my children, Ben Ruah. In addition to four grown foster children, two step sons, and one birth son, I have three adopted special-needs sons, of whom Ben is one:

- *Conner, 23, mentally retarded and with severe Posttraumatic Stress Disorder, had been moved twenty-one times in the five years he was in State custody before I got him on the day before his tenth birthday. He still lives at home and goes to work with me.*

- *Ben, who will be 18 prior to the court date, is a ninth grader who suffers from Reactive Attachment Disorder, Oppositional Defiant Disorder, and Bipolar Disorder with psychotic episodes. This hearing is regarding his child support.*

- *Edward, 16, has Polycystic Kidney Disease which will eventually require a kidney transplant, ADHD, Obsessive Compulsive Disorder, and is a ninth grader at his high school. It is because of his need for a transplant that I have always maintained private insurance on the boys, regardless of its expense. This was true even prior to my being ordered to do so by the Court this spring.*

All three were adopted with Adoption Assistance contracts which I was told would cover all their needs in connection with their pre-existing conditions. This has not been so.

- *In the fall of 1995, I went bankrupt when it took two and a half months to get the Department to approve the treatment Conner needed, which had already been written into his contract. During that time, he was incapable of going to school or daycare, and I had to stay home with him, missing work until I appealed the request far enough up the DCS ladder that it was approved. As a result, my house also went into foreclosure.*

- *In March of 2001, it took my coming here to Juvenile Court to file aggravated assault charges against Ben and attempting to return him to State custody before the State would approve the treatment all his providers agreed he needed. This program was less expensive than another program that his doctors had already anticipated he might need, which was already written into his contract.*

- *For the past eight years, since Ben and Edward's adoptions were finalized, it has been written into the Adoption Assistance contracts that the State would pay $1,920 per child per year so that I could have one weekend a month of respite*. After I was finally able to find someone who was willing to stay with Ben, which in and of itself was a difficult feat, that person quit after three months due to difficulties in being paid by the State. Because I was unwilling to ask someone else to do something that I had reason to believe they would not be paid for, I have never had any respite in the almost eight years since. When I requested that Adoption Assistance pay me directly so that I could pay the respite providers myself, the request was refused.*

Since it could be argued that for the past seven years and nine months I have provided the one weekend a month of respite care myself, that the State has not paid me for, at ninety-three months for Edward that would come to $14,880. Even assuming that Ben has been in one treatment facility or another for half of the time I have had him, that would still be another $7,440 due in respite funds for him. That would mean I have provided, in addition to the services I contracted with the Department to provide, a total of $22,320 worth of services that when I did ask, they refused to pay me for. It certainly makes the $860 I am four months behind on my child support look insignificant in comparison.

In spite of that, over the past three months, I have:

- Been reported to Credit Agencies for being behind in my obligation

- Had my Adoption Assistance check garnisheed, insuring that the amount I receive from the State is now less than the cost of the insurance the State requires I maintain

- And now I have been reported to the Federal government so that my income tax refund will be withheld and I will eventually be unable to get a passport.

I am not asking that I be excused from paying for Ben's foster care. It is important to me that he knows I am continuing to be his mother. I am confused by a formula which says I have to pay out more than I have coming in, but I absolutely believe that formulas are the only way to insure that rich people who can afford expensive lawyers pay as much as poor people who have no way to defend themselves. What I am asking is that I be granted as much leeway in the timing of my payments as the Department is allowed.

- Conner's tutors have gone as much as nine months at a time without payment.

- The boys' psychologist has twice gone over two years at a time between payments, in spite of the fact that he has seen all three of these boys a minimum of twice a week for all the years I have had them.

- The only person I could ever convince to provide the respite contractually promised was paid a year later for the first weekend of respite, and as of this morning, nine years later, has never received payment for the other two weekends.

I am asking the Court to give me an unlimited amount of time to pay the State for providing services to Ben, just as the State has taken an unlimited amount of time to pay those who provide services to its children. I am asking the Court to require the State's attorney to have my credit record cleared, to immediately stop the garnishment of my children's support check, and to clear my record with the Federal *government. I am also asking the Court for some assurance that I will be free from further persecution by the Department, so that I can stop worrying about the possibility of being sent to jail while I still owe this obligation. Only then will my children and I feel safe.*

Thank you for your consideration of this request.

Sincerely, Sophia Ruah

I mail the letter off to the judge, and hope for the best.

I saw an article in the paper this week that a new television show was going to hold a casting call looking to grant wishes "of deserving individuals who always think of other people and never think of themselves." *As suicidal as I have been, I have nothing left to lose by asking for any help at all.* On July 10, I do something I would never have believed I could. I go to the hotel where the casting call is being held. "I have a wish," I tell them. "You said that people who had always tried to do the right thing and take care of others could make a wish for themselves. I've been a VISTA volunteer, a chaplain, a pastor, a counselor, and I've worked for a child abuse hotline. I've taken care of people who were dying. I've fostered four children and adopted three more. Then when I couldn't take anyone else home, I started a non-profit to try to get even more children out of foster care and into permanent adoptive homes. Please," I said, "my wish is that I do not want to lose my farm." *I don't care if the farm is paid off, or if they give the non-profit a start-up grant so that I can pay my salary and make the payments myself. If I am going to survive, and maybe I will, I just don't want to lose the place the children and I love to live.* The real miracle is just in saying the words. I have a wish, for myself. I want to live. And I want to live, for the rest of my life, at The Refuge.

As my energy starts to return, I go to the juvenile court to see if my friend Tim, who works as the court administrator, can find out anything about my child support case. I have not heard anything in response to my letter, but he pulls my file and finds out that the young attorney did file an appeal after all, though I was never notified. It turns out the appeal was continued three times before it was dismissed for lack of prosecution. Choking back tears, I explain that I cannot afford to pay to file another appeal. He has the fee waived so that I can file a new appeal, still terrified that when I go to court I will be going to jail. The court date is set for two weeks later.

Within days, I receive another letter, this one saying that three years after the fact, my old insurance company has finally settled with the psychiatric hospital in the other state over Ben's remaining bill. From me, they had wanted almost $17,000. From the insurance company, they have settled for $5,000. It is another thing off the list of burdens which daily wears away at me.

During the last week of the month, the television reporter who did the feature on the store comes in shopping. She asks how it is going, and I tell her not very well. She talks through some possibilities, and then suggests that she could invite a decorator to come walk through the store with her. That way, they could discuss how items from one department could be combined with items from other departments to create decorating possibilities. She thinks that might be a way she could help. It is another little sign of hope. *Don't give up. Hold on just a little longer.*

In the meantime, we continue to be financially destitute. I keep writing fund-raising letter after fund-raising letter to anyone I can think of. I keep writing letters to car dealers begging for the donation of a truck that actually runs. I send off a few more résumés to promising job opportunities in the paper. I keep giving flyers to everyone who comes into the store, asking them to share with friends. My friend Deborah keeps calling from Florida encouraging me, but there seems no end in sight. And in between all those other things, I continue typing this manuscript.

At the end of the month, there is once again no money for child support or health insurance. All I can do is keep begging friends for loans. Nothing seems hopeful. In the end, when my month-long grace period is up and I haven't been able to pay what I owe, I write a check I know I cannot cover to buy just a few more days of time before the COBRA insurance is cancelled. When I get home at the end of the day, I find out that my joint checking account with Jack, the one on which I have just written the check, has been closed for exceeding the overdraft limit for too long.

The first of August, I am once again able to talk to Ben, who has been moved out of his treatment program and into a therapeutic foster home for support while he tries to get a job and an apartment. Once he is eighteen, paying for an apartment will be cheaper for the Department than continuing to provide the level of care he needs. Since he has admitted he still fantasizes about blowing things up and going on killing sprees, and especially about ways to kill me, all agree that it is still not safe for him to come home. He has already told us he has decided to stop taking his meds once he is eighteen. *Still, I am sad that the young man I love so dearly is unable to be at home, and is so far from me in body and spirit.* At least on this one night, the night before his birthday, he calls and is happy to talk to me. I am delighted he is voluntarily talking to me at all, and I wish him a happy birthday from the bottom of my heart. On Tuesday, the second of August, Ben is eighteen, legally an adult at last.

The court hearing that will decide my fate will be tomorrow. My mind has been made up for quite some time. *I'll take the kids to friends' houses this evening, and line up folks to check on the dogs and horses. I can straighten up the house tonight. Tomorrow morning, I will kill myself before it is time to go to court.* But now, Doc is telling me he doesn't think I *will* go to jail tomorrow, which is ironic; he doesn't even know that I am planning on killing myself before I go. He says even if I am going to be arrested eventually and sent to jail, it wouldn't likely happen tomorrow. He says my arrest is more likely to come as a result of an action the state files than as a response to an appeal I have filed. "You have no idea how mad I will be at you if you are wrong," I reply. *He can't even imagine.*

When I finally get to court, my friend Susan sits behind me. She and I worked together in this court almost twenty years ago, though under a different judge; and she's been working here continuously ever since. "I've got your back," she says. I don't know that she can actually *do* anything, but it sure makes me feel better just knowing she's there. The judge has received my letter and accepts it as a motion. She hears my testimony; the Department's witnesses are not there.

When I have finished testifying, the judge suspends any child support I might owe until the Department can produce its witnesses. After court is adjourned, she talks to Susan in the hallway, and suggests off the record that I sue the Department for breach of contract. She is the second judge who has made that recommendation. I don't think she will send me to jail after all. Court is continued. Life is continued. I am still alive.

My mind is in a million places. My mind is no place. The voices in my head circle round me, an echo of all the things I have told myself since the New Year's Eve when my understanding of the world fell apart. I am a different woman from the one I was before all this began, and yet I am the same. I struggle with the notion of Job, and the question of what that story might mean for me.

Ever since Easter, when I began to type, I have wondered what – *if* – the happy ending would be for me. Job's life ended well. He was given a new crop of children to replace the ones he had lost, and possessed even more material goods at the end of his days than he had owned to begin with. If my life really were to turn out like Job's, it too would embody some sort of restitution at the end.

But what would that restitution look like for a woman? If we work at home, we women may find ourselves sustained not by *stuff*, but by delayed gratification until that small victory we've been hoping for gives us just enough strength to last until the next one. If we work outside of the home, we may be inclined to mark our accomplishments not by huge milestones and promotions, but by the relatively minor successes we achieve day-to-day. If we are mothers, our lives may be less linear and more circular, going from caring for children, to caring for grandchildren, to caring for our own parents, so that more children at the end of our days may not necessarily make our lives any easier or better off than they were without them. What would it mean, then, for Job – as a woman – to be restored and to have even more than she ever had before? What gift, I wonder, would make a woman rich?

Afterwards

In the weeks that followed my court date, I was finally able to accept that I would not be able to afford to buy feed for the equines over the winter, and found them all a new home, even Oaty-Belle. I kept thinking about Betsy's e-mail that said donkeys can kill you. She was right – they can completely break your heart. It was anguish to lose them, but it was better than watching them starve. For weeks afterwards, I kept finding myself standing at the gate to the empty meadow, weeping. Sunday mornings, time I usually spent with the animals, were the worst. I started trying in earnest to find homes for our dogs. And I decided that since many days I did not make enough money at the store to pay for gas there and back, I would shut it down. Maybe if I eliminated everything I could, I would at least be able to buy food for the children over the winter, when the utility bills started to rise.

The only thing I could figure was that what I had believed was my calling must not be. I decided that I was unwilling to continue to force my will on what seemed to be an unwilling world. There had been other times in my life when I made decisions and everything fell into place. With the store, everything seemed to be doing the opposite. I could not make it work, no matter what I tried. When I could not pay the children's health insurance one too many times, I decided I would give it one last shot, and if I could not raise enough money to pay the insurance and the rent by the last day it was due, I would give the entire contents of the store away. It was clear to me I could not make it a success.

When I started telling people that I was giving up, Craig, the vice-president of the board, convinced his parents to donate $5,000 to the non-profit. The money came literally on the last morning I had to pay the insurance to have it reinstated before Ben and Edward would lose coverage altogether. With their pre-existing conditions, there would have been no hope of getting any other coverage for them until their eligibility period for COBRA ended and they could apply for state insurance. They would have gone over six months without any coverage at all. We would have had no way to pay for meds or doctor's visits, much less Edward's transplant if it was needed during that time. Instead, on the very last morning, the money came, and the cash was deposited into the store's account. I was able to pay myself part of what was owed me in back salary, cash the paycheck, race the cash to the insurance administration offices where COBRA payments were made, and have it reinstated.

Another day, I received a call from a flight attendant on one of the airlines. She said that during a safety inspection for one of their planes, she had found a copy of Conner's book. Finding my address in it, she had flown with it back to the closest airport. She brought it to me at the store, saying she had read part of it (along with a letter that was with it), and had decided it was important and needed to be returned. When she called, I couldn't imagine how a copy of the book had made it onto a plane. There were not many copies around, since we only had a couple dozen bound to give as thank-you gifts to Connor's friends, but when she got to the store I recognized what she had. Some months before, I had written a grant request and had given it to one of my customers, who had delivered it to her boss. Her boss had written a cover letter and had attached her own copy of Conner's book. She had then given the packet to the parents of a possible financial donor, who had given it to the potential donor herself. That person had put all the materials into an envelope on which she had written a note to another possible funding source, and had given it to him. He was the one who lost it on the plane.

I immediately wrote another letter explaining how it had come back to me, and took the entire package back to my customer and her boss. They again delivered it to the possible donor's parents. Just as the parents received it, their daughter called long distance to say that the packet had been lost, and her mother explained that once again it was in her hands. Her daughter sent a courier to get it. The timing was stunning. Surely the Spirit was at work.

Within a week after that episode, someone came into the store and said that the agency he headed might be interested in partnering with us to start a sheltered workshop for mentally challenged adults. One of the young people they were providing services to was Conner's younger brother. We met to discuss possibilities. Craig brought in the road manager for one of the local country music stars. It turned out that the man was himself adopted, that he had a special-needs child, and that he was "really into" recycling. He said he would do whatever he could to help. The couple who had passed my grant application and Conner's book along to their daughter sent me the message that the materials were "now in the right hands of someone who could help." I prayed for the miracle that I hoped would come.

I got a call from Jack that he had been released from prison and was on probation. A few days later, I heard from his probation officer that the only reason he had let Jack call me was that Jack had lied to him and had told him we were still married. It turned out that since he was a convicted sex offender, he could no longer have any contact with any former victim – or the family member of any former victim. That includes me. The probation officer also told me that for a few weeks Jack and Gabriel, who is now serving seventeen years for his crime of sex with an underage female, had been housed at the same processing center. Since that time Jack had been claiming Gabriel had "forgiven" him. *Yeah, right,* I thought. *How could Gabriel say anything else? Jack abused him for so long that even as an adult Gabe is afraid of him and feels powerless to say "no" to his abuse.* The probation officer reminded me that the state was unable to do anything about the years of abuse Jack had perpetrated on Gabriel, because the statute of limitations had run out. Without the name of a victim still a minor, they could not charge Jack with any of the other molestations to which he has already confessed. Jack knows exactly what he is doing. Not until after Ben's eighteenth birthday did Jack add him to his list of victims.

After getting out of jail and re-entering the community, Jack rapidly deteriorated, much like any addict who relapses. For years, I have heard people in Al-Anon tell stories about how the disease of addiction continues to progress even while the addict is sober. If and when the addict relapses it is as though the disease fast-forwards to the point it would have been if there had never been a period of sobriety at all. I know it happens, but I have never personally seen it happen as graphically as with Jack. It was as though he perceptibly plummeted to the low he would have sunk to had he never stopped acting out at all.

That was most vivid in the circumstances surrounding his being asked to leave multiple halfway houses in just a few months.

The first time it happened, his probation officer let me know that he was sexually acting out with other residents behind the dumpster of the homeless shelter where he was staying, and that the staff believed he was turning tricks because he wanted the money for cigarettes. In spite of his being put back out on the streets, the consequences of his actions did not make much of an impression on him. The last time he was asked to leave a placement, it was because he would not leave the younger residents – who he had been warned to say away from – alone. In all, Jack has been kicked out of three different placements for making "inappropriate sexual advances" to the other residents.

When I said to Jack's probation officer, "Well, at least they were adults," his reply was, "Yeah, but they weren't exactly consenting adults. It's hard to consent when you're asleep." Jack was asked to leave each placement in part because there was some concern that if the staff didn't get him out of there, the other residents "might take matters into their own hands." Perhaps even that, horrible though it might be, would not be as bad as his molesting another child; Jack may never be able to keep his hands to himself.

And in the end, it was the kind police officers – my landlords at the store – who set the deadline for the end of my prolonged suffering there. They gave me until New Year's Eve, exactly two years from the date of Jack's confession, to vacate the premises. The timing of their notification was poignant. Officer Chuck let me know I needed to vacate only hours before the first adoptive family we could help came into the store to get the building materials they needed to complete their new, larger home. Their home's completion would make it possible for our farrier and his wife to adopt more special-needs children in addition to the three they have already adopted. Perhaps that one family, maybe just one child, redeemed the previous two years in their entirety.

That my family has survived is not *because* of Jack, but *in spite of* him. "Jack is," as one of our friends said, "his own worst enemy." No matter what his *intentions* were, the result of his *actions* has been that he has embodied our adversary, too. Over and over I have discovered ways in which he sabotaged me – not only with the boys, but also at the store. For instance, I didn't find out until after we had already shut it down that my struggles in making the store a success were in large part because Jack told all his old customers never to buy from me, but only to do business with him. I could only assume he set me up in every other way, too, all along.

Jack *was* telling the truth about one thing, though – his admission on the day of his first lie detector test that he had lied about virtually everything he had said to me from day one. By his own choice of actions, he effectively eliminated any last possibility of our remaining friends. There were some people and things, I learned from him, that I just couldn't save.

Larry, a friend of Jack's as well as of mine, paid for a rental truck and helped the boys and me deliver what was left of Jack's belongings to a storage unit where he would be able to retrieve them. With his remaining possessions returned to him and the closing of the store, the last of my ties to Jack was severed. After whittling away at them for twenty-four months, I paid off the remaining bills from our marriage. A month after that, my bankruptcy from Conner's old medical bills from his hospitalization ten years before was off my financial record. Two years prior, I would never have believed I could do it, but the boys and I marched into the future completely broke, yet unencumbered. We still didn't have enough for tomorrow, but every single day we had been provided Manna enough for that day's needs. And every single night I went to bed knowing that more than likely, whether I worried about it or not, the same thing would happen again the next day, too.

A Lamp unto My Feet

◆ ◆ ◆

"The theological starting point
is that
we are not God."

PEGGY WAY
Vanderbilt Divinity School Lecture

◆ ◆ ◆

THE GODDESS

Then, the internalized voices of her culture and her friends circled round in Job's mind, challenging her assumptions about herself and her world. Despairing and longing for death, she heard voices that reminded her of all the good she had done and the value of her life. She heard rumors that if bad things were happening to her, then she must have deserved it, it must be her fault, she must have done something wrong. She heard the clamoring that insisted that good would be rewarded and evil punished, yet she knew evil ones who triumphed and good ones who suffered seemingly for no reason at all. She thought of all the times she had tried to do the right thing, only to have it fall flat in front of her eyes. She thought of the struggle to determine what her calling was, what the loving thing was. She thought of how many times she had sobbed that the only thing she had done wrong was to believe the one who lied to her. She told herself that he had never loved her, that everything he had told her was a lie. Then she heard the voices of her friends telling her that what she was telling herself was the lie, and that he had loved her all he could. She recognized the voices of the young asking how God could be all-powerful and all good when yet there still existed evil in the world. She heard the whisper of the thin Silence asking, "Where were you when I gave birth to the world? Where were you when I labored with Creation?" And she knew, for the first time, what she had never fully understood: that she labored along with the Goddess, giving birth to Creation every day.

Truth within Human Limitations

The entire time all these events were going on, I struggled with the very same questions humankind has asked since reason made questioning a possibility. The deepest and most immediate of these questions, after Jack's confession, was the problem of truth within the limitations of our finitude. I had believed I knew the truth, but I wasn't even close.

I immediately began to question everything Jack had ever told me, and eventually, I began to question everything I had *ever* believed. What was the truth? When could I believe him? When could I believe myself, even? The change that had occurred in my life when I believed I was loved by Jack in the same way I loved him was nothing short of miraculous. I believed I was worthy of being loved, I believed my life was worthwhile in a way I never had before. Instead of making myself the measure of my own Truth, I put Jack in my place. Sure, I had made a difference in the lives of clients who came for counsel. Sure, I had gotten kids who would otherwise have spent their lives languishing in foster care out of the system and into a home of their own. Sure, I made a difference in the lives of others. But I had never mattered to myself until I believed I mattered to Jack.

Once he confessed to me that New Year's Eve and I realized that so much of what I believed was a lie, I could not believe even that my life had value any more. I didn't know what the Truth was. Not just truth. *Truth.*

I remember when I was a kid the first time I realized that at the end of *The Wizard of Oz*, when the Scarecrow spouts out the mathematical equation, "The sum of the square roots of any two sides of an isosceles triangle is equal to the square root of the remaining side," that the way he said it, the equation is all wrong. The correct equation is the sum of the *squares* of the two sides of a *right* triangle is equal to the *square* of the *hypotenuse*. I was shaken to the core. For years, I had believed that the Scarecrow was given some kind of wisdom when the Wizard gave him his diploma, and therefore his confidence. Even as a child I knew that a medal and a ticking heart on a string didn't change anything for the Tin Man and the Lion. Well, it didn't change anything except what they believed about themselves. But because what the Scarecrow said sounded so impressive, I had always thought the Wizard actually did something for him. Really, all the Wizard did was make him believe in what was within himself all along – right or wrong. It was HIS truth. For the Scarecrow, it was Truth.

Every time I realized Jack's story had changed yet again, I had to begin my search for Truth one more time from scratch. I didn't know what *my* Truth was any more. Eventually, I realized that was because I had made someone outside myself the measure. Jack, who had become my measuring stick, was himself so confused that he did not even have any idea what *his* Truth was. For the first fifteen months after his confession, he could not come to terms with the fact that he was, in addition to being a child molester, gay. He would change his mind not just daily, but sometimes by the hour or minute. "Yes, I am; no, I'm not" became his refrain. Jack had internalized the hate he believed his parents could have developed for him to such an extent that he could not accept himself for who he was.

But if Jack had not been the basis of the change that occurred within me, then I was perplexed as to what it was that *had* generated the change I felt. In the end, the answer that came to me was that the only thing that was really different when I fell in love with Jack was that I believed differently about myself. I believed I was lovable. I believed things were going my way. I believed Creation was a safe and friendly place to live. Nothing in the world had actually changed. What had changed was the world inside my head.

It wasn't that my nightmares went away when I was in Jack's arms because he would have protected me and I was safe. My nightmares went away because I *believed* that I was safe. I believed that it was true that he would protect me. I felt safe because that belief became my Truth.

Finitude (the concept that finite beings are limited in their possibilities, i.e. that we are not God) comes into the equation when we make anyone or anything that is human or worldly the measure of an Ideal. If I make a measure out of someone human – *any*one human – I am in trouble. Jack was no more the measure of Truth, than my doctor was the measure of Sanctuary.

I had for a long time hoped that Doc would be there for me until the last of my kids left home, and for an equally long time in my life, his office was the only place in the entire world where I felt safe. Eventually, when he was put in the position of having to weigh what was in the best interest of the hundreds of people involved in his practice – people who could reasonably be threatened by my son's behavior – and the needs of his own family for his continued livelihood, I had to deal with the fact that he of course had to choose the greatest good for the greatest number. Only I was responsible, in the end, for the children I had chosen. They were not Doc's responsibility, but mine.

There was no way I could argue with his choice. I am quite certain that if I had to choose between providing for my family and providing for his, I, too, would choose my own. It had never occurred to me that there would ever be a reason for him to choose, but the choice was reasonable. I am the only person responsible for my children; he is the person responsible for his. The important thing is not to confuse what we are humanly capable of with the Ideal itself. As humans we have human limitations. We are finite, and we can only do the best we can.

Just as our doctor had to abide by the decision of his practice about what was in the best interest of the greater number, I had made choices just like that for years. Ever since I was in college, it had plagued my decision-making process that if I chose to donate money to one cause, it meant not donating to another. If I fed one person, or took one child home, that meant there was another person I could not feed or take home. No matter how I tried, I could not do it all.

There is no Ideal that any one human can live out completely, though some do get closer to some Ideals than others. Doc, who has faithfully provided services to our family in spite of the sporadic nature of his remuneration by adoption assistance, has seen us through thick and thin, when we certainly were unable to pay him ourselves to do so. There are few providers who would – or even could – have done what it took him to gain our trust and to make us feel safe in what we perceived to be a dangerous world. But no matter how dependable or reliable he was, even he could not embody the ultimate Sanctuary, always there, no matter what, no matter when. To expect that of anyone human is not reasonable. No one could. However, it is because I have known him that I can believe God is trustworthy. It is because I have learned to trust at all that I can imagine what it is to trust completely. And it is because Doc has done everything he possibly could for my family that I can believe in a God with our best interest at heart, One who can do anything at all.

And so it is with Love. Laura, who kept trying to teach me that I needed to learn to lo-o-ove George Wallace, lived out that Ideal to an amazing degree. Her love so permeated her being that it teaches me still. When she looked at me the love I felt was so tangible it changed my world, but even Laura was not Love incarnate. Close to the Ideal, so transparent you could see it through her, she was still not the Ideal itself.

That is how I have always thought of the Christ – so transparent you could see Love through him. I can imagine that because I have known Laura. I have known other people like that, people through whom you could see Love to a certain degree. People who make Love tangible in a human world.

The hard thing is often to trust the Truth that tries to make itself known though our own lives. It is much easier to trust others. It is easier to give others' opinions value than to believe in our own. But we will never know Truth if we make others the measure of what is true in our own lives, because others will always be finite, just as we are, too. What is not finite is the Truth that lives within us. It is that to which we must listen. That Truth is stronger and larger than any reality we can create, for it was before us. It is within us. And it will remain in infinity long after our finite selves exist no longer.

Memories

It is bad enough that we cannot always be sure what the Truth is, but there are also times we cannot even count on our own memories. Sometimes I can't even be sure of where I left the keys ten minutes ago, much less what happened to me in my childhood. So I can understand how difficult it would be for my mother to believe me. If I *am* telling the truth, it would mean she failed to protect me. If what I say *is* true, she married not just one but two men who were abusers.

I know I sure don't want to believe that I exposed my own children to men who would abuse them, or that the things I believe I remember from my childhood really happened. I don't *want* either of those things to be true about myself, but I *believe* they are. My mother, on the other hand, cannot believe my story; she cannot even believe her own. Memories are complicated, and they are interrelated. Until we come to terms with our own demons, we cannot recognize and accept the demons of others. "I don't *want* it to be true" is not the same as "I *won't* believe it is true."

There have been a number of studies done on memory which generally conclude that rarely do participants remember events in the same way. People remember the things that are important to them, with the way someone looked, how another smelled, or even what was said being remembered differently by diverse individuals at separate times. Settings are remembered in different ways. Backgrounds, the time the events occurred, what else was going on at the same time – all are subject to interpretation. Each is subject to the slant of the one who is remembering. Memory is fallible, just as are the humans who remember.

And that's not all. Not only is human memory imperfect, but it also comes and goes at some very inconvenient intervals. We can almost always remember something when we don't need to, but frequently not when we do. It is a common experience to forget something while under duress only to remember it the minute the information is no longer needed. The name of someone to whom you would like to make an introduction is a common temporary memory lapse. Phone numbers, addresses, and the like – all are things we frequently forget at certain times only to remember them at others.

We also know that memories are repressed when the events are too distressing for the individual to process. Not quite the same as simply forgetting, repression* is the mind's built-in protective mechanism. Repression has been documented in many studies. Linda Meyer Williams found that 38% of the adult women in her study denied any memory of having been abused as children, even though hospital records documented that 100% had been.[4] Lawson and Chaffin documented that only 43% of the children in their study acknowledged memory of being abused, even though 100% had sexually transmitted diseases.[5] It is as though the mind puts traumatic events into a file drawer, which may or may not be opened later. Frequently, the drawer will not be opened until the individual is at a point in his or her life when it is safe to do so. Often, this will be after the victims of abuse have reached adulthood and are no longer in danger from their perpetrators.

One of the most fascinating things to me about memory I learned at a conference many years ago. The speaker, an art therapist whose name I no longer remember, told the audience about a long term study she had been involved in. In the study, children who had been abused were asked to draw pictures of the scene and what had happened. The fascinating thing was that as time progressed and the children aged, when they were asked to draw pictures of the same scene, the pictures became *more* detailed, with the additional details being verified by the forensic evidence. Things the children had omitted in their earlier drawings and disclosures were found to have actually been documented at the scene of the crime. No matter how young the children had been when the events occurred, many of their depictions of the events improved, rather than deteriorated, over time.

From these studies and others like them, we know that people do not always remember what happened to them immediately after it occurred, there are times when we forget things altogether, and there are other times, especially regarding important events, when our memories become more detailed as we age. It is an almost universal experience to forget the answer to a question on a test only to remember it the minute after the test is turned in. And almost everyone can think of some event they remember, even if it is as slight as telling their children something the children say they don't remember being told, which demonstrates that frequently people remember the same events differently.

In the real world, unlike movies or television, we have to live with different remembrances of the same events. Most of the time those differences are mildly troublesome, but it gets much more complicated when the events are emotionally laden! In those cases, not only are the events remembered differently, but also the interpretation of what actually happened affects the relationships between those whose lives are involved.

Because our memories differ, sometimes the things we say hurt the ones we love who may or may not remember things the same way we do. They may not be at a time or place in their own lives that they can safely entertain even the *possibility* that what we are saying may be true. It is not because we want to hurt them that we speak our Truth, but because we are compelled to speak in order to heal ourselves. And when we speak aloud the things we have kept hidden, it sometimes causes anguish for those who are not prepared to believe that perhaps what we say is, in fact, Truth.

Speaking one's own Truth does not necessarily mean that the aggrieved party is not loved. But it does, sadly, sometimes mean that loved ones may cause each other less pain if, for a period of time (whether for days or months or years), they stay very far apart.

ISSUE THREE

Power and Control

Another issue I struggled with on a daily basis was the issue of power and control. For over a year, I prayed many times daily. *Please just give me the wisdom to know what the next right thing to do is. Please, just give me the courage to choose that thing. Please, give me the strength not to give up, but to do the right thing, and to see it through to the end.*

It was well over a year before I heard the other side of that, which was also something I had been saying every day, but hadn't realized was connected: *I admitted I was powerless over Jack and my life had become unmanageable.*

It was in praying for Knowledge and Courage and Strength that I was able to hold on to the illusion that I could be in control. If You just give me those things, Creator, I can take care of this on my own. If You will just share a few of those Ideals with me, I'd be glad to take care of this for You myself.

When I would forget how out of control I really was, Children's Services would remind me. The example that kept beating me mercilessly over the head all year, encouraging me to acknowledge my powerlessness, was my inability to get Ben's social worker to agree to anything that the rest of his providers thought was appropriate. It was all because of the letter written by the administrator of the out-of-state Level 3 facility where Ben had been to the local juvenile court judge. The letter contained the euphemism that Ben had "achieved maximum therapeutic benefit" from their program. Since it served as the cover letter for a thirty-page report documenting how, over a two-year span, Ben had failed to meet even a single therapeutic goal, no one fell for it, least of all the judge. Well, no one except the social worker, that is. He must have quoted that letter in every meeting we went to. "Ben is a good boy," he would say. "He completed the program," he would insist. Either he couldn't get it, or he wouldn't.

In one meeting, when he quoted it one more time and I just couldn't stand it anymore, I burst out, "Oh, give us a break. *Everyone* knows what that means!"

A representative of the agency that was currently refusing to allow Ben to come back because of his disruptive behavior just looked at me and sighed. "No," she said, rolling her eyes and nodding towards the Children's Services worker. "We don't *all* know what that means."

When in meeting after meeting, the worker continued to express his confusion and surprise that Ben had just self-mutilated, or attempted suicide, or run away, "when he seemed to be doing so well," all I could do was tell him that he was the only one who was surprised. No one who had known Ben for any length of time was surprised at all. But I could not, absolutely *could not*, make his worker get it. When all the MD's and PhD's involved in Ben's care agreed he needed Level 4 care, but his Children's Services worker decided that since Ben wanted to be in a foster home that he would lower him to a Level 2, there was nothing any of us could do to convince him of the absurdity of his position. No one else could convince him, and I couldn't either. It was totally out of my control.

No matter how much I would have liked to, I couldn't take care of everything myself. Reality is too much for any one person to bear. It was the whenever I recognized that and begged in prayer for Mercy that my life would turn around.

ISSUE FOUR

The Pollyanna Take on Sin

Pollyanna had a way of looking at the world that would drive most of us crazy. It all started when she received a pair of crutches she didn't need, and developed a worldview to accommodate them: "At least I can be grateful I don't need crutches." As time went on, "At least it wasn't..." became her refrain. You know the type: "Just be grateful he's with God." "She's better off now." *At least they are not alive and miserable* is one of the most obnoxious offenders. It belittles our pain, saying we should be grateful for our losses instead of giving us permission to grieve.

People use that attitude in relation to sin, too. "Well, you may have been fondled, but at least he wasn't a rapist." "Well, you may have been raped but at least he wasn't a batterer." "Well, he may have broken your arms and legs, but at least he wasn't a murderer." Being thankful for all the things that didn't happen does not diminish our anguish about the things that did. And to inflict Pollyanna's mantra on the victims of abuse does them a great disservice. Victims need room to experience and process the full gamut of emotions. They need to be able to express their feelings without the additional infliction of guilt for having them at all.

If you, as a companion, find some solace for your own powerlessness and inadequacy in thinking such platitudes, keep them to yourself. The victim would be better served by your keeping silent. If you can't think of anything else to say, mirror what you hear. "That really hurt" at least validates the victim's experience. That is *infinitely* more helpful than empty platitudes. Sin is sin. Violation is violation. Being grateful it wasn't worse does not make what actually happened any better.

✸exuality

As these events unfolded, I was surprised at the number of people I came across who equated homosexuality with pedophilia. That Jack was disclosing proclivities regarding both the age and sex of those to whom he was attracted at the same time made it more complicated, but sex and age are two distinct categories. Adult heterosexuals prefer as sexual partners adults of the opposite sex. Adult homosexuals prefer adult partners of the same sex. Pedophiles, on the other hand, are adults who prefer children as sexual partners. If the diagnosis is the mental illness of pedophilia, the children are prepubescent, and generally speaking, those who prefer pre-adolescents gravitate to an age range rather than a sex (such as four-year-olds of either sex). If the attraction is to children who are pubescent or post-pubescent, the criminal activity is ephebophilia, and those who prefer adolescents in this developmental stage generally prefer one sex over the other. In Jack's case, for instance, his preference was newly pubescent males.

As used in the common vernacular, the attraction for pedophiles is to anyone who is younger than the age of consent. Some child molesters are always sexually attracted to children. Others find it possible to maintain sexual relationships with adults for short periods of time, only to return to children as safe objects of sexual gratification under stress or duress. Some, like Jack, invest years in relationships with adults in order to have access to their own or their partner's children just when their victims reach the desirable age. Others are completely impotent in relationships with equals and are consistently able to perform sexually only with those over whom they have power.

And that is the issue at stake: power. A child is unable to give full consent, because a child lacks the power to say "no" and have that "no" respected. Adults are larger, older, more knowledgeable, more powerful. Children, who have no way of understanding the full ramifications of sex in any event, are simply not in a position to say "no" to them. Jack did not respect it when Gabriel told him he did not want to do what Jack wanted.

He did not respect it when Edward said he didn't like it when Jack touched him. He did not even quit when Edward hit him. He just kept going, bulldozing over their feelings, blindly going after his goal of self-gratification.

In the same sense, an adult who is being raped is put in the position of having his or her "no" negated. The one who is raped has less power – either due to age, size, job, physical strength, weapon, relation, or any number of other issues. If one party is in a position of power over the other, whether he or she is a teacher or is simply larger, the younger, smaller, less powerful person is not in a position to say "no." When that is true, "yes" always has no meaning, and sex under those circumstances is always a crime.

Sex offenders choose victims who are either unable or are unwilling to give fully informed consent, and the perpetrator is disdained in almost every society. Activities in which there is an imbalance of power are formally criminalized in many legal codes, including our own. Almost across the board, sexual activities between adults and children are forbidden by custom if not by law, especially when the adults and children are related and the result is an incestuous relationship. But even that is not true in every country at every time. There are even a few people widely scattered who lobby loudly for the right of adults to be involved sexually with children, regardless of the effects on the child.

This behavior is quite distinct from those who choose to be involved in equal relationships with others who *are* fully able to consent, whichever sex they might be. The issue of sex with someone who is able to give informed consent is the question of sexual relations between consenting adults. In that regard, there are no easy answers about what is good or bad, right or wrong.

Heterosexual marriage between consenting adults is the acceptable outlet for sex in many countries, but there are other legal outlets in many others. Some countries do not consider sex between consenting single adults, married or not, to be a problem, while others will not even allow marriage between consenting adults of differing sexes unless they are also the same race. Prostitution between consenting adults is legal in many countries but not in others. Polygamy between consenting adults is not only condoned but also encouraged in many places in the world, while it is abhorred in others. Even within each individual country, the laws have changed over time, with acts that were illegal at one point becoming legal at others and vice versa. The legalization of interracial and homosexual marriage and changing laws regarding the legal age of majority would all be cases in point.

Many are those who have debated long and vigorously whether or not homosexuality is normal or abnormal, a sin or not. Debates have raged over whether or not bisexuals, gay men, and lesbians choose their sexuality and whether or not they have any control over the objects of their attraction at all. Transgendered individuals live in a legal netherland. Laws regarding relationships change with the winds. This book is not equipped either in length or scope to address the issues that spring from these questions, which historian John Boswell and others have already aptly addressed.

All I know is that I cannot speak for anyone else; I can only speak from my own experience: I cannot think of a time in my life when I chose to be heterosexual. I have been this way, as far as I know, all my life. I can think of several adults I know whose homosexuality has been apparent since they were children. Even Jack's proclivity for children has been a powerful force in his life since he himself was a child.

It seems that in each of these cases, sexuality was something innate to the individual. Each of us seems to have been oriented in one direction or another not because of the choices we have made, but because of the makeup of our being and the events which have shaped our lives. And if our sexuality is something over which we have no choice, I cannot in good conscience adhere to the position that sexuality – in and of itself – of any type is a sin or evil, any more than I would advocate that skin color constitutes a sin. I do not believe we can be held accountable for what we did not choose. I do, however, hold firmly to the belief that to inflict *whatever* one's sexual orientation is upon those who have no power to say "no" is, in fact, a sin. I do believe that to victimize the marginalized and powerless is, in reality, evil.

I certainly am not in a position to speak for God, but it is hard for me to believe that any two people trying to love each other, no matter how imperfectly or humanly, could possibly be as grave a sin as eating too much while others die of starvation, or having two coats hanging in a closet when others freeze to death on the sidewalk outside, and we don't think anything about admiring, electing, or ordaining people who do both of those. Denying the full rights of humanity to adults trying to love other consenting adults is appalling; it makes criminals of those in the minority who are asking for nothing more than the right to be held to the same relational standards as the majority.

One of my old pastors used to say, "If you are going to err, err on the side of grace." I choose to err, if it is doing so, on the side of those who are trying to love each other, no matter how imperfectly or how offensively to other people. If heterosexuals are striving to love each other in relationships of equality, I am not in the position to throw stones. The same is true if the persons trying to love each other are homosexual, bisexual, or transgendered. I have not had to walk in their shoes, and I am not in the position to pass judgment upon them.

I think that for people to try to act lovingly towards others is a good thing, and we should do the best we can at it. God knows I have never done it perfectly myself. The gay and lesbian couples I know who have been together twenty, thirty years or more have certainly done a better job of loving each other than I have done in any of my three perfectly legal marriages. Although I do not envy them the disdain they suffer from those who think they are sinning, I do certainly envy the longevity of their relationships. I only wish I had made as good a choice in any of the partners I have chosen for myself.

Good against Evil

The question of how there could be a good and all-powerful God and still exist evil in the world was put forth in the biblical book of Job long before I asked it. It doesn't make sense to us. If the All-Powerful were really All-Good surely that power would be used to stop pain and suffering. If the All-Good were really All-Powerful surely the evil ones would be stopped in their tracks. But what we know is that suffering and evil do exist in Creation. So what does that say about the Creator?

The only way I can get my thoughts around an issue this big is to think of an incident that happened over twenty-five years ago, involving my own creation, of a sort. It involves my one birth child, John.

Our family was standing outside First Church on a cold, bright, clear winter day, talking with friends after worship. John and several other toddlers were playing in the driveway, while we parents were trying to decide where to eat lunch. It was an activity in a location that had occurred hundreds of times before, and would again.

Suddenly, for no reason that I could see, John darted for the street. He was after something; I have no doubt even though I could not see anything there, and he was too far away for me to reach him before he reached the street. A car was coming. If he kept going at the same speed, and the car kept going at the same speed, it was going to hit him in front of my eyes before I could get to him. I knew all this in an instant, but there was absolutely nothing I could do. Nothing.

Nothing, that is, except call him. I shouted out his name, hoping desperately that he would stop, turn around, and come back to safety. I called him by name, because it was all that I could do. I called him, begging him to return to me. And I realized that day, that calling us is all our Creator can do, too.

When John ran headlong towards the street that Sunday morning almost thirty years ago, I was not making him do something frightening and dangerous. I was not making him do something that might leave me grieving and suffering the rest of my life, though I did, in a sense, make him. Once he was created, he was out of my control. All I could do was beg him to come back and do the right thing. All I could do was plead for him to return to safety.

And I believe that is how it is with the Goddess. She creates us, all of us, in her womb, the Earth. She loves us with all her heart. She may be All-Good. And She may be All-Powerful. But once She has created us as beings with choice, She no longer maintains control over our choices. She may call us, begging and pleading with us to return to safety. She may send us messengers telling us what the Good thing to do is, what the Right is. But once we are created, asking is all She does. She leaves to us the choice between Safety and Danger, Good and Evil, Right and Wrong.

As a consequence, some people choose badly. Some people choose to hurt others. Some people will always choose their own good over the greater Good. Thankfully, the opposite is also true.

ossibilities and Predestination

Some people think our every move is predestined, but I don't agree with that. Just because our Maker may know us so well that She knows what we will choose before we choose it, that doesn't necessarily mean She makes it happen. I, too, have friends I know so well that I can frequently predict what they are likely to say before the words leave their tongues, and I have no control over them at all. Rather than being predetermined, life is more likely like our experience with our own children: once we are out of the womb our Creator begins to lose control of us. By the time we have left the womb and are mobile and able to make choices of our own, She controls us no more than we can control our own children. She chooses to give us freedom to choose, too.

What that means for us is that there is always the possibility of novelty. Because we have the freedom to make choices of our own, sometimes our lives *do* change. We see possibilities revealed in history. We discover that our own or others' lives have been converted, turned back, turned around. Just as our children grow up and leave home, so do we. We graduate. We get new jobs. We retire. Sometimes we even fall in love. No matter how old we are, we can still develop and grow, even changing our ways of thinking and responding to life's opportunities.

When I met Jack, I believed I had finally processed the aftermath of my childhood and had made a better choice. I believed I was stepping outside the patterns of my youth. Unfortunately, I believed that because he lied to me and I trusted him. And while I don't want to believe in predestination, that is how it seemed at first when I found out that once again I had repeated my past. It felt like I was going down the drain in a whirlpool from which I would never escape.

But in spite of the fact that on that occasion I repeated a choice I had made before, I don't think it always has to be that way. Each time I have relived the patterns of my youth, I have gotten closer to the promise of a new life, the possibility of a new future. I may have repeatedly chosen men who were much the same, but my responses have changed over time. I am not willing to tolerate as much abuse. I get out quicker. I heal faster. I hold out the hope that God is a God of infinite possibilities, and that the day will come when my choices will be not just better, but good ones.

Little by little, we victims of abuse unlearn the lies we have been taught. We come to value our own lives. We learn to make better judgments. There are always new possibilities for us. As long as we live, there is hope that we can change. And there is always the hope that we will.

The Nature vs. Nurture Debate

Many abuse victims have asked how it is possible for them to be good, if one or both of the people who made them was evil. I was driving down the road one day when the answer came to me on the radio. "Why is it," she asked, "that when you mix flour and water, you get glue, but when you mix flour and water and sugar and eggs, you get cake?" For the life of me, I can't remember the name of the comedienne whose joke about cake opened me up to a new way of looking at the relationship between nature and nurture. I'm not even sure I remember the punch line correctly, because I was so taken by the implications of the joke's setup. "That's it!" I thought. And in an instant it was all clear.

Our biological parents are flour and water. Mix the two together, and you get this sticky stuff that has no shape or form of its own. That's nature. But when that stuff goes through the process of a life, you get something else altogether. First, you add the egg, the unique combination of DNA that makes up each of us. That egg grows into each of us as an individual being in our own right. Mix an egg with the product of flour and water and you get flatbread of life to sustain you, maybe, but not necessarily something yummy.

Fortunately, though, as we roll through life, other things stick to us as well. Friends, schools, teachers, communities of faith, events, jobs, and families of our own all get folded into the mix, too. The love of others is the sugar and spice and yeast of our lives, and love is always the best form of nurture. For each of us, the ingredients that flavor our lives, hold us together, and help us grow are different. Mix them together and bake, and *Voila!* No matter how bad the parents you start out with, *you* can still get to be cake.

Each of us, including everyone we love and everyone we hate, is a combination of nature and nurture, inseparable. Not either/or, but both/and.

ISSUE NINE

Mental Illness or Just Plain Meanness

Many times over the years, Doc has said to me, "That is a normal response for when abnormal things happen to people." The more I've thought about it, the more complicated the issue of normalcy has become for me. First of all, there is the question for me of whether or not Jack was indeed mentally ill or just plain mean and evil, and then there is also the question of whether or not a diagnosis of mental illness in one's partner should prolong the amount of time one stays in an abusive relationship. I wanted desperately to be fair. I would not have left Jack if his illness were a physical one. Was it fair to leave him if his illness was mental? If he had no choice regarding the object of his attraction, how much control did he actually have over his actions? If he was mentally ill as a result of something that happened to him, were his actions his responsibility, or the responsibility of his abuser? And if they were his responsibility, when did the age of accountability occur?

Then I wondered, if abuse creates certain symptoms in the victim, is it even fair to label the victim with a diagnosis at all, or does that just foster the illusion that the victim is the one who was sick to begin with? How come the victims are the ones who are sick if the abuser is just plain mean? And at what point does the transformation from "sick victims acting out what happened to them" to "mean abusers" occur?

A therapist I know who works with abusers has told me predators can spot a victim walking down the street a block away. Just by posture, eye contact or the lack thereof, and the way someone walks, an abuser can tell if a person is someone they can prey on and get away with it. Does that mean that once we have been victimized we advertise that we are ripe for re-victimization? Are we then responsible for bringing additional abuse upon ourselves? In my immediate family, did I set the boys up without knowing it or even being able to help myself? In the larger world, if we use provocative illustrations of young people to entice people to buy products they do not need, do we ourselves participate in the victimization of the children upon whom the abusers then act out their fantasies?

Pedophilia, the sexual attraction to prepubescent children, is listed in the most commonly used diagnostic manual as a mental illness. Ephebophilia, the attraction to post-pubescent children, is not. While the acting out of either of those attractions is a crime, it is still considered normal to be attracted to youth at the height of their blossoming sexuality. That reality is taken advantage of by advertisers who use the innate appeal of children to sell whatever product they are being paid to hawk. Even our society programs us to be sexually attracted to youth. Every visual medium caresses our inclinations in that direction and stimulates those feelings, even in those who choose to obey the laws.

Surely we as a society make it worse by legally stimulating those who would *like* to break the laws, and who would abuse rather than protect the young. We, as a society, participate in criminals' temptation. We say that *being* sexually attracted to young people is understandable, but that *acting* on that attraction is bad, or even evil. Yet we, ourselves, make the temptation worse. We put the stimulation out there, and then say that to respond to temptation is against our laws. And it is always against the law. Jack's actions were unquestionably criminal, even if I am still not sure if they were the manifestation of mental illness or just plain meanness.

The line between mental illness and just plain meanness is a fine one, but one thing is absolutely clear. No matter what *anyone's* feelings are, it is always the responsibility of the older, larger person to protect the younger, smaller one. *Always*. Even if that means protecting someone from himself or herself. And even if it means protecting him or her from the ones we love.

ISSUE TEN

Responsibility, Reward, and Punishment

I have always, since I was a child, hated the story of Job, for one very simple reason. All Job's children die, for no reason, on a whim. And then, at the end of the story, God gives Job a new crop of children, and Job is happy, like that is supposed to make ANYTHING better. God had to be kidding.

All I have ever been able to think is that no mother would go along with that. Sure, Job, as the father, could calmly say, "God gives, and God takes away, Blessed be the name of God," but I was sure no mother would take the same events with such calm. A mother would be ranting and raving and doing whatever it took to get her children back, or at least to make God aware of her distress. No replacement would suffice. A mother would be like Rachel, weeping disconsolately for her children. A mother would never so easily forget. A mother would remember. A mother would fight back.

I struggled with all these issues as the events of this book unfolded. One of the biggest issues for me was the question of responsibility, with its dilemma of reward and punishment. These things that happened to me, were they all my fault? Was it really my fault when I could not figure out some way to stretch our meager resources further so that I could afford Ananda's meds to keep his seizures from returning? Was it really my fault, as I believed it was, that I was unable to stop Conner from his explosion on the second New Year's Eve, the one that resulted in our being fired by the practice? Was it really my fault that the boys had been placed in danger because I believed the things Jack told me, fell in love, and asked him to marry me? What really was my liability? And if it was my fault, could I somehow beg, plead, cajole, curse, rage God into giving me my life back, the one I had before?

I kept trying to balance what was my responsibility and liability against the responsibility and culpability of the others in the story. In the biblical story, once Job's friends entered the picture, they kept saying to Job that none of the things that happened to him would have occurred if he had just been better. If only he would admit his sin, the deluge of misfortune would come to an end. The good are not punished. The evil are not rewarded. That would not be fair, and since God must be fair, then it must have been something Job did. "It is your fault, Job, somehow, because it could not be God's."

Job doesn't fall for that for a minute, and though it was often repeated by the voices inside my own head, too, neither should we. We are not, no matter how much our voices tell us we are, responsible for the choices of others. We are not, no matter how deeply ingrained it is within our souls, culpable for things out of our control. We are human, we are finite, and we are limited in power.

While I have always been convinced a mother would fight back, even a mother cannot save her children from circumstances beyond her control. And even though I hate to admit it, time does ease the pain of most wounds, though it never entirely takes the pain away. The loss of children, in particular, for both mothers and fathers, is a loss from which we never fully recover.

Someday, however, no matter how hard it is to believe that it will ever happen, we do dare to love again. Eventually, something or someone breaks through our defenses and we discover that we care about something new. In my case, the first time I noticed that feeling, it was a horse.

Almost exactly a year after Liberty died, Wilma sent me her sister, Gaia. I kept telling Wilma it wasn't a good time for me to take on anything else, but Wilma and her husband, Bill, brought her to my house and left her. I didn't want to love her. I was afraid I would lose her, too. And sure enough, eventually, I did. We had wormed all the horses, and apparently she had a reaction to the wormer. She got sicker and sicker, and over the span of a very few days, she died. When it happened to her, the vet thought that might have been what happened to make Liberty sick, too, that perhaps they had some hereditary allergy to the wormer, but knowing that didn't help any. Her death was just one more loss I wasn't ready for.

The more time I spent with the little filly, the more I handfed her and pumped medications into her, the more I discovered I loved her, too. Up until that point, I had not had any feelings for her in particular. I had only accepted her because Wilma's husband wanted her gone, and because she was Liberty's sister. She didn't move like Liberty, she didn't love me the way Liberty had. But still, once she was there, I had taken care of her along with all the others.

During those last few days, when I slept in the stall with her and we were together night and day, I felt the ice within me begin to melt. By the time she died, I knew that she truly was mine. She was no longer just one of the horses out in the pasture. She and I were bonded in a way I didn't think I could ever feel again.

It made me mad to think that the part of Job I had always hated might be right. But it might. While it is true no horse will ever be Liberty again, and no horse will ever again be her sister Gaia, someday, if the Goddess is willing, I will love again. Nothing will ever take their places in my life, just as no new child could ever take the place in the heart of any parent who has ever loved. But someday, it is possible, that I may have those feelings again. And that is true for the feelings I had for Jack, as well.

The Sins of the Fathers

It isn't fair, and there's just no way to get around it. No matter what the consequences are for the offender, the victim ends up paying for being abused. Victims pay for abuse emotionally, through nightmares and flashbacks and unrelenting fear and self-doubt. We pay for it mentally, as a result of diminished concentration and capacity to cognitively make sense of the things that happened to us. We pay for it physically, as a result of the stresses to the body due to events we did not instigate. We pay for it relationally, as a result of a life of insecurity and second-guessing our every choice. And we pay for it financially, both as a result of being stuck with the responsibility of paying for therapy and medications to address symptoms we did not create, and as a result of diminished earning capacity due to the trauma we have experienced. The abuser abuses us, and we end up paying for it. It isn't fair.

But, fair or not, that's what happens. The sins of the fathers (usually) are visited on successive generation after generation, and it is the children who bear the burden. It is not even clear whether or not it is reasonable to hope things will get any better as time goes on, but hope we do, anyway. It is hard to tell if any given one of us will ever escape the pattern, or if we, too, are inextricably caught up in the web of Sin.

All we know is that sometimes, some people do escape. Some people choose not to pass the abuse on to the next generation. Some people do battle with their own demons, and win. We don't know why some survive and others do not. We don't know why some are able to fight off the inclination to repeat what we have learned. But we do know that any given one of us *can* choose to stop the cycle with ourselves and our own children. We may need help to pull it off. We're even likely to. But there is no shame in asking.

ISSUE TWELVE

Justice, Vengeance, and Restitution

Throughout this period of time, one of Jack's refrains was, "I just want to make it all up to you. I just want to get all this behind me and come home." He was absolutely certain that he would be the exception to the rule and would zip through therapy and come home sooner than anyone expected. I couldn't tell that he spent much time at all thinking about whether or not we would want him to, and he certainly didn't seem to think a lot about what would be the best way *for us* to have him make it up to us. Like so many of us, he wanted to give the gift he wanted to receive.

I remember well the day he shouted at me, "You act like this is all my fault," and all I could respond was, "Well, that's because as far as I am concerned, IT IS." I do believe that. I believe with all my heart that while I am responsible for having married Jack, what happened to the boys and to me after the wedding as a result of Jack's abuse and his lies *was* his fault, just as I believe that whatever happened to Jack was *his* abuser's fault, whoever his abuser might have been. Jack is long past the age of accountability. He knew what he was doing. He knew it was wrong, and worked hard to hide his actions from anyone who might stop him. And if what Jack did was his fault, then the question of what would be an equitable restitution for him to make to his victims is a reasonable one. Not retribution, not vengeance for actions performed by a person suffering from a mental illness – if in fact that's what it is. But restitution, justice for the victims who have been hurt by his actions. Just as Jack deserved justice, so do the boys, and so do I.

We deserve justice because we have been hurt by his actions. Our trust has been betrayed and our self-esteem has been damaged. The boys deserve justice because they now have to unlearn everything Jack tried to get them to believe about the relationships of fathers and sons. Their sense of their own sexuality has been impaired. They sometimes feel powerless to protect themselves. We second-guess ourselves even more than we did before. Much as it was with Ben's rape many years ago, it may be difficult to sort out which symptoms belong to Jack's abuse, but that we have been damaged by his actions cannot be disputed. We feel all these ways because of his actions, and while none of us want him punished, all of us want Justice.

My friend Deborah has pointed out many of the things Jack did that fell into the category of "intentional tactics" to get what he wanted, from his using his size to intimidate the boys to his threats of suicide to get me to hang in there with him a little longer, so the first thing he could do to "make it up to us" would be to be just as intentional about keeping other children safe. He could use the tools available to him to keep from acting out on other victims. Up until now, he has steadfastly refused to be honest in the log of behaviors and actions he is supposed to keep that would help contain his activities. He constantly "forgets" to carry with him the ammonia capsules that sex offenders are supposed to inhale when they begin to slide into the cycle towards abuse. He "forgets" the monitor that goes with his ankle bracelet. As his probation officer has said, "Jack likes the game." He doesn't want to do the things that would help keep children safe, and he does not choose to do them. So he could start by just following the rules, and he could do so consistently.

He could quit lying to himself, starting with the big one, which is that he is just a nice guy who likes children "and it isn't his fault some of them trigger him." Jack is *not* just a nice guy. He is a child molester who likes the game so much that he has been willing to invest *years* in relationships in order to make sure he has access to young boys just as they reach the beginning of puberty. He spent *years* getting to know me and appearing to be whoever I wanted him to be, until he broke down my defenses and enticed me to trust him. In retrospect, I sometimes wonder if asking him to marry me was my idea at all, or if it was really *he* who set *me* up. He spent *years* developing his relationship with Gabriel's family so that just at the opportune moment he could step in and appear to be the hero. He spent *years* grooming the boys so that by the time Edward hit puberty, he would be their father and confidant.

Jack has structured his entire life around having access to prepubescent children just so he could be with them when they were the most sexually attractive to him. He has intentionally targeted abused and abandoned children with severe emotional and medical conditions and, as he demonstrated with Gabriel, has been willing to intentionally abuse their trust from the first time he met them. He was also willing to daily expose me to AIDS by telling himself the lie that I wasn't really in danger because "Gabe's viral load is really low right now." He acts in a way that communicates that he clearly believes it is acceptable to use people in any way he chooses in order to get what he wants. He conveys that, as far as he is concerned, it is permissible to do anything as long as you hide it, it is tolerable to lie to get what you want, and it is convenient to put oneself in positions of sacred trust in order to have access to needy children. And all of those are lies. Thus, the second thing he could do would be to start telling the truth about his actions, about his intentions, and about his beliefs.

The third thing that would be helpful would be to make financial restitution to his victims. Like every family of victims, every day we have expenses that are related to our years with Jack. These range from the expense of gasoline to drive to therapy, because believe me, we are still talking about him, to trying to make the payments on The Refuge, because while I do love living there, it is certainly an expense I would never have taken on without his assurance that he would do whatever was necessary to make the payments. And if we ever get out of therapy and get the farm paid for, Jack could keep making financial restitution to agencies such as Rape and Sexual Abuse Centers, which provide services to many victims, some of whom, including Gabriel's family, are victims of Jack's.

He could choose to learn from his own experience so that he could change his behavior, his life and maybe, in the long run, help others change their lives as well. At one point, during the early days after his initial confession, he brainstormed about converting my dream for The Refuge into a center for the treatment of sexual abusers. It was not clear if he did or did not think through the ramifications of having sex offenders adjacent to a church camp that provides childcare to children. While that will never happen, he could still make use of the consequences he continues to suffer in order to make other perpetrators aware of the potential consequences of their own actions. I am sure none of them thinks, as they are grooming that very first child for abuse, that they will someday end up like Jack, being caught prostituting himself with street people behind a dumpster.   I doubt that many of them think on the front end they will end up as decaying old perverts, spending their lives further victimizing the marginalized and vulnerable. Using what he could learn from his experiences to change first his own life, and then, only after doing that, working to change the lives of others would be a fourth thing he could do.

Yes, there are things Jack could do "to make it up to us" but none of them include being involved in our lives. Each time a few months go by without our having any interaction with him, we all start to feel better, and then, just when we're not expecting it, something brings him up, the wound rips open once more, and we all have to heal again. Sometimes, the most loving thing you can do for someone is to stay very far away. While even Edward and Gabriel did not want vengeance, Justice would still be nice.

Longing for Candyland

Many days, even hoping for Justice feels like longing for Candyland. It is a nice concept, fun to think about and even to entertain fantasies of, but not likely to ever happen in reality. Justice just doesn't usually seem like a very realistic possibility.

But, in all fairness, sometimes novelty does break through into our history of doing the same thing over and over again. New ideas erupt through our habitual ways of thinking. Individuals do sometimes act in unexpected ways. Non-violence brings about changes that generations of violence could never effect. Change does happen, to us as individuals and as a people. And Justice, even Justice is possible.

Gabriel never got Justice for what Jack did to him, nor is he ever likely to. I am not likely to ever get Justice for what happened to me as a child, and neither is Jack. But sometimes, the just thing does happen. Gabriel's underage victim saw the criminal justice system act on her behalf. Edward saw his abuser stopped, jailed, and kept away from him. I was able to write this book, tell my story, and maybe, if I am lucky, be a part of some other victim's healing, or be a tool in stopping some offender from striking again.

Just because Justice sometimes feels like such a remote possibility that it might as well be Pie-in-the-Sky-By-and-By, that doesn't mean we shouldn't work to make it happen.

Providence and Want

There is a parable Jesus is reported to have told, that goes like this:

One morning, a group of a group of day laborers is hired and promised decent wages for a day's work. They agree to the offered amount. By midmorning it is clear more help is needed, so additional workers are hired for the balance of the day. At noon, again in the afternoon, indeed all the way up to the end of the day, workers are added to the morning crew. When the day ends, even the last is paid the same as the first. Those who have been working the longest are disgruntled: "We worked longer and harder, so why don't we get paid more than they do?" they ask. To which their employer answers, "What are you griping about? I paid you what you agreed to. Who are you to complain about my generosity?"

The story of the workers who all get paid exactly the same regardless of the amount of work they do has always given me trouble. So has the fact that throughout this story of my own, my family has always received whatever it needed to survive, and no number of panic attacks on my part ever seemed to influence Providence in the least. We never got more than we needed, but we never got less that was necessary, either – even when I thought I knew what was necessary, and it was more than we actually got. No matter *what* I thought, the amount we received was always enough to survive on until the next day's Manna from heaven arrived.

It wasn't fair. And I don't just mean that it wasn't fair to me; I mean it wasn't fair to all those who every day do *not* receive what they need – from children who suffer from hunger or brutality, to nations massacred in acts of apparently pointless genocide. Every day there are those who do *not* receive enough.

So who am *I* to be the recipient of our Creator's generosity? Why should my family survive when others don't? While I may not want to feel guilty about others' poverty, at the same time I don't want it to be my own children who are hungry. How can I make sense of the fact that, as the morning workers said, "It just isn't fair?"

I don't know the answer to that question. There has never been a single theological stand I have come across on this issue that has ever made sense to me at all. Well, none but the faithful steward: whether we receive just what we need, more than we need, or less, the only thing that does make sense is for us to be faithful stewards of whatever it is that we have received from our Creator's bounty.

When John was eighteen months old, he and I were traveling in the car one day when I heard a radio plea for foster parents. At the time, I was a VISTA volunteer, living on welfare and food stamps and $63 a week, but we still had more than the people I worked with. We had a roof over our heads, food to prepare, and a kitchen to cook it in. My child had a jacket, though we had no money for two. Compared to many who lived in want, we lived in plenty.

The radio announcement changed the direction of my life. In comparison with those in the housing projects where I worked, we were rich. By inviting a child into our home, I could be a faithful steward of what I did have. The balance of my life tipped, and as a result many lives were forever changed.

I don't know why it is that some have much and others have none. I don't know why our family has always received enough when I could see no way to make it happen and was powerless to make it happen myself. I only know that the only thing that makes sense to me is to keep thanking Providence, because the woman watching her child starve to death could have been me. I am certain I have no right to complain if I do not also give thanks for everything I have received.

I once saw a poster that read: *There is nothing I can do. I am just one person… Do you really think God is going to let you get away with that?* No, I really don't. Neither do I know why it is that my family has bread enough for today. It certainly is not because we have deserved it, while others have not. But since by tomorrow this bread I have will mold or go stale, won't you let me fix you a sandwich today while it's still good? It would be an honor if you would let me share with you this Providence which is not my own. Please, be God's guest. I believe I am.

Faithfulness and Fidelity

Before one is ordained in most denominations, there are rounds of interviews; usually starting with the pastor, proceeding to the local church board, and (depending on the denomination) frequently going on to the conference or diocesan level. During the ordination itself, the candidate pledges to be faithful to certain vows. In many churches, these vows include some variation of the one used by my own denomination, "Celibacy in Singleness, and Fidelity in Marriage."

These vows are the formal commitment to a faithfulness we expect of most who are in positions of leadership. We expect leaders to be trustworthy. We expect them to keep safe those in their care, whether it is their flock, their patients, or their students. And we absolutely expect it from those responsible for the care of our children, from the hospital nursery staff to the high school principal.

Sexual perpetrators make use of that trust to work their way into the lives of those upon whom they would prey. They take advantage of others' need for safety and structure to put themselves in positions from which they can take advantage of others' vulnerability. For this reason, many states have higher penalties for violations of trust committed by caregivers and authority figures. We don't simply *expect* caregivers to live up to society's customs and laws. Whether they take a formal vow or not, we *demand* it, and rightfully so.

ISSUE SIXTEEN

Does Everyone Really Have a Place?

As a kid, I used to listen to two radio talk shows with great amusement. Both the hosts were preachers. Though representing the same denomination, each of them insisted not only that salvation was limited to the members of their *denomination*, but also each claimed salvation for only the members of his individual *congregation*. The preacher from the church in town claimed that the folks who worshipped at the lake would not be welcome in heaven, and the preacher from the lake declared the opposite was true. God's table, each wanted me to believe, could not possibly be big enough for all.

The question of whether or not everyone really does have a place at God's table is not an easy one. Every person wants to be right in his or her beliefs, and to human eyes it seems that for some people to be right and welcome, others have to be wrong and excluded. Fortunately, God's Grace breaks through our humanness: some churches now "adopt" prisoners upon their release, helping them to resettle and welcoming them to worship with their sponsors. Many congregations now pride themselves on being both racially integrated and culturally diverse. And almost every church these days has a wheelchair ramp.

Openly gay, lesbian, bisexual, and transgendered congregants who were once excluded from places of worship are now welcomed by congregations that have joined the Welcoming Church Movement. There are now hundreds of openly gay clergy in a variety of denominations, and the Episcopal Church USA has also ordained an openly gay bishop. First in Massachusetts and now in other states as well, same-gendered couples can be married in churches and in civil ceremonies, and even more states offer them civil unions. Slowly but surely, religious institutions are breaking down their barriers. Many who were once considered "outsiders" are now invited "in."

So far, however, known pedophiles and child molesters have not been included in those who are welcome. Known sex offenders continue to be excluded from communities of faith. Still, that does *not* mean that pedophiles and child molesters are not present within worship facilities, any more than it means that pedophiles and child molesters are not present in the world. What it *does* mean is that *if* we know who they are, we exclude them. And statistically, current research shows that by doing so we only increase their danger to the community. Child molesters are not *less* likely to reoffend if they are exiled from their support systems; they are *more* likely to do so.[3] Moving offenders from where they are known to where they are unknown may create the illusion of safety for the communities they have left, but it increases their potential for danger in the communities they enter, as the recent revelations about sexual abuse by priests have amply shown.

Few congregations are prepared to protect children from dangers both known and unknown. It is easier and by far more comfortable to pretend that if there are no *known* offenders within a congregation, then its children are safe. It is much more painful to acknowledge our vulnerability to *unknown* dangers. It is more difficult to develop systems that keep children safely supervised at all times than to tell individuals they are not welcome at worship.

Many I know and love do not agree with my position that we must welcome known sex offenders to our places of worship, but I believe that in order to be faithful, we have no choice. All sinners have a place at the table of God. And while I certainly have a great appreciation for those who want to keep children safe (goodness knows, I have spent my entire life trying to do so myself), I cannot get past the fact that I believe through to my deepest core that even Jack has a place at the table of God. I truly believe that if offenders go to church with a chaperone, stay with that person throughout the service, and then leave with them after it is over, then children can be safe. Several states even have training programs for these companions. There are offenders in many places of worship, just as there are at many job sites and many recreational facilities, who are not treated as criminals simply because others do not know who they are.

When Jack first confessed, Doc encouraged us to continue to go to the church where we had been precisely because it *was* a church where everyone knew what he had done. He told us that *knowledge* was the way to safety, *not*, as so many recommended, going where no one knew us. With everyone at First Church watching Jack like a hawk, it probably would have been one of the safest places he could ever have worshipped. Our staying away only meant that as long as we were not present at First Church, the congregation was free to demonize Jack and to put off dealing with the issue that he, too, was a child of God. As long as Jack was gone, everyone left behind could hold fast to the illusion that his absence alone assured the safety of the children who were left.

One member of First Church even wrote me a letter suggesting that the Catholic Church (though neither Jack nor I has ever been Catholic) might be willing to start an "adults only" congregation and that Jack could go there. She wanted him so far away that she didn't even want him in her own denomination, much less congregation. This is in spite of the fact that Jack is not the only person in the congregation to have been accused of molesting a child, though he is, as far as I know, the first who has confessed. Several years before, the congregation eagerly welcomed back one member who was arrested on charges of molesting a child but denied that his child accuser was telling the truth. Though no one in the congregation can ever know for sure whether it was he or the child who was lying, everyone was eager to believe that the one they knew was innocent. And, had Jack denied that he had abused Edward, I am sure that the same would have been true for him. In all fairness however, we have no way of ever knowing that *any* member of the congregation is trustworthy, whether they have been accused or not. The larger issue is how to keep children safe, no matter what, and no matter whom they are with.

Some denominations have already developed "safe sanctuary" guidelines such as the one that First Church was attempting to develop. In some instances, congregations have been encouraged to incorporate these guidelines even before any known sexual abuse has occurred. Other denominations and congregations are in the process of developing policies to address these situations as they arise.

For the sake of the families these policies will ultimately affect, time is of the essence. Insofar as it is possible, "safe sanctuary" guidelines need to be developed *prior* to any known sexual abuse. They need to address the needs of all involved, not only taking into account the need of the congregation for safety, but also the need of the family for pastoral care. Guidelines need to be developed with sensitivity for the conflicted feelings the children will have about their abuser (if the abuser is known to them), especially if the abuser is a family member. The guidelines also need to be developed with consideration for the trauma experienced in the life of the non-offending parent, and the difficult position that parent will be in – not only financially and legally – but also in relation to societal support systems and to the other members of the congregation itself. If God is the first and great Healer, then surely the church, of all institutions, should be a place where we live out the physician's Hippocratic Oath: "First, do no harm." It might as well be "Love your enemy."

Somehow, I think First Church's rejection of Jack would have troubled me less if the congregation had at least been honest with themselves and with others about their position. "*Not* everyone has a place at the table" might be less inspiring, but at least it would be telling the truth. It is the lie that is perpetrated week after week which continues to trouble me the most. The congregation certainly has the right to decide that not everyone has a place at their table, but if that is the decision, don't lie about it. Just tell the truth. Just go ahead and acknowledge it. Say it out loud: "We say this is God's table, but really it is *our* table, and while we wish everyone had a place at our table, sometimes we just aren't comfortable with them here. Everyone has a place at the table in theory, but in reality we can take that place away, and sometimes, we do."

There must be a balance between Safety and Grace, but locking sinners out of the house of God is not the answer. It is precisely in the house of God that sinners do belong.

Issue Seventeen

Hope vs. Despair

Whether to succumb to despair or cling to hope was an issue I had struggled with long before the events in this story took place. There were events in my childhood that left me believing that death is not the threat that life is. Instead, in many cases, death is better than life. I have never feared it, except for one aspect.

My fear regarding death has been that, rather than life ending, it does not. My fear has been that once your body is dead, your soul remains conscious, like closing your eyes at night, in a dark and silent room. What if, when I die, I am left alone with my thoughts, my nightmares, my terrors and fears, and there is not even anyone else there to talk me through them. What then?

That fear has stopped me from choosing suicide on many occasions. Three times only, it did not. On those three occasions, I believe deep in my soul I was stopped by the Goddess. I believe that in part because one of my graduate school professors brought it to my attention that if I had been stopped by the (masculine) God, matters would likely have been handled differently.

Though I had actively wrestled with the idea of suicide since my twentieth birthday, before I was even pregnant with John, I did not outright decide to kill myself the first time until he was about six years old. At the time, the demons in my head were overwhelming me. Daily, I was reliving the horrors that had happened to me when I was John's age, and I was having an impossible time separating the reality of what I was living in my daily life from the reality I was remembering in my internal life.

Finally one night, the pain became so great that it entirely encompassed my world. I was so deep in despair I could not have even told you I had a child, much less that I had friends I could have called. I decided that the only place the demons still lived was within my own head (both of the the perpetrators of my abuse had long since died), and that by killing myself I could kill them. That I would be dead was of no consequence. It was worth my death if my memories, which were all that kept them alive, could be destroyed.

I had been so invested in death as a way out of my distress that I had framed up the ceiling above the staircase in my house in such a way that I would only have to make a small hole in the drywall to get a rope around a joist to hang myself. Ever since I was twenty, I had known at all times of a location where I could hang myself and had kept a rope available, in case the occasion ever arose. Having finally decided to carry it out, for the first time that I could remember in my life a huge wave of calm and relief washed over me. Finally, my misery would be over. I would be dead, but the demons would be, too. It would be a bargain.

I was lying in bed, experiencing the relief, trying to remember where I had last left the drywall knife to make the hole, when John started screaming. And I don't mean crying. I mean *screaming*. I was startled, because in my agony I had completely forgotten that he existed. The only things in all Creation that existed were the demons in my brain and the rope that could free me from them.

Furious at being stopped in the middle of what had, for a few moments, promised to be my deliverance from a lifetime of pain, I went in to see what was the matter with John, who was sobbing harder than I can ever remember him doing before or since. "I was having a nightmare," he gasped. "And you were dead."

As he described the nightmare, I became more and more angry with God. How dare God interfere in my child's dreams? He was MY child. MY CHILD. And God was interfering in MY child's dreams. God had no right. And it had to have been Divine interference, because John's nightmare was this: "You were dead," he sobbed. "And I had to leave my school, and all my friends, and I had to go live with Janet and Bill, and you were dead, too," he repeated. I sat in the rocking chair and rocked him for what seemed like hours, raging at God all the time in my head.

By the time he had stopped crying and fallen back asleep, I, too, was calmer and could go back to sleep. Somehow, I made it until morning. And in the morning, I called my MD, got the name of a psychiatrist, and made an appointment to be evaluated for anti-depressants; I was still alive, and I had been reminded that I had a child I needed to provide for.

When I told my advisor about the incident, she said that of course it proved that the Intervener must have been feminine. I asked why, and she pointed to the way I was stopped. "If God were masculine only," she said, "someone would have called the police, who would have come and broken down the door, or there would have been some other show of power. But in this case, the intervention was gentle, still leaving you with the choice. You could have chosen, once John was asleep, to go back to what you were planning, but you did not. Instead of taking control and stopping you, the Goddess used John's dream to gently remind you of some things you had forgotten – you do have a child, you do have friends, you do have resources you could call on the next day – and then She left you alone, so that you could rethink your choice."

The second time I decided to give up my fight against the powers of Death, I had decided to do something I had sworn all my adult life I would never do. In March of 2001, I was so overwhelmed with fighting the state on Ben's behalf that I decided to give up. I could not get an approval for the care he needed, and I could not pay for it myself. After five years of nonstop fighting the state on his behalf, I was worn completely out. I gave up. It was too much, and the battle had gone on too long. I took Edward and Conner to people who would care for them, and I took Ben to juvenile court with the intention of returning him to the state. Only in that way, I believed, could I force them to provide the care the contract guaranteed him. If he were back in their custody, they would have to do it. But I could not force them to while he remained in mine.

My plan was to surrender custody, leave him in their care, and then go home and kill myself, because I could not live with having given him up. I had repeatedly promised the kids that I would always be their mother, that no matter what, they would never be able to get rid of me. Yet there I was, making a lie of what I had told them. I couldn't live with it. The state had won. I gave up.

On that occasion, too, the Goddess had something else in mind. When we got to court, the judge, sensing my distress, would not let me transfer custody to the state. He said it wasn't right that I should have to give them custody in order to get Ben the care he needed. He wouldn't let me.

He arranged for a Children's Services representative to meet with me to try to come up with a placement they would pay for. I had no hope they would be able to do so, because we had sent Ben's packet of information to every place on the approved list in the state, and all of them had turned him down. They kept trying to find a placement for a temporary respite – something the contract had said I was entitled to all along – but no one was willing to provide it. Ben's particular combination of diagnoses made him difficult to treat, and there was no provider in the state who specialized in his primary diagnosis. The issue was that the state was unwilling to pay for an out-of-state provider, even though one had been found.

I sat in the upstairs hallway of the juvenile court building with the Children's Services representative until the end of the day, by which time they still had been unable to find a placement. He asked if I would give them another day to find one. That night, and for the thirteen nights that followed, I slept with Ben either in the car or anywhere else we could find to sleep overnight, because he was at the time so violent and such a threat that I could not have him sleeping in the house with the other children. They were not safe from him. I wasn't either, but at that point my only thought was to keep his brothers safe.

It took a total of two weeks before Children's Services could find a placement that was willing to accept Ben and for which they were willing to pay. With all the resources at their command, with an entire staff to deal with the issue, it took them fourteen days to do what I had been unable to do on my own. In the end, they put him, though still in my custody, in a state funded facility that normally only provided services to children in state custody. And by the time that was done and he was finally safe, and by the time the other children in my household were safe, and by the time adoption assistance had agreed to pay for the service while he remained in my custody, my reason to kill myself had washed away. Again, I believed it was due to the intervention of the Goddess that the judge would not play the part I had assigned him. Nothing physically stopped me from carrying out my plan. It was just that the reason for it was removed.

On the third occasion, towards the end of this story, I had decided once again that I was completely depleted. I could not fight the state any more on these children's behalf, and I gave up. I simply couldn't do it any more. It was too much. And I don't just mean I adopted a cute baby, he turned out to be a rebellious adolescent, and I wanted to give him back. I mean everything was too much. The battle to get the state to do what it had promised to provide for their care was too much, and I could not provide for them alone.

When I discovered that I could go to jail for being unable to pay my child support payments – a responsibility that meant that my financial obligations exceeded my income – it was more than I could bear. I couldn't face being locked in a place so reminiscent of the terrors of my past. It was absolutely the last straw. I gave up, once again.

I decided what the parameters would be for my suicide, and for the third time, things did not work out as I had planned. I thought I knew what would happen. I made the most efficient of plans. But the scenario I had decided would determine the timetable did not occur, due to a couple of divine interventions. First, Doc told me that even if I was going to be arrested, he did not think it would be the next day, and I took a chance on his being right. Then, the judge who was hearing the appeal removed my reason for suicide completely when she made it clear to me at the hearing that I wasn't going to go to jail at all. The Goddess was at work again.

The issue of Hope versus Despair will always be a difficult one for me. Three times, out of fifty years, I have decided that the forces of Evil in the world were too powerful, and I have given up. Three times, out of fifty years, the Goddess has stopped me in my tracks, given me the opportunity to rethink my decision in the light of the changed events and has then left me to weigh the equation again. I can't be sure it won't happen again, that I despair. I can't be sure that if it happens again, that She will intervene. All I have ever been able to do is the best I can to fulfill the calling I hear from Her, to love the life She has given me, and to choose for myself to live.

Issue Eighteen

Choosing Life or Death

I have always, it seems, been more aware of the powers of Death than Life, and that has always made it look to me like Evil was more powerful than Good. As long as I can remember, I have been aware that in an instant, a cruel action or a careless word can do damage that takes a lifetime to repair, if repair be possible at all.

After Jack had gone to jail, something started killing our chickens. One by one – literally one every single day except for the one day we found two – they were killed, the heads were eaten, and the carcasses left in the chicken coop. The boys and I tried everything, closed every possible hole that we could find, but we still could not stop the power of Death. The killing continued until only three were left. That night, we crated the three to take them to Wilma's the next morning to give them away. Before we could get them in the car, two were killed in the crate, and only one was left. We gave that one away.

We never did figure out if it was a raccoon, a possum, a fox, or a cat, but something was getting in the coop every night and killing its dinner. Our inability to protect the chickens we relied on for our eggs epitomized the powerlessness I had felt since I was a child, when Evil felt so powerful and Good so inadequate. Death, in my mind, could beat Life any day.

Sometimes the powers of Death overwhelm the powers of Life not in a physical sense, but a spiritual one. One such example for me was the experience my first foster child had with the foster care system. First, after years of being rented out by her birth mother for men to do whatever they wanted to her, Lucy was removed from her mother's home because her mother told a Department representative that she had in her possession a gun with which she intended to kill her own daughter if they did not find another place for the child to live. Then, after living with me for a year, Lucy was returned to her birth family – sadly, in her case, to an uncle who abused her further.

When Lucy married and had two children of her own, her birth mother wanted access to those children, as well. She reported her own daughter to Children's Services over and over again, claiming Lucy was abusing her children, and trying to get custody of them. Repeatedly I went with my foster daughter to court, and witnessed the Children's Services investigator tell the judge that there was absolutely no evidence that Lucy was harming her children in any way. When the judge in one county finally told Lucy's mother to leave Lucy alone, and that if she ever made another report on her daughter again the judge would hold her in contempt of court, Lucy's mother just moved to another county with another judge.

In that county, Lucy's mother was smarter. This time, when she made her first report, she gave her own address as her daughter's. In that way, when the summons came, it came to her own address. Naturally, she never gave it to her daughter. When Lucy did not appear in court in the new county to defend herself against the charges, her mother won by default. She went with police officers and a court order, and took my foster daughter's children away.

By the time we were able to get the Department to investigate the children's grandmother and the children were removed from *her* care, both of the boys had been both physically and sexually abused in their grandmother's home. Still, the Department would not give them back to their mother, even though there had never been any evidence she had ever been inappropriate with them in any way. Workers from the new county had not been a part of any of the earlier court battles and had only reports from the previous county to go on, reports which gave the details of the number and type of former accusations but not the accuser's name; those were stricken from the record. Though Lucy had always been found not to be at fault, the enormous number of allegations outweighed what we were saying. The children were placed into foster care.

After years of trying to get them back, my daughter eventually decided that the only way she would ever be able to protect her children from her own birth mother was to give them up for adoption. She and her husband asked me to adopt the boys to keep them away from her mother, but I knew that as long as her mother knew where they were, we would never be safe from her constant harassment, and declined. Lucy and her husband finally surrendered the children directly to another couple who agreed to adopt them on the condition that the adoptive parents would allow them to have continued visitation with their birth parents.

When allegations were then made against the adoptive couple prior to the adoption being finalized, the children were removed from that home, as well. When my daughter tried to get them back, she was told that her parental rights had been terminated, and that she could not. For the next twelve years, she never gave up her search to find them, but the powers of Death seemed too powerful. She heard that the younger one had been adopted. The older one was always just out of her reach.

When I started working for the Department of Children's Services after my wedding to Jack, I started asking around, trying to locate Lucy's older son. Eventually, I was able to do so, and was able to get the permission I needed to meet him and to reintroduce him to his own birth mother.   That experience became for me an example of what Doc had been telling me for years. I believed that Evil was more powerful than Good. If that was true, I had to admit that in this case, at least, Doc was right: Evil might be more powerful, but Good had proven itself to be more persistent. The Life that their reunion brought to both of them was remarkable.

Another time during this story that Death felt more powerful than Life was not long from its beginning. It was after Jack had moved out the first time and had lost his job, but before the store opened and he had hope of another one. At the time, I was still appointed as one of the associate pastors at First Church, where I had worked for fifteen years with no financial compensation at all. I had no way to pay for Conner's deductibles on his meds, and we were so broke that a friend from First Church got permission from the church council to collect donations on our behalf.

After fifteen years of my volunteering without pay as one of the associate pastors in that place, the collection she took up came to less than three hundred dollars. That said to me, right or wrong, that my contributions as a pastor had been worth less than twenty dollars a year to the congregation. It didn't matter how bad things were with the current pastor, or how many people had left.   All I could see was the fact that I was worth less to the congregation than I had spent out of my own pocket on the confirmation class in any one of those fifteen years. Death was overwhelming my ability to hold on to Life. It was adding insult to injury, at a time my self-concept could not bear it. As far as I was concerned, Death won.

The powers of Death also seemed to win when the abuse that Jack said he had suffered as a child was passed on to the children who then lived with him. After he finally stopped acting that abuse out, he began having flashbacks and nightmares of things he said happened, just as I often did. I wrestled what seemed like forever with the question of why he had reenacted the abuse he described, while I spent my life trying to keep what happened to me from ever happening to anyone else. I just couldn't get it.

In my life, the powers of Life somehow eventually won. In Jack's life, the winner so far has been the power of Death. I still hold desperately to the hope that my doctor is right, and Good is always more persistent than Evil. I hold on to the hope that the Goodness of Life will eventually win out in Jack's life as well as Ben's. It can, I do believe it can. I just don't know if it ever will.

Love, Hate, and Redemption

I'm not proud of it, but in spite of Laura's admonition that I needed to learn to lo-o-ove everybody, there have been people in my life I have hated. One in particular stands out in my memory – a pedophile I dated many years ago when John was just a child. When I discovered the man was dating me with the intent of abusing John, I truly hated him. When the man was later arrested for kidnapping and raping another little boy, I was grateful for the life of my friend Harmon, whose witness kept reminding me that I was against the death penalty. It would have been easy to forget. The instinct within me to protect those I love at all costs is strong.

When John found out about what Jack had done, he, too, remembered the man from his childhood, and commented about how "really sick" it was that I had fallen for two of them. He had no idea that those were just the only two he knew about. The legacy from my childhood is even more far-reaching than that. One of the men I chose to be in a relationship with choked and threatened to hit me. Though I did not have him arrested, it only happened once; before it could happen again, I was gone.

Years later, my foster daughter, Lucy, told her social worker that yet another man I was involved with had sexually abused her. He was able to convince anyone she'd told about what happened that she was lying. Sadly, I had believed him, too, in spite of the fact that I once found myself paralyzed to intervene, having caught them in a compromising situation which he explained away by assuring me that my fears and accusations were groundless. The Department found that there was not enough evidence to successfully prosecute him (which did not necessarily mean, as he claimed, that he was innocent), and it was because of the possibility of his guilt that Lucy was removed from my care.

It was not until Lucy was an adult herself and told me details she could not have made up about the man, that I realized it was he who was the liar, and not she. Sometime after he abused her, but before I realized the truth, he told me late one night that, "I never did abuse Lucy, but I did take [another child's] penis in my mouth when he was just a baby, just because I always wondered what it would feel like." At the time, he had me convinced that I could not testify against him and that the statute of limitations had run out. By the time I found out differently, the boy was already an adult, and the abuse really was too far in the past to report. Years later, I met another victim who named the same man as her childhood abuser, not having any idea that I knew him. She said he had told her that she was not the only one. In spite of all my good intentions, I had not believed my daughter when she was telling the truth, and had failed to protect her just when she needed it most. I had completely unintentionally repeated my past.

Though I do not know what the long term effects of Jack's abuse will be for Edward, I often look at my own history and worry about what his future will be like. Sometimes, I have hated my own father for the fact that I have chosen men like him. Other times, I have hated the men. Most of the time, though, I have just hated myself for choosing them over and over again and exposing my children to them. I was so sure Jack was different, but I was wrong there, too. Like I said, I'm not proud of it, but I do feel hate from time to time.

The admonition to love everybody – even oneself – is hard. It was hard for me to hear the words when Laura said them to me, and from what I can tell, it has been a hard lesson to take from every theologian who has ever passed it on to those who followed. I can *say* it, but I have no idea how in the world we can possibly pull it off. It sounds in theory like it would be easy, but living it is not easy at all.

What helps me is just to keep trying to hold on to George Wallace. "Lo-o-ove George Wallace," Laura said. Love the man who epitomized everything evil for a woman of color from Tuskegee, Alabama. Love the man who was the icon of segregation in September 1963, when he called out the state police and the Alabama National Guard in order to keep students and faculty in Huntsville, Mobile, Birmingham and, yes, Tuskegee from being able to go into school buildings there. Love the man who thought it would be better, after the courts ruled to force integration of Alabama schools, for *no one* to learn or teach than it would be for *everyone* to learn and teach. "Love," Laura said, "George Wallace."

George Wallace was the epitome of evil for me, as a small girl in 1963, just as he was for her. Even though he was not the governor of my own state, George Wallace was the one my schoolmates spoke of, wide-eyed and with hushed voices, whispering his name as though he were the boogie man or evil incarnate. George Wallace was the one I heard my caregivers discuss in voices trembling with fear and anger, full of anguish and concern. It was George Wallace whose actions threatened the safety of people who were cared about by those I loved dearly, even if not within my own state lines. It was only many years later that for me evil took the form of someone much closer to home – the man who would become my mother's second husband. Later still, I was a young mother with a child of my own before evil became any force which might hurt the child I loved. And eventually, evil for me became those who would physically harm or sexually abuse *any* child, regardless of color, sex, or creed. "Love," Laura said, "George Wallace."

And then, in 1982, George Wallace made a remarkable statement. Speaking of segregation, he said, "We thought it [segregation] was in the best interests of all concerned. We were mistaken."

Was it possible that even George Wallace could be redeemed by Love? Perhaps. The terrifying part for me was that if that was true, then I could never be sure that anyone was beyond redemption. No one was beyond the conversion that might turn a life around. I could never be sure that anyone who was the "bad guy" would remain so. If Laura was right about George Wallace, then she was also right about those who had hurt me. She was right about those who would hurt other children. She was even right about those who wanted to hurt my own children. They were, all of them, children of God. Each and every one of them was deserving of Love. All of them had been given places at the table of God. And it was not my right to deny them, because I had a seat there, too.

That doesn't mean I don't think most child molesters belong in jail; I do. That doesn't mean I believe that they should be excused for their behavior, any more than I believe Jack should be excused. In order to keep children safe, there are many people, I believe, who should never be released from the prisons and jails in which they are held. But no one, I believe deep in my heart, is beyond redemption. Or else there is no hope for you and me.

ISSUE TWENTY

Humor as a Means of Grace

This period of my life was not all grim, not by any means. Humor has broken through my despair right from the beginning, when I took Jack to be arrested and discovered the jokes about Children's Services posted on the police department walls. There have been other times, too, when this was also true. Grace has often permeated my despair in the form of humor, whether the other person meant it to be funny or not.

The two most notable of those occasions were one of each example, one intentional and one accidental. In the first case, Conner said something he never meant to be funny, but it did touch me at a time I was in absolute anguish. After Jack confessed, Liberty died, I knew I couldn't make The Refuge payments any longer, and the chair of our church council had suggested I go to church somewhere they did not know me, I was at one point sobbing uncontrollably in the car while driving Conner and Edward somewhere. I was talking to someone on the phone, which was admittedly not a very good idea. Sobbing, driving, talking, I was so anguished I could hardly function.

Finally, in response to what the other person said, I replied that everything that brought me joy in my life had been taken away. I had lost everything that made me happy. And Conner, bless his heart, said, "You still have us, Mom. You still have Edward and me."

He had no conception of how much energy it takes to care for them. He had no way of understanding that the other things fed and nourished me, thus giving me energy, while caring for my children drained me and used up my depleting sources of energy as I provided for them. All he knew, in his sweet innocence, was that he wanted to make me feel better, he wanted to make things easier for me, and he wanted to be a source of nourishment for me, too. Eventually, I could laugh at the absurdity of what I was saying versus what he was trying to say, because of course the boys and their sisters bring me joy. Not exactly the way I meant it at that moment. But they do. More than I can say.

The other example of humor that stands out from this year was from a day my car was broken down on the highway, when I was on my way to babysit for my grandson, Zach. Bridgett needed to be somewhere in about an hour, and it was looking like I wasn't going to get to her house in time for her to leave. I called for roadside assistance from Sam's Club, and was told that they had discontinued roadside assistance and towing as member benefits. They said a letter to that effect had gone out in February. I guess I missed it.

I called Bridgett, apologizing for being late, and she called AAA to ask if she could get my car towed as a member of her family. When she did so, she discovered that her membership had expired, so she couldn't even have gotten her own car towed. At that point, she offered to come get the boys and me from the side of the road. I accepted.

When she got to us, she got out of her car laughing. After a year of joking about my being Jobette, Jobina, Jobella, and Jobelliah, her first words were, "Okay, I'm just doing a reality check here. Did ALL of Job's sons and daughters die?" Together, we laughed about the notion that everything in my life that we could imagine could possibly go wrong seemed to be doing so. If my life really was paralleling Job's, what did that say about her life expectancy, after all?

Later that week, when I had my regularly scheduled lunch with Jim, I was telling him about Bridgett's question, and his reply was equally funny. "Oh, no," he replied. "This is the *feminization* of Job. If you are the mother, and you have to take care of them, then all of your children LIVE."

There are times when humor can be used to be cruel. There are other times it is used just for fun. But blessed are the times it brings relief and perspective and joy.

ISSUE TWENTY-ONE

Speaking of Things We Do Not Understand

Even to discuss these matters at all presumes that we can understand anything about the infinite possibilities of Creation. Perhaps I cannot. Perhaps all the things I tell myself about how Good can come from Evil are just an attempt to make myself feel better. My mother summed up that possibility for me one day when she said, "Not everything has a reason." I sure don't want to believe that, but she may, of course, be right.

For the entire time these events were going on, I kept telling myself there had to be some Good that could come of it. There had to be some reason, some greater part of a plan I could not understand, that would make sense of all the things happening to me. There *had* to be. I needed desperately for there to be.

But, in all fairness, my mother may be right. Maybe there just isn't. Maybe every time I told myself there had to be some reason none of my résumés found me a job, I lied to myself. Or maybe, the reason was that I needed to stay at the store. Maybe I couldn't find us another place where I could bear to live because I didn't try hard enough. Or maybe it was because in the end, the Goddess would provide a way for me to stay in the place I loved. Maybe every time I voiced my frustration that – in spite of the fact that we were getting great donations – so few customers came into the store, there really was no reason for the lack of traffic. But then again, maybe no one came in on those days because what I was really called to do was type this story.

Maybe there really was no rhyme or reason behind my losing my job at the church down the road. Or maybe, as my neighbor Sara put it, the reason was that I belonged somewhere else. Maybe there was no reason the things that happened to me as a child occurred. Or maybe the changes they brought forth in my life could be used to give Life to others. I just don't know. Maybe it is Truth. Maybe it is wishful thinking.

I don't know how to speak of things too great for me to understand except to put them into the framework of things I *do* understand: the framework of being a mother, a woman, a creature of the Creator.

Where was I when She labored in creation? Where was I when the germ of the Earth spun within Her womb?   Nowhere. Everywhere.

These events brought home to me that not only does the Goddess live within me, but also I live within Her. At the end of the biblical story of Job, God forgives Job's friends only because Job has intervened. Their fates are interconnected; their lives, intertwined. When the Goddess was giving birth to the Earth, where were you?

AFTERMATH

Words of Grace

◆ ◆ ◆

"I will not allow my life's light
to be determined
by the darkness around me."

SOJOURNER TRUTH

◆ ◆ ◆

WISDOM

And the Goddess made Job aware
Of something always within her reach,
An insight worth more than all that she had lost.
She gave Job a greater blessing than a pearl without price,
A more valuable benediction than all she had possessed.
The Goddess gave Job the gift of Wisdom.

Thus, the Goddess blessed Job's life
Even more at its end than at its beginning.
And Job still had three daughters and seven sons.
She still lived in Gaia, but now knew she, herself, was filled
With Spirit, Breath, Ruah, Wind, and Wisdom
Worth more than the fortunes of men.

In all the land, there were no women
More beautiful than Wisdom's daughters,
And the strength that was within them was equal
In every way to any power their brothers' money could buy.
And many years later Job died, full of Faith and Grace,
Old and Blessed for all her years.

Amen.

EPILOGUE

As devastating Hurricane Katrina hit New Orleans, the Gulf looked on the outside the way I felt for a year and a half on the inside. Raped, ravaged, exhausted, depleted. The city and my psyche were in ruins. The aftermath of the storm in the part of the country where The Refuge's valley lay was remarkable. The rains and warm weather brought more wildflowers that fall than I had seen in any spring since we had moved there. One Sunday morning, about the time church would have been going on back at First Church, I counted almost a hundred different varieties. Taking pictures of them as I wandered around the farm, I realized that I had never seen such a miracle.

I sat on my deck in awe and called people who had helped me to survive, to share with them the glory of the place where they had helped me stay. One of them, my friend Deborah, reflected that what was going on in my valley was a metaphor for the wondrous blooming going on within me as well as outside. I, too, had been blossoming as the fall approached. Instead of the expected dropping of leaves, the world was experiencing a rebirth of spring. The unexpected flowers growing along the creek in my valley were a reflection of the unexpected spring within my soul, where instead of flowers, Wisdom grew.

Throughout all the chaos and confusion of this period in my life, I struggled with what it meant to be a woman, a mother, and to be faithful. I struggled to hold on to hope when all I felt was despair. I struggled to do the things that needed to be done, when I had no energy to do them.

When my friend Judy's son was murdered, for instance, somehow Creation shared with me the energy to reach out beyond my own despair and check on the family to let them know how much they meant to me. The unexpected gift I received in return was finding out how much I had meant to the young man and to his friends, some of whom let me know at the funeral about the difference I had made in their lives. At a time I felt my life had no value, I was reminded that to others, at least, it did.

When I would have those sacred moments, and moments were usually all I could spare, to sit on my deck and listen to the creek gurgling, or to listen to the frogs and watch the heron and the horses, I was each time reminded of the sacredness of all Creation. Creation would rejuvenate my spirit on those occasions and make me whole. Every once in a while, we would be in the part of town where the boys and I used to live, and I would feel my chest constrict, my blood pressure start to rise, my distress begin to accelerate… and I would be reminded that for me, everything I had sacrificed to hold on to The Refuge was worth every day we stayed there. The place pours life-giving Creation into my soul, and creates me as much as my act of love once participated in the Creation of the child who grew inside my womb, the child of my body.

While it is not true that I love John any more than my other children, it will always be true that I treasure the time he grew within me, the time he was an infant in my arms, the time he taught me how to love and grow into my own adulthood as his mother. But it is no less true that I have participated in the Creation of the lives of the others. I have watched them grow into adulthood, as well. I watered, perhaps, the gardens others had planted; but those children, too, are part of Creation, and just as I am part of Creation, I am part of them. Even Ben, who has struggled ever since his adoption with the notion that I am not his "real mother," and that he wants her and not me, was and is a part of the same Creation that I am also a part of. Together, we are still a family, and whether we ever live together again or not, I will always be a part of him, and he a part of me.

Another thing I struggled with was how my own despair, should it end in suicide, would affect the children remaining at home. Conner, with his limited ability to understand, would worry about who was going to take care of him. If I died, he was not likely to trust anyone else to do that for a long time. Edward's struggle would be a different one. He has always believed himself to be responsible for everything, even when he denies any culpability at all. He has always thought everything was his fault. Parts of this book actually began as the letter I was writing to him when I was planning to kill myself, trying to explain that my suicide was not his fault, and that in fact *none* of what happened was his fault. I was trying to tell him all the things that happened and to explain that it was just too much for any one person to bear. In the end, his letter became part of this book, and writing this book gave me something to do when all I really wanted to do was die.

There were moments during these months when I received gifts of Grace from others. The night before Easter, when Bridgett gave me the impetus to write this book, was one. So was the conversation with my own mother, who said that if what I really wanted to do was write, I had better get started, because I was almost fifty and had no more than half of my life left. She told me I could do it, and that I had better get busy. And so I did. That, too, was a moment of Grace. My other-mother, almost-mother Martha touched my life as well, especially as this book blossomed and grew within me. For twenty years now, she has been one of my dearest friends and a vehicle of the Love that permeates my being.

Many things I heard and read over these months lifted me out of the mire of my own thoughts and anguish, and helped me stay on the path of growth. Our family's psychologist has helped and continues to help us to make sense of the confusion of our lives. Year after year, Doc puts words to the chaos I cannot sort out on my own. His spoken words have brought calm and order to the disorder that has reigned with me.

Deborah has called several times every week for years, and she kept it up all through this period, even when all I could do was cry. We ranted and raved, celebrated and grieved, laughed and cried, all over the phone. Each and every time I talked to her, it was reassuring to know I was not alone. It makes the world a friendly place just knowing she is in it.

Written words have also been a blessing. Most notable this year was *The Dance of the Dissident Daughter* by Sue Monk Kidd. It was a gift from my friend, Julie, which touched me deeply and resonated with my every internal vibration. All throughout the years Julie has stood by me. How she knew I needed just that book, at just that time, I will never know.

Other friends touched my life and changed it, as well. Bonnie, healer and friend, gave me the image of myself filled with golden butterflies, an image of transformation and light. She said there were two different kinds of them within me, and I mulled over that description for a very long time. *What could it possibly mean*, I wondered. Finally, I came to the notion that I kept looking for something outside myself to make me whole, as though I was one thing, and out in the world there was another thing I needed to complete me. It was in pondering the butterflies that I finally realized that if there are two forces in the world, they are already both within me. I am already whole, a part of Creation with Creation seeping through every pore. It is not what is without me that will save me; it is what is already within.

When Susan and Martha first read the initial manuscript of this book that started as Edward's letter and ended with the poem *Wisdom*, each of them pronounced in her own way the writer's equivalent of what every expectant mother wants to hear, "Congratulations. You've got yourself a book." As time went on, Allison, Ann, Barry, Bridgett, Deborah, Doug, Jennifer, Jim, John, Judy, Julie, Lauren, Morty, Nathan, Peggy, Rolanda, Ronni, Sarah, and Tracee all read versions of it as well, and each of them brought my attention to an important piece I had not noticed before. When Andrea read it, she suggested I rewrite it completely – four times in a row, which I did. Then I even rewrote it a few more times again. When I thought I was done, Tracy mercilessly proofread and edited my efforts. Thanks to all of their encouragement, suggestions, and support, this is a better book than it was when I began.

Earline shared her meager resources, when she could barely afford it any more than I. Bobby resurrected my car each time I thought it was irreparably dead. When I was exhausted from moving the store and did not think I could go on any longer, Tracee would come and help me unpack not just boxes, but the clutter in my mind. Bianca, Cassius, Craig, Debby, Dillon, Don and Bettye, Ed and Kathryn and their son Edward, Jim, Joan, Mary, Matt, Melissa and Wes, Merryl, Michelle, Nathan, Pat, Sharon, Tom, and others kept me from giving up at the store on countless occasions, when I thought I could not possibly last one more day. Some days, in spite of myself, they even made it fun.

Craig and his wife Laura deserve a special award for faithfully pledging a tithe to the store, a commitment they have continued to honor each and every month, even after the store itself closed. Each monthly gift from them has reimbursed me in part for a little more of my long overdue salary, and has made it possible for me to survive and feed my children a little longer. Their kindness is overwhelming. Craig and Laura, I thank you.

Many old friends have been a part of my struggle to make sense of my family's rejection by our old church. Mauni, especially, stood quietly by, taking onto herself the full brunt of my anguish. Although her position and mine regarding Jack's attendance at the church which proudly proclaims, "Everyone has a place at this table" are diametrically opposed, she still called Jack faithfully, week after week after week.

When I was losing faith in the community I loved, All Saints Community of Faith took my family in and loved us. They have truly been a family of faith for the both the boys and me. Our ringleader Jim, especially, has held my hand and helped me keep my balance this year when I felt sure I would fall. His was the gift of Wisdom, and just when I needed it. All of them, channels of moments of Grace.

And last, but not least, there is my teacher Jack. On my better days, I do believe he loved me, as much as he could. And, on those days, I also believe that he was victimized as much by his own past as we have been by the legacy he left *our* family. My love for him, fortunately grown and blossomed before I found out that he was not exactly as I believed he was, was what made it possible for Laura's admonition to "lo-o-ove George Wallace" finally to get through to me and teach me that even the perpetrators have a place at the table. Not just in theory, but in reality.

Loving and losing Jack taught me something else, too. Before I loved him, I thought I needed no one. I thought I could do everything myself. And for years, I had. If the plumbing broke, I fixed it. If the kids knocked a hole in the wall or broke a door, I repaired it. If I couldn't reach something, I got a ladder. I surely wasn't going to ask anyone for help. When I allowed Jack into my life, though, in many ways, it turned my life around. I allowed him to do things for me that I would never have let another do. I learned to ask for help when I needed it. I learned to trust. Misguided, though it was in many respects, there were things I could trust about him, and did. There were many times he and I joked about the fact that loving him was turning me into a girl.

If that is true, then losing him turned me into a woman, in a way I had never been before, for it was in losing him that I learned my new place in the world. No longer did I see myself as an independent creature who needed nothing and no one. Instead, I have come to see myself as an interdependent creature who is a part of everything and every one. My work at the store has been a part of that. My life as a mother is part of that. And my efforts to continue befriending the man who in so many ways betrayed me, but who is also a part of Creation, has also been a part of that. Many of my old friends do not understand it. But some of them do, as do the new friends I am making every day. And perhaps my friend the heron, understands it as well.

It is when I listen to the voice within me that I embody the Wisdom that flows through the creek outside my window. It flows through the voices of the wise, the wind, the horses, and the trees. It flows through the heron when she stands solitary in the creek, and also when she flies. And when I am faithful to it, Wisdom also flows through me.

◆ ◆ ◆

At this point, Edward is still in high school; last semester he made the best grades of his life. A typical argumentative teenager, he is blossoming into a kind and considerate young man. Conner is doing well and is happy to have his disability check after all the years of fighting against it. On good days, he helps me out in any way he can. On bad days, he stays in bed. We have not yet been able to find him another doctor, but a month before the deadline the other doctors in Doc's practice set for him, they decided to give him a year's extension. Their willingness to do that was based in part on the enormous effort he put forth this past year to learn to control his anger. I doubt that he would have worked so hard even for me, but his relationship with Doc is so important to him that he has made greater strides in that area in just one year than in his entire life before now. He is still, as Doc said one day, doing better than any of us have a right to expect him to be doing.

Ben is in a transitional living situation, trying to save money until he can get an apartment of his own. I have written a letter to the juvenile court judge in his case asking to be released from my obligation to pay for his medical expenses. If granted, that will cut the last financial tie that binds him to me, and will at last grant him, at eighteen, the freedom he so desperately desires. For better or worse, he will finally discover the cost.

Gabriel is serving seventeen years in the state prison system for passing Jack's legacy on to the next generation. Gabriel was charged with one victim; Jack has so far confessed to over two hundred victims, but he, too, had only one identifiable victim within the statute of limitations. With Gabriel's combination of Hemophilia and AIDS, he is not likely to live long enough to get out. The inequity of his serving what amounts to a life sentence for doing what Jack taught him, while Jack was sentenced to only two years probation, is appalling. The day I realized Gabriel would likely die in jail as a consequence of what Jack had done to him was the day I was the angriest I have been with Jack throughout these entire two years. I truly believe that if Gabe dies in prison, Jack should be charged with having murdered him.

John has at long last come home from England, and since his return I have been grateful to see him at least once every week. I do not know how long he will remain in the States, but while it lasts, for me each time I get to see him is a Mother's Day.

My mother, Allison, and my stepfather, David (who has proven to me every day for twenty-five years that there really are some good men in the world), have supported me in every way they could. They have helped me survive this difficult time, even when I have not made it easy for them to do so. I am certain I am not the easiest of their children for them to parent. It is thanks to their financial investment that this book has reached this format.

My dear friend, Martha, and I just celebrated the twentieth anniversary of our sharing our birthdays with each other. For twenty years in a row, we have eaten lunch together at the same bookstore. This year will have been our last, as she and Hoyt are moving to California to live closer to one of their sons. The first year, I was exactly half her age. In ten more years, I will be the age she was when we began.

I am grieving the loss of Martha's company already, but in this respect, too, Manna has been given to me. Two weeks before Hoyt and Martha were to leave town, I discovered Peggy had retired and returned. For those two weeks, the four of us ate lunch together, and now just as I acknowledge one loss, I am grateful for another friendship's resurrection. My needs continue to be provided for, day after day. *Manna for each day.*

My beloved companion, Ananda, has continued to hold his own. He has survived over two years since the week of his diagnosis and Jack's confession, a year longer than his best prognosis. He has lived a long time, and I have been blessed to share over ten of those years with him; he has been my companion from a few months before my fortieth birthday until after my fiftieth. Lately, the most exciting part of his day has been his morning walk down to explore the spring, after which he returns to rest on the couch until bedtime. At this writing, over two years have passed since his first seizures. There has been no fairytale cure, but he does not seem to be in pain – just happy to see us each time we come home, and content to live out his life with us here on this small farm.

It remains to be seen what is coming. Not a single one of the many leads, each of which gave me just enough hope to last till the next one, has panned out. Still, it feels as though something is just around the corner, though I have no idea what. I stand facing the future, like Job, with my past behind me. Unlike Job, I have not been given a new home, a new fortune. I have not (thank goodness) been given ten more children in addition to the ten I already love. Instead, every day I have come to cherish even more dearly the treasures with which I have been blessed.

Some of these riches are tangible ones. I have in my room a shelf, which I can see from my bed. On the shelf are beloved treasures, tokens that remind me of my place in the strand of women woven through my life: an angel from my mother, a seashell from my grandmother, a card on which women are dancing, sent by my son John, a small statue Martha bought for her daughter Mary, before Mary's untimely death, tiny gifts handmade by little girls whose lives I have touched. For my fiftieth birthday, my Aunt Kathie sent me the telegram my father sent her announcing my birth. I had it framed, and placed it on the shelf. I put it there to represent my Aunt's love for me, but after I placed it on the shelf, I realized that now, I, too have a place in the progression of women who have been important in my life.

Some of the gifts I have received are not so tangible. Job was rewarded for his faithfulness to his God with gifts that came from outside of himself. I have been rewarded for my own faithfulness to the call I hear from the Goddess with gifts from within – Courage, Knowledge, Patience, Faith, and Wisdom: a new understanding of Love. I find myself standing at the door to the future open to life's possibilities, daily being filled with Faith and Grace, growing Older and sometimes Wiser, and being Blessed by each and every one of my years.

Sophia Ruah
Valentine's Day
14 February 2006

POSTSCRIPT, MAY 2007

ANANDA died peacefully on the third day after Valentine's, 2007.

BEN has, with his latest arrest, met the final criterion for diagnosis as a sociopath. On the day of this writing, he is in jail.

CONNER continues to live at home, and is working part-time at the camp next door. In April, Doc's practice gave him permission to stay in therapy with Doc for yet another year.

FIRST CHURCH never did let Jack know what he would have to do to come back to worship, though someone did hang a large sign just inside the door. It reads, "Everyone has a place at this table."

GABRIEL remains in prison.

JACK has been able to maintain staying out of jail, is on an ankle monitor while on probation, and has written to Oprah asking her to pay for chemical castration as part of his treatment. He has not yet received a reply.

EDWARD will be a senior in high school next year. His recent eighteenth birthday effectively ended Sophia's twenty-nine year relationship with the Department.

JOHN decided to stay in the States, fell in love, and married. He and his wife have a newborn son, with whom they live in a house about thirty miles from Sophia's farm.

AND SOPHIA was able to negotiate a deal with the camp next door which makes it possible for them to use thirty acres of the farm while guaranteeing her the right to live out her days on the remaining ten. She is currently working on her next book, a novel.

SUPPLEMENT

Study Guide

◆ ◆ ◆

"Always hold firmly to the thought that
each one of us can do something
to bring some portion of misery to an end."[1]

"GATHERING"
Syracuse Cultural Workers

◆ ◆ ◆

STATISTICS

In the United States:

In 1994 (the most recent year for which statistics are available on the Department of Justice website) there were:

234,000 "offenders convicted of rape or sexual assault under the care, custody, or control of corrections agencies."

60% of these (approximately 140,400) were "under conditional supervision in the community" in programs such as probation or parole.[6]

♦ ♦ ♦

99% of sexual offenders against children are male.
Most of them started molesting before they were age 15, demonstrate deviant behavior, and average 117 victims.

53% were never themselves sexually abused.
They committed an average of 37 acts against 7 victims.

47% *had* been sexually abused. Those abused 50 or more times committed an average of 142 acts against 25 victims.

51% consider themselves to be exclusively heterosexual,

19% predominantly heterosexual, and

9% equally hetero/homosexual, abusing an average of 52 girls.

7% did not have any adult partner preference at all, and only

8% considered themselves to be exclusively homosexual. Those who molested boys abused an average of 150 each.[7]

♦ ♦ ♦

68% Non sex offenders who are rearrested for *any* offense

43% Sex offenders who are rearrested for *any* offense

5.3% Sex offenders of all types who are rearrested for another sex crime within 3 years of their release from prison

3.3% Child victimizers who are rearrested for another sex crime against a child within 3 years of release from prison.[6]

♦ ♦ ♦

17.6% Child victimizers who *re-offend* within 3 years of release from prison *without* any type of treatment

13.2% Child victimizers who *re-offend* within 3 years of release from prison *with* treatment

7.2% Child victimizers who re-offend within 5 years when maintained in a relapse prevention program

In the absence of a relapse prevention program, at the end of ten years the recidivism rate for offenders is approximately the same whether the offender has completed treatment or not. [8]

Of the Victims:

67% of all victims of sexual assault were under the age of 18.

34% were under the age of 12.

1 in 7 was under the age of 6.[6]

◆ ◆ ◆

Girls have a 1 in 3-5 chance (20-33% depending on the study) of being sexually abused prior to their eighteenth birthday.

Boys have a 1 in 6 chance (5-16% depending on the study) of being sexually abused prior to their eighteenth birthday.

In the majority of cases children know their abuser prior to the assault.

GLOSSARY

Adoption Assistance

The federal program that provides adoptive parents of special-needs children with funds to pay for the treatment of the children's pre-existing medical and/or psychiatric conditions.

"Aging Out" of the Foster Care System

The termination of services provided to a child in foster care when that child reaches majority, in most states at the age of 18.

AIDS

The fatal constellation of symptoms that results from the collapse of the immune system after infection by the HIV virus.

Arrested Development

The slowing or complete cessation of normal emotional development, typically following a traumatic event. In some circumstances this condition may improve with treatment.

Attention-Deficit/Hyperactivity Disorder (ADHD)

The inability to function within normal parameters due to increased physical activity and decreased mental attentiveness, frequently to such a degree that the behavior interferes with normal day-to-day activities such as school or work.

Bipolar Disorder

A condition formerly referred to as **Manic-Depressive Disorder** in which the mood swings cyclically between manic and depressed states. Bipolar Disorder is treatable with medication which is frequently refused by patients willing to experience suicidal lows in order to enjoy the high of mania.

Child Molester

A person who has committed a criminal sexual offense against a child under the age of consent (typically 18 in most states).

Clinical Pastoral Education (CPE)

A supervised internship done by pastors and chaplains, frequently in an institution such as a hospital. CPE is an almost universal requirement for employment as a chaplain. Some denominations also require such an internship prior to ordination.

Community Service Worker (CSW)

The term used for an individual who has been sentenced by the court to perform some form of volunteer work as part of his or her sentence or probation requirement.

Conduct Disorder

The most severe manifestation in childhood of aggression to people and/or animals, destruction of property, stealing and dishonesty, and a complete disregard for rules.

Department of Children's Services (DCS)

The term used in this book for the division of state government that provides services to children. Other states have different names for this department, such as Child Protective Services, Child Welfare Department, etc.

Ephebophilia (Hebephilia)

The sexual attraction of adults to adolescents, typically, between the ages of 13 and 18. When this attraction is followed by criminal sexual activity involving pubescent or post-pubescent children, the adult is commonly referred to as a "pedophile."

Failure to Thrive

The sometimes-fatal failure of a child to grow and develop physically, due to any combination of physical, medical, and emotional reasons frequently including abuse and neglect.

Farrier

A person who shoes horses.

Foster Care

The provision by a state for the care of children who have been removed from their own parents and home because of neglect or abuse, but who have not yet been placed in a permanent new home.

Guardian ad litem

An attorney appointed by a judge or court referee to represent the best interests of a minor child during a court proceeding.

"Hard to Place"

See Special Needs

Hemophilia

An inherited blood disorder characterized by the absence of clotting factor, making it impossible for bleeding to stop once it has started. Someone with this disorder may bleed to death from receiving minor scratch or even developing a bruise.

HIV

The virus that causes the breakdown of the immune system and possible subsequent constellation of symptoms known as AIDS.

Intermittent Explosive Disorder

The intermittent inability to control anger and destructive impulses that are out of proportion to the precipitating events, frequently resulting in physical or property damage.

Level 1

The designation for a foster care placement with the lowest level of supervision, such as might be found at a private home.

Level 2

The designation for a foster care placement in which children are housed together in a facility staffed by several trained personnel.

Level 3

The designation for a foster care placement in which children are supervised round-the-clock in a facility either located or designed so that escape or harm of self or others is unlikely.

Level 4

The designation for a foster care placement in which children are housed in a locked facility and are monitored 24 hours a day.

Manna

Food said to have been provided on a daily basis to the Israelites in the wilderness. Manna could not be stored or even kept overnight without spoiling.

Mitzvah

An undeserved act of kindness meant to be passed on rather than repaid to the giver.

Multiple Personality Disorder

A condition now known as **Dissociative Identity Disorder** in which, subsequent to abuse, the personality fragments into multiple divisions, each of which exercises control over the body in turn and is largely unknown to the other parts.

Obsessive-Compulsive Disorder

The intrusion of repetitive thoughts and behaviors so time consuming that they become socially disruptive.

Paranoid Schizophrenic

Someone who experiences a combination of symptoms including auditory and/or visual hallucinations, disorganized thinking, and delusions that others are "out to get them." Usually the beliefs of persecution are more pronounced than the overall impairment from hallucinations (when present).

Pederasty

The criminal activity of sexual intercourse between an adult (usually male) and a newly pubescent child of the same sex.

Pedophilia

The sexual preference of an adult for prepubescent children, typically those under the age of 13.

Polycystic Kidney Disease (PKD)

A fatal, hereditary medical condition in which cysts grow in the kidneys, reducing kidney function. PKD has no known treatment other than kidney transplant.

Posttraumatic Stress Disorder (PTSD)

A mental disorder developed subsequent to a traumatic event, characterized by symptoms including intrusive memories and nightmares of the event, fears that the event will repeat, behavior designed to avoid any reminder of the event, an exaggerated startle response, and other such indications.

Reactive Attachment Disorder

A mental disorder that develops in children as a result of lack of care during infancy and early childhood, resulting in the child's inability to emotionally attach to people, animals, or objects, and consequently resulting in the lack of development of a conscience.

Repression

The natural ability of the mind to protect itself from events too painful or traumatic to experience by involuntarily storing those memories in such a way that makes them largely inaccessible to the individual.

Respite

The provision of a temporary placement for a child (typically for a few days or a weekend), which makes it possible for both the child and the parent to have a break from the conflict between them.

Safety Plan

A spoken or written contract between two or more parties that sets out rules designed to maintain the safety of one of the parties or of another person.

Sitting Shiva

To participate in a seven-day period of ritualized mourning for the dead.

Schizophrenia

A disorder characterized by visual and auditory hallucinations, delusions, grossly abnormal behavior, bizarre speech, and disorganized thinking. There are several subtypes, of which the Paranoid type is one.

Sociopath (Psychopath)

An adult, typically charming and manipulative, who has never developed a conscience and is capable of engaging in any sort of criminal behavior without feelings of guilt or shame. This disorder is known as **Antisocial Personality Disorder** and typically develops subsequent to a childhood diagnosis of Conduct Disorder.

Special Investigations

The unit within the Department of Children's Services that has the responsibility of investigating allegations of abuse involving schools, daycares, public figures, its own employees, and their family members.

Special-Needs Children

The designation given to children in foster care who are considered "hard to place," including Caucasians over the age of five, minority children over the age of two, sibling groups of three or more, and children with any type of handicapping condition.

Wraparound Services

Case management services provided by a social services agency to facilitate the functioning of an individual in an outpatient setting. These services are usually provided for a short period of time during transitional periods, and may include working as a liaison with schools or employers, providing transportation and counseling, crisis intervention, and/or other services.

RESOURCES*

For Child Abuse Survivors, Parents, and Professionals:
The Child Abuse Prevention Network has an exhaustive list of resources on their website http://child.cornell.edu. Click on the tab for "Links."
The Darkness to Light website (regarding child sexual abuse prevention) also has an detailed resource list which can be found at: www.darkness2light.org
The National Children's Advocacy Center website (concerning child abuse response and prevention) is found at: www.nationalcac.org

For Resources Related to Justice and Activism:
Syracuse Cultural Workers "Tools for Change" catalog is 40 color pages of feminist, progressive, multi-cultural resources to help change the world and sustain activism. The Peace Calendar, Women Artists Datebook, over 100 posters on social, cultural and political themes, holiday cards for Solstice, Christmas, Chanukah, plus buttons, stickers, T-shirts, notecards, postcards, and books. Great fundraising products. Box 6367, Syracuse, NY 13217, 800-949-5139, Fax 800-396-1449. 24-hour ordering by Visa/MC email: scw@syracuseculturalworkers.com

For Relatives and Friends of Lesbians and Gays:
Support is available through Parents, Family, and Friends of Lesbians and Gays (PFLAG), at: www.pflag.org

For Those Affected by Mental Illness:
The American Psychological Association website has information about mental illness and treatment at www.apa.org
The National Alliance on Mental Illness (NAMI) provides support for those suffering from mental illness, as well as family and friends of those who are afflicted. Their website is found at www.nami.org and their phone number is 888-999-6264 (888-999-NAMI).
The National Mental Health Association website is www.nmha.org. They can also be reached at 800-969-6642 (800-969-NMHA).

For Those Seeking Sex Offender Treatment:
Most states have listings for sex offender treatment providers and their licensing boards on their state web pages. For additional information, contact The Association for the Treatment of Sexual Abusers (ATSA) at: www.atsa.com

BIBLIOGRAPHY*

Child Sexual Abuse and Pedophilia:

The Sexuality Information and Education Council of the United States has an excellent bibliography at: http://web.archive.org/web/20071203110724/http://www.siecus.org/pubs/biblio/bibs0002.html

For Child Abuse Statistics, please see Jim Hopper's comprehensive website: www.jimhopper.com/abstats/

Homosexuality and Gender:

"Answers to Your Questions About Sexual Orientation and Homosexuality," American Psychological Association website: www.apa.org/topics/orientation.html

Christianity, Social Tolerance, and Homosexuality, John Boswell, Univ. of Chicago Press, 2005. (This book received the National Book Award in 1981.)

Homophobia: How We All Pay the Price, Warren J. Blumenfeld (ed.), Beacon Press, 1992.

Jesus, the Bible, and Homosexuality – Explode the Myths and Heal the Church, Jack Rogers, Westminster John Knox, 2006.

Made in God's Image (Discussing Gender Differences) *And God Loves Each One* (Discussing Sexual Orientation), Ann Thompson Cook. (Intended for church discussions but informative and useful in many other settings, as well.): www.godloveseachone.org and www.madeinimage.org

Inclusion and Pastoral Care:

Created by God: Pastoral Care for All God's People, Peggy Way, Chalice Press, 2005.

Please keep in mind that homosexuality is not equivalent to pedophilia or to child sexual abuse. All three of these topics are covered on these two pages since they are all related to this story, but they are distinctly separate issues. Information about them is found in separate sources.

QUESTIONS

Chapter One

1. In what ways have the patterns of abuse been passed on in this family from generation to generation? What are the similarities and differences that can be seen between generations?

2. Frequently, children who have been abused repress the events that have traumatized them. By the time they are adults, this blocking out of their own abuse has developed into a blind spot that hides from them the abuse that is perpetrated on the next generation. Consider how the inability to recognize and admit one's own victimization affects the ability to protect the next generation.

3. Often, when victims grow up, they repeatedly choose – and are chosen by – partners those who will victimize them or their children. How does the mind of the victim turn from avoiding thoughts of abuse to yearning for relationships that turn out to be abusive?

4. Consider the various psychiatric diagnoses the members of this family developed as responses to abuse each of them suffered as a child. How is it that personalities develop such different responses?

Chapter Two

5. What can the community at large do to protect children from abuse? What considerations go into decisions regarding the cost effectiveness of these interventions?

6. What did the foster care system do to each of these children to exacerbate the trauma that each had already experienced? What steps, if any, could be taken to ameliorate these effects?

7. If any private enterprise had as poor a success rate as the foster care system, it would not likely survive. Why would anyone want to work for a system that is so irreparably broken? How can its success rate be improved?

Chapter Three

8. How does abuse within the familial context make the members of this family even more vulnerable to abuse from outside the family, such as that perpetrated by clergy and other authority figures?

9. What characteristics, other than the ability to recognize and latch on to people who have already been abused, does Jack exhibit that might be shared in common with other child molesters?

10. How does Jack use these traits to work his way into the lives of those who are possible targets for his abuse?

Chapter Four

11. In Greek, there are three different words for love. In English, the one word has an abundance of definitions. How can any of us concretely love those who are "unlovable?" Should we? What would it mean if we did?

12. In this family, each generation produced children who perceived that it was their responsibility to protect their mothers and other family members. These children became the caregivers of the generation that should have been caring for them. How did that happen, and how can it be prevented?

13. Police officers told Sophia, "Real life is not like it is on television. It can take up to a year for charges to be filed." By the end of that year, the church had still not decided what response, if any, to make to keep their sanctuary "safe." The jokes and disparaging remarks made by various law enforcement personnel reveal that they knew that the Department of Children's Services was faulty. Discuss the ways in which our systems are "broken," and possibilities for "fixing" them.

14. Edward did not understand that "bad touch" had anything to do with what Jack was doing to him. How can it be made clear to children that this type of behavior is not acceptable, without unnecessarily frightening them?

Chapter Five

15. In her desperation, Sophia prays to "anyone she thinks will listen." What is your response to those with other belief systems than your own?

16. Can any group of volunteers adequately police the actions of one abuser in a setting such as a church or synagogue? If the abuser escapes from supervision and is able to harm another child, where does the responsibility lie?

17. There were people who stated their intention to leave First Church because of Jack's presence. Would the disapproval of some members of a congregation be a sufficient reason to deny someone a place there? How important is it to obtain the approval of others when deciding upon the right course of action?

18. Consider your position regarding the idea that it is necessary to "love everyone" in order to be able to "love anyone." Who are the George Wallaces in your life? What would loving them mean to you? What is your position regarding a creative spirit that "loves" all of its creation, versus there being limits to divine acceptance?

Chapter Six

19. Consider your understanding of God and what "everyone has a place at the table" might mean for you in the context of your faith. What is your position about sin within the community? What about people who are dangerous? What about people who are not trustworthy? What about those who express regret for their actions, but whose actions do not reflect an effort to change?

20. Frequently groups of various kinds work hard to gain new members, but rarely is there any follow-up when anyone leaves. What can be done to determine why members leave, and to retain members of a group?

21. Sophia chooses her commitment to her family over loyalty to the church to which she was appointed. How is a clergyperson's calling to minister to his or her family distinguished from the calling to serve a congregation? How does *anyone* go about balancing the often-conflicting needs of family and workplace? How do *you*?

22. Many of the members of First Church came there because they had been made to feel unwelcome at the churches they had before. The church considered itself to be open, affirming, and liberal, and yet it was just as unwilling as the more conservative churches to let Jack worship there. In many ways the two types of congregations are different. In what ways are some liberal and conservative congregations alike?

Chapter Seven

23. Hypocrisy and inconsistency are rampant in every system. Frequently those who are "cogs" in the system will do anything needed to maintain the system and discourage change. Employees not only lie to protect their employers, but also often believe the lies they promote. Is significant change within systems possible? How would one go about instigating such change?

24. Institutions embody both good and evil. Our society cannot survive *without* them, but in many ways individuals cannot survive *with* them. How would you turn their capacity for evil to good?

25. What can individuals and institutions do to address the anguish experienced by people who have been wounded in the ways this family has been? What responses are helpful to make, and which are destructive?

Chapter Eight

26. The rules set up by the courts should, in theory, have been sufficient to protect children, but Jack demonstrated his willingness to violate them. What actions could be taken that would, in fact, keep children safe from people like him?

27. It takes approximately eleven months for Children's Services, the investigating lieutenant, and the district attorney to make the decision that they will not charge Jack with the abuse of Edward as long as he complies with every requirement of the safety plan. This decision is based in part on Edward's mental status. How do *you* make a decision weighing certain harm to one party against possible harm to many others?

28. In your state, what is the legality of forbidding someone who has not been convicted of a crime to enter into a place of public worship? What if the person *has* been convicted, but has already served a sentence and been released? How do the rights of the individual coincide and conflict with the safety needs and rights of the congregation?

29. If Jack had lied and denied his abuse of Edward and Gabriel, he would have been welcomed at all three of the churches that exiled him. How does our society conspire to discourage the acknowledgement of responsibility, and to encourage dishonesty?

Chapter Nine

30. This family's commitment to stick together "no matter what" resulted in both positive and negative consequences for the various family members. How realistic is such a position, and what are its realistic limits?

31. How can mental healthcare safely be provided to severely wounded adults like Conner, who have minds like children but bodies the size and strength of adults?

32. People who have been abused often lead lives of chaos. In what ways are the events of this family's life unforeseen and unpreventable, how much is due to the events of their pasts, and how much is the responsibility of the individual family members?

33. Sophia, like Job, suffered greatly – in no small part because of her fear of what might be coming. Is her fear realistic, or the result of the conditioning of her youth? Is fear itself an expression of lack of faith? Is it the manifestation of mental illness? Of sin?

Chapter Ten

34. The formula for making a sociopath is said to be almost as predictable as the recipe for baking a cake. What goes into that formula, and how does it go about causing a personality that is lacking in conscience, guilt or shame?

35. Frequently, organizations have members – or the children of members – who exhibit this lack of conscience. How should they balance the needs of the family for care and the need of the community for safety?

36. Of all the churches in this story, the one that most clearly ministers to this family is the congregation made up of people that most other congregations would condemn. How is it that the members of All Saints embody Grace?

37. If the members of this family came to you looking for a place to worship together, how would you go about making your decision regarding what to do?

Chapter Eleven

38. Consider how the interplay between the various hospitals, insurance companies, and the slow workings of the judicial appeal processes worked together to further victimize this family. What can be done to address human needs and improve the healthcare system?

39. Sophia's desperation about the possibility of going to jail leads to her write checks she knows she cannot cover. Discuss the ways in which victimization and desperation affect the decision-making process.

40. Repeatedly, this family receives what it needs to survive while many others – equally deserving or even more so – do not. Explain why and how it is that happens.

Chapter Twelve

41. For years, therapists have been taught to demonstrate "unconditional positive regard." How is it that the genuine compassion of others is healing for the wounded?

42. Consider the possibility of the pervasive nature of evil in a world where its existence is denied. How does the psyche of each individual interact with circumstances to perpetuate the evil each has experienced?

43. Consider the parameters of the debate between the possibilities of free choice and predetermination. How much control do any of the members of this family actually have over their own choices? How can you be sure you came to your opinion of your own free will?

Afterwards

44. Jack chose to endanger children "to prove to himself" that he could be around them without abusing them. What *faulty beliefs* did Jack have? What *decisions* did Jack make that increased the likelihood of danger to the children with whom he came in contact? What preventative *actions* could Jack have taken that would have helped to contain his destructive tendencies?

45. Many states have laws allowing for the "involuntary commitment" in mental institutions of any sex offender considered at risk for re-offense. Does your state have such a law? Does the concept of involuntary commitment following the completion of a criminal sentence amount to double jeopardy? Is the resulting insult to an offender's civil rights worth the potential benefit to society?

46. Dr. Hans Selye is reported to have told the story of two brothers who grew up in an alcoholic, abusive household. Years after each left home, the same researcher interviewed them both. One had become a drunk like their father. The other had become his opposite. When asked by the psychologist why he turned out like he did, each of them gave the identical answer, "What else would you expect when you have a father like mine?"[9] In the same way, Sophia and Jack had opposite responses to the experience of being abused: Sophia grew up determined to stop abuse wherever she could; Jack grew up to be a perpetrator of abuse whenever he could get away with it. Discuss the factors that might have led to this discrepancy in their responses.

Issues

47. **Issue 1**: How can we ever really understand ideals such as truth and love given our human limitations? If we can begin to comprehend them, how can we then begin to live them out?

48. **Issue 2**: How do *you* define the "truth" in a world in which not everyone remembers things the same way?

49. **Issue 3**: What does it mean to have power over your own life? Is it ever a good thing to relinquish that power to others? How do you decide when to do so?

50. **Issue 4**: What can you do or say to concretely validate the experience of those you know who have been wounded by others?

51. **Issue 5**: Take a stand on sin and sexuality. When *is* using one's sexuality a sin? When is it a sign of grace?

52. **Issue 6**: How do good and evil manifest themselves in your life?

53. **Issue 7**: What difference would it make in your life if you knew you were governed by predestination as opposed to free will?

54. **Issue 8**: What is the balance between our innate nature and the circumstances that have nurtured our lives? How do those interact in our decision-making process?

55. **Issue 9**: Consider the concepts of good/evil and mental health/mental illness. How do you draw the line between mental illness and evil? How are they alike? How do they differ? Does mental illness in any way excuse abusive behavior, and if so, when?

56. **Issue 10**: How do you make decisions regarding the individual's responsibility and the issues of reward and punishment?

57. **Issue 11**: How is the repetition of abuse from generation to generation a manifestation of the concept of "the sins of the fathers?" In what ways does your own life demonstrate the intergenerational aspect of "the sins of the fathers?" Is there any escaping the cycle? How?

58. **Issue 12**: What would you consider reasonable restitution from someone who probably ought to be spending a lifetime incarcerated in a correctional facility?

59. **Issue 13**: What do you long for in your life, and what would you be willing to do to realize it?

60. **Issue 14**: How do you balance the needs of your own family and friends against the needs of the poor who are always with us?

61. **Issue 15**: What behavioral expectations do you have of those in positions of power? Why do you or do you not have the same expectations of yourself?

62. **Issue 16**: Consider who you welcome to your table, and why. Who is it that *you* do not welcome there?

63. **Issue 17**: Dreams are interpreted differently depending on one's philosophical/theological foundation. How would you explain the timeliness and meaning of the dreams experienced in this story? Where do you find signs of hope you can hold on to or offer to others when you yourself are deep in despair?

64. **Issue 18**: What aspects of your own life are life-giving to you, and how can you use your gifts and skills to bring life to others?

65. **Issue 19**: What does conversion mean to you, and what does it mean to you to be redeemed?

66. **Issue 20**: How can you develop your own sense of humor so that it might be restorative to others?

67. **Issue 21**: What language can and do you use to communicate truths too deep for words, and to speak of things you do not understand?

Systemic Implications

68. Consider the external manifestations of Jack's internal conflict. What signs could have been recognized at an earlier stage, prior to his confession? What, if anything, could have been done earlier to head off this disaster?

69. Before the decision has been made about whether or not to even charge Jack with a crime, someone from First Church calls his employer to make sure he is fired. He has not, at this point, been found guilty of any offense. What is an appropriate response to institutions and/or individuals who circumvent the criminal justice system? Is it ever appropriate to do so, and if so, when?

70. Sophia's commitment to her children was that no matter whether they went to treatment or jail, her home would always be their home. That commitment results in an unusual understanding of "family." How do you define your family system? Who is included, and why?

71. What requirements are placed on sex offenders by the state in which you live? What are the restrictions on residences and association with others? How should these requirements be incorporated into various settings in order to keep children safe?

72. Jack says that he is sorry for what he has done, but that he cannot help himself. Consider people who express remorse but who do not change their behaviors. If one is truly remorseful, will that person necessarily exert whatever effort is necessary to change? If one claims to be truly sorry but does not change, what value, if any, does remorse have? What, then, is an appropriate response from society?

73. Gabriel, a young black male, was sentenced to seventeen years in prison for offenses against one victim; Jack, who is Caucasian, confessed to two hundred victims but received only two years probation. Discuss what can be done to make the criminal justice system more "just."

74. In spite of Sophia's determination not to repeat the trauma of her past, she repeatedly chose men who were abusers as partners and inadvertently participated in the passing on of abuse to the next generation. Discuss this dynamic, and the possibilities for ending the intergenerational cycle of abuse.

75. How can support systems be utilized to reduce the potential for further abuse by molesters of children?

NOTES

[1] www.SyracuseCulturalWorkers.com. For additional information, see the section on Resources, on page 272.

[2] For additional discussion regarding the differences in homosexuality, heterosexuality, pedophilia, ephebophilia, child molestation, and pederasty, see page 115; Issue Five, Sexuality, beginning on page 195; Issue Nine, Mental Illness or Just Plain Meanness, beginning on page 204; and definitions of some of these terms in the glossary.

[3] Levenson, J.S. (2006). *Sex offender residence restrictions.* Sex Offender Law Report, 7(3), 33; 46-47.

[4] Williams, Linda Meyer (1994). *Recall of Childhood Trauma.* Journal of Clinical and Consulting Psychology, Vol. 62, No. 6. 1167-1176.

[5] Lawson and Chaffin (1992) in London, Bruck, Ceci and Shuman, *Disclosure of Child Sexual Abuse* (2005). Psychology, Public Policy and Law, Vol. 11, No. 1, 194-226.

[6] Department of Justice website: www.ojp.usdoj.gov/bjs/crimoff.htm

[7] Abel, Gene G., M.D. and Nora Harlow. *The Stop Child Molestation Book.* Xlibris (2001).

[8] Alexander, M.A. *Sex Offender Treatment Efficacy Revisited.* Sexual Abuse, A Journal of Research and Treatment, Vol. 11, No. 2, (1999), 101-117.

[9] www.nightingale.com/tAE_Article~A~HowtoreacttoStress~i~313.asp

ABOUT THE AUTHOR

In the early 1970's, Sophia Ruah was a sixteen-year-old driving along back roads on the way to Memphis when she witnessed two youngsters on a motorcycle being hit by a truck. Leaving another passerby to deal with their injuries, she went desperately from door to door trying to find anyone who could call for help. Eventually, she found a garage where one couple said they had a phone; but before they would agree to call an ambulance, they wanted to know if the children were black or white. Her life was irrevocably changed, and she has been committed to working for justice ever since.

She began by doing food stamp advocacy, worked in the successful campaign to start the school breakfast program in her state, coordinated a sliding-scale family counseling program, and participated in the development of her state's child abuse hotline. For over thirty years, she has been caring for foster and adopted children with special needs. In all that time, until the turn of events described in this book, she had never imagined that she would ever have to advocate for herself.

Job of Arc is the remarkable first-hand account of Sophia Ruah's life for the two years following her discovery that her husband was a child molester. Containing a study guide complete with questions appropriate for use by individuals, classes, and discussion groups, this book chronicles the almost universal experiences of the non-offending parent, as well as the author's personal struggle to stay true to her faith – a faith which she believes calls her to love all of God's children, even the man who betrayed her trust in him – regardless of the cost.

Friends and family members of those traumatized by abuse, clergy, social workers, mental health and criminal justice professionals – even perpetrators themselves – will find this remarkable book to be a startling revelation regarding their often unintended impact on the victim's entire family. Non-offending parents who have thought, "I cannot possibly survive," have found her story to be a beacon of hope. Ruah not only survived, she thrived. And if she could live to tell the tale of the onslaught her family experienced, then it is possible for anyone to do so.

www.ingramcontent.com/pod-product-compliance
Lightning Source LLC
Chambersburg PA
CBHW020840270326
41928CB00006B/500